TURKISH–GREEK RELATIONS

Edinburgh Studies on Modern Turkey

Series Editors: Alpaslan Özerdem and **Ahmet Erdi Öztürk**

International Advisory Board
• Sinem Akgül Açıkmeşe
• Samim Akgönül
• Rebecca Bryant
• Mehmet Gurses
• Gareth Jenkins
• Ayşe Kadıoğlu
• Stephen Karam
• Paul Kubicek
• Peter Mandaville
• Nukhet Ahu Sandal
• M. Hakan Yavuz

Books in the series (published and forthcoming)

Turkish–Greek Relations: Foreign Policy in a Securitisation Framework
Cihan Dizdaroğlu

Policing Slums in Turkey: Crime, Resistance and the Republic on the Margin
Çağlar Dölek

Islamic Theology in the Turkish Republic
Philip Dorroll

The Kurds in Erdoğan's Turkey: Balancing Identity, Resistance and Citizenship
William Gourlay

The Politics of Culture in Contemporary Turkey
Edited by Pierre Hecker, Ivo Furman and Kaya Akyıldız

Peace Processes in Northern Ireland and Turkey: Rethinking Conflict Resolution
İ. Aytaç Kadioğlu

The British and the Turks: A History of Animosity, 1893–1923
Justin McCarthy

A Companion to Modern Turkey
Edited by Alpaslan Özerdem and Ahmet Erdi Öztürk

The Alevis in Modern Turkey and the Diaspora: Recognition, Mobilisation and Transformation
Edited by Derya Ozkul and Hege Markussen

The Decline of the Ottoman Empire and the Rise of the Turkish Republic: Observations of an American Diplomat, 1919–1927
Hakan Özoğlu

Religion, Identity and Power: Turkey and the Balkans in the Twenty-first Century
Ahmet Erdi Öztürk

Turkish-German Belonging: Ethnonational and Transnational Homelands, 2000–2020
Özgür Özvatan

Contesting Gender and Sexuality through Performance: Sacrifice, Modernity and Islam in Contemporary Turkey
Eser Selen

Turkish Politics and 'The People': Mass Mobilisation and Populism
Spyros A. Sofos

Erdoğan: The Making of an Autocrat
M. Hakan Yavuz

edinburghuniversitypress.com/series/esmt

TURKISH–GREEK RELATIONS

Foreign Policy in a Securitisation Framework

Cihan Dizdaroğlu

EDINBURGH
University Press

Edinburgh University Press is one of the leading university presses in the UK. We publish academic books and journals in our selected subject areas across the humanities and social sciences, combining cutting-edge scholarship with high editorial and production values to produce academic works of lasting importance. For more information visit our website: edinburghuniversitypress.com

© Cihan Dizdaroğlu, 2023, 2025

Edinburgh University Press Ltd
13 Infirmary Street,
Edinburgh, EH1 1LT

First published in hardback by Edinburgh University Press 2023

Typeset in 11/15 Adobe Garamond by
IDSUK (DataConnection) Ltd

A CIP record for this book is available from the British Library

ISBN 978 1 4744 9210 2 (hardback)
ISBN 978 1 474 49211 9 (paperpack)
ISBN 978 1 4744 9212 6 (webready PDF)
ISBN 978 1 4744 9213 3 (epub)

The right of Cihan Dizdaroğlu to be identified as author of this work has been asserted in accordance with the Copyright, Designs and Patents Act 1988 and the Copyright and Related Rights Regulations 2003 (SI No. 2498).

CONTENTS

List of Tables — vii
List of Abbreviations — viii
Acknowledgements — x

1 Introduction — 1

Part 1 Turkey's Securitisation of Greece (1991–99)

Part 1 Introduction — 23
2 The Disputes in the Aegean Sea — 31
3 The Cyprus Problem — 64
4 The Issue of Terrorism and the Capture of Öcalan — 82

Part 2 Desecuritisation in Turkish Foreign Policy: The Rapprochement between Turkey and Greece (1999–2016)

Part 2 Introduction — 97
5 The Root Causes of Rapprochement — 103
6 Instances of Rapprochement and Forms of Desecuritisation — 125

Part 3 Reverting to the Default Settings in Turkish Foreign Policy (2016 Onwards)

Part 3 Introduction   149

7   Conclusion: What Does the Future Hold?   165

Bibliography   177
Index   197

TABLES

5.1 Military Expenditure of NATO Countries in Percentage
of GDP (1990–99)   111
6.1 Trade Volume of Turkey and Greece (1990–2021,
in USD 1,000)   133

ABBREVIATIONS

AKP	Justice and Development Party
CBMs	Confidence Building Measures
CIA	Central Intelligence Agency
EAST-MED	East Mediterranean Gas Forum
EEC	European Economic Community
EEZ	Exclusive Economic Zone
EMU	European Monetary Union
EOKA	National Organisation of Cyprus Fighters
EU	European Union
EYP	Greece's National Intelligence Agency
FETO	Fethullah Gülen Movement
GDP	Gross Domestic Product
HLCC	High-Level Cooperation Council
ICJ	International Court of Justice
JHET-SDRU	Joint Hellenic-Turkish Standby Disaster Relief Unit
MHP	Nationalist Movement Party
MIT	Turkish National Intelligence Agency
NATO	North Atlantic Treaty Organisation
NSC	National Security Council
PASOK	Pan-Hellenic Socialist Party
PKK	Kurdistan Workers' Party

RoC	Republic of Cyprus
TGNA	Turkish Grand National Assembly
TPAO	Turkish Petroleum Company
TRNC	Turkish Republic of Northern Cyprus
UK	United Kingdom
UN	United Nations
UNCLOS	UN Conference on Law of the Sea
UNHCR	United Nations High Commissioner for Refugees
UNSC	United Nations Security Council
US	United States

ACKNOWLEDGEMENTS

The idea and research for this book began while I was a PhD student at Kadir Has University. It evolved over the years, and many people have contributed to this journey. I am grateful to numerous professors, including Sinem Akgül Açıkmeşe, Mustafa Aydın, Serhat Güvenç, Mitat Çelikpala, Özgür Özdamar, İnan Rüma, Balkan Devlen, Kostas Ifantis, Dimitrios Triantaphyllou, Haluk Karadağ, Başar Baysal and Onur Kara, who have provided crucial guidance at different stages. I am extremely thankful for each and every one of their contributions. I would like to offer my sincere thanks and gratitude to my mentor, colleague and friend, Professor Sinem Akgül Açıkmeşe, for her excellent guidance, encouragement and insightful critiques since the beginning of this journey.

While I was working as a Marie Curie Fellow at the Centre for Trust, Peace and Social Relations (CTPSR) at Coventry University between November 2018 and October 2020, my colleagues and friends – Professors Alpaslan Özerdem, Bahar Başer Öztürk and Ahmet Erdi Öztürk – strongly encouraged me to transform this project into its current book form. I would like to acknowledge the series editors, Professor Alp Özerdem and Professor Ahmet Erdi Öztürk, for allowing my work to be part of the Edinburgh Studies on Modern Turkey series and for their patience, as it took almost two years to bear fruit. Many thanks to Emma Rees, Kirsty Woods, Louise Hutton, Eddie Clark and Isobel Birks from Edinburgh University Press for their kind assistance throughout the process.

I am also thankful for the insightful comments of the anonymous reviewers, which improved the quality of this work.

The course on *Turkish–Greek Relations and Cyprus*, which I have been teaching at different universities for the last couple of years, and workshops such as the *Greek–Turkish Young Leaders Symposium*, which has been conducted by the Center for International and European Studies (CIES) at Kadir Has University, have greatly helped me to observe first-hand both Greeks and Turks' perceptions of each other; thus, I am very thankful to all students and attendees of these courses and workshops. I completed the last chapters of this book after I began to work at Başkent University, and I appreciate all the support I received from my colleagues and students there. Special thanks are due to the Dean of the Faculty, Professor H. Nejat Basım, the Head of the Department of Political Science and International Relations, Professor H. Yelda Ongun, and my colleageas in the department for their support in completing this book.

A warmest thanks to my love, Hande, since it would not have been possible to bring this journey to its end without her infinite support, love and encouragement. She always supported me without questioning and gave me time to study, write, learn and teach. Her willingness to share her valuable comments, criticism and feedback helped me a lot. Last but not least, I am greatly indebted to my father, mother and brother, who have always supported me, no matter what I wanted to do. I am sad that my father, who passed away while I was writing this book, will never get to see the completed work. I hope that he rests in peace and continues to be proud of his son, wherever he is now.

Ankara, July 2022

To my beloved Hande

1

INTRODUCTION

As neighbouring countries, Turkey and Greece share an extensive past. Their historical ties date back to the fourteenth century and to the Ottoman Empire's conquest of Constantinople in 1453. However, the beginning of their contemporary relationship can be traced back to the early nineteenth century, when Greece became a sovereign and independent state as result of its struggle against the Ottoman Empire. This historical background between the two nations has always shaped the priorities on both countries' foreign and security policy agendas.

Historically, one may identify the Turkish–Greek relationship as a vicious cycle of improvement and deterioration. Both nations view each other as a 'source of threat' or as 'enemy', a mutual perception that mainly stems from the historical context. Although the problems between them have generally been interpreted through the lenses of security, politics and, to some extent, economics, it would be naive to over-estimate the burden of the past – the main source of feelings of enmity and mistrust. History, thus, has conceivably played a significant role in shaping not only their foreign policies but also their national identities. Historical legacies and feelings of mutual antipathy between Turkey and Greece have also influenced their bilateral relationship and the mindsets of decision-makers ever since the two nation-states were founded. As such, an understanding of the nature and present state of the Turkish–Greek relationship would be incomplete without its historical context. As Gürel (1993a, 10) has pointed out, for both Greece and Turkey, '[h]istory is not past, [since] the past continues to live in the present'.

Likewise, Clogg (1980, 141), noting the impact of historical heritage on national identity and historical consciousness, has written:

> . . . even if a rapprochement between two governments is achieved, it would be a much more difficult and arduous process to overcome the mistrust between two peoples, mutual stereotypes and fears that are fundamental for existing confrontation. Until a fundamental change in mutual (mis)perceptions has achieved, we will continue to see a mutual proclivity towards suspicion and crisis in the relations between two states.

It is still possible to observe the same pattern, as Clogg has argued in the 1980s, in the level of trust between the two peoples due to the historical background. As reflected in surveys conducted in Greece and Turkey, even at the elite level mistrust has continued to dominate the mindset of people on both sides. As Triantaphyllou (2017) has reported, according to the elite surveys conducted by Triantaphyllou, Ifantis and Dizdaroğlu in 2015 and 2016, 'the level of trust towards the "other" is especially low – at some 28% for Turkish elite and 11.4% by Greek elites'. Accordingly, a brief investigation of the historical background of Turkish–Greek relations will help readers comprehend today's disputes between the two.

Turkish–Greek Relations: A Bird's-eye View

The modern relationship between Turkey and Greece began with the Greeks' revolt on 25 March 1821 to end the four centuries of Ottoman rule over Greece. In July 1832, the Kingdom of Greece became a sovereign and independent state, emerging from a struggle against the Ottoman Empire. The popular Turkish image of the Greek 'War of Independence' is that of rebellion, instigated and supported by the Great Powers of the nineteenth century (Aydın, 1997, 111). Furthermore, according to Clogg (1992, 47–99), '[t]he establishment of an independent Greek state meant divided loyalties among the Greek subjects of the Ottoman Empire; as a result, Greeks could no longer be trusted to hold official positions and those in the Ottoman diplomatic corps were purged'.

This perception coalesced with the goal of Greek politicians to unite all Greeks under a single flag and country, an ideology known as the

Megali Idea. The 1850s, following closely behind these political ambitions, saw some territorial expansion,[1] which reached a peak during the Balkan Wars of 1912–13. With the support of Bulgaria, Montenegro and Serbia, Greece conquered vast swathes of territory in Macedonia and Thrace, seizing the opportunity presented by a weakened Ottoman state (Ker-Lindsay, 2007, 12–13). After the defeat of the Ottoman Empire in World War I, the Greeks turned their attention to their ethnic peers living in Asia Minor and Constantinople (Ker-Lindsay, 2007, 13). But the Greeks' invasion of Western Anatolia after World War I and their subsequent defeat, followed by the foundation of the Republic of Turkey, caused difficulties in both countries. What the Greeks remember as the 'Asia Minor Catastrophe', Turks call their 'War of National Liberation' (Aydın, 1997, 111). Fuelling the contentious relationship, Greek and Turkish delegations on 30 January 1923 signed a protocol during the Lausanne Conference, leading to the compulsory population exchange in the 1920s and reinforcing the notion of ethnic separation between Greeks and Turks (Evin, 2005, 395; Ker-Lindsay, 2007, 13; Demirözü, 2008, 309).

That the two nations were founded out of a slew of viciously fought wars helped to craft certain perceptions of the 'other' and of the national enemy in historiographic and literary texts, in order to consolidate national identity (Millas, 2004, 54–61). Millas (2004, 61) has stressed the general trend of communities perceiving their counterpart as the 'other', an 'unreliable neighbor' or 'potential danger'. He has written (2004, 54):

> Greek textbooks portrayed Turks as an enemy with barbaric characteristics – rude warriors, uncivilized, invaders, etc. – an anathema that caused the slavery of the nation for many centuries; Turkish textbooks are almost a mirror image of the above: the Turks are perfect and the Greeks, who hate and massacre the Turks carry many negative characteristics: they are unreliable, unfaithful, cunning, insatiable, etc.

From this sweeping history came stereotypes of supposed ethnic behaviours, locking Greeks and Turks into an 'age-old' enmity and clash of civilisations (Carnegie, 1997, 3). As such, the current disputes owe much of their divisive nature to the threat perceptions and the symbolic or historical significance that both sides attach to them (Siegl, 2002, 42–43). Accordingly, studying Turkish–Greek relations requires a thorough consideration of the decades of distrust and prejudice between the two nations.

The course of this bilateral relationship has been dominated by conflict and rivalry rather than collaboration. As Gürel (1993b, 161–90) has posited, the history of Turkish–Greek relations has more chapters on competition than on cooperation. In addition to the latest rapprochement process, which began in late 1999 and lasted until late 2016, the relationship has had two periods of concord that were shaped around the common threat from a third country, first Italy and later the Soviet Union.

The first period started with a letter exchange between Greek Prime Minister Eleftherios Venizelos, who had won a recent electoral victory in his country, and his Turkish counterpart, İsmet İnönü, in 1928. Accordingly, the two countries signed the Ankara Agreement in 1930 to solve the remaining problems from the population exchange of 1923. This was followed by the Treaty of Friendship which was signed in August 1930 between Turkish President Mustafa Kemal Atatürk and Greek Prime Minister Eleftherios Venizelos, who conducted a historic visit to Ankara between 26 and 29 August 1930. This treaty brought the two countries closer in the political, military and social spheres. Two months after Venizelos' trip, on 30 October 1930, the two countries signed three more agreements: a treaty of neutrality, conciliation and arbitration; a protocol on the limitation of naval armaments; and a commercial convention (Heraclides, 2010, 68). During that period, both Turkey and Greece were aware of the threat from Italy and therefore broadened their friendship (along with Yugoslavia and Romania) by establishing the Balkan Entente[2] in February 1934. The spirit of friendship was also reflected in the leader's statements and attitudes. While Atatürk, articulating the cordial relationship, stated that 'Turkish–Greek friendship is eternal', Venizelos sought to nominate Atatürk for the Nobel Peace Prize and sent a letter to the Norwegian Nobel Committee on 12 January 1934 (Heraclides, 2010, 68; Tulça, 2003, 54). The rapprochement that began in the 1930s was interrupted by World War II but resumed in the early 1950s.[3]

The second period of cooperation was defined by the Soviet threat against the Western bloc, and both countries met under the NATO umbrella at the encouragement of the US (Aydın, 1997, 113). In the aftermath of World

War II, both Turkey and Greece faced threats from the Soviet Union due to Soviet claims over Turkish territory and Soviet influence on domestic Greek politics. As a result, the US began to support both countries to secure its regional interests and to retain Turkey and Greece in the Western bloc.[4] The US-Greece-Turkey trilateral relationship was consolidated by the accession of both countries to the NATO in 1952. Between 1950 and 1955, both countries correlated their national interests with the needs of the alliance (Fırat, 2010, 354; Larrabee, 2012, 472). As Güvenç (2004, 3) has pointed out, these threats, first from the Italians and later the Soviet, provided the glue necessary to bind Turkey and Greece together during two separate periods of cohesion.

Following the emergence of the Cyprus problem in the mid-1950s, the cordial spirit of the relationship between Turkey and Greece quickly dissipated.[5] Subsequent conflicts on the small island in the eastern Mediterranean had serious repercussions for both the island's residents and the broader Turkish–Greek relationship, to be discussed in the chapters below. Over time, the two communities on the island have sought a comprehensive and equitable solution to the issue, although all efforts thus far have failed. The Cyprus problem, with its enduring partition of the island, remains on the foreign and security policy agendas of both countries.

While the Cyprus problem has been a persistent thorn in the side since the mid-1950s, other issues in the Aegean Sea have created problems for the two nations. Since the mid-1960s, differences over the delimitation of maritime borders and the continental shelf, the breadth of territorial waters and airspace, and the Greek fortification of the Eastern Aegean islands have been tenacious challenges for Greece and Turkey on their path to establishing greater rapport. Even the number of conflict areas across the Aegean Sea has been a dispute between the two. Greece has only perceived the continental shelf issue as a challenge, whereas Turkey has claimed several more. For the past six decades, ever since the problems in the Aegean Sea arose, these issues have influenced, in parallel to developments in bilateral relations, international politics and international law. Although the Treaty of Lausanne demarcated the Turkish–Greek border, developments in bilateral relations and international politics sparked a previously dormant issue. Tözün Bahçeli (2004, 98) has written: 'The equilibrium established by the Treaty of Lausanne in the Aegean did not pose any large problems for the two neighbours for half a century'.

Several incidents in the course of this bilateral history very nearly brought the two countries to the brink of war. The worst crisis erupted when a Turkish ship ran aground on an islet in the Aegean, on 25 December 1995. These disputes in the Aegean still loom on the horizon and continue to trigger crises in bilateral relations. Thanks to a process of rapprochement that commenced in 1999 – or, perhaps, because each imminent disaster has been carefully handled by the decision-makers – there has been no armed conflict between Turkey and Greece.

Nevertheless, a diverse array of issues has plagued the relationship: the rights and status of minorities in Turkey and Greece, border disputes, the status of the Halki Seminary in Istanbul, Greece's political blockage of Turkey's EU relationship and Greece's support for terrorism, to name just a few. Although the two countries at times teetered on the edge of conflict, the burden of assuming responsibility for a full-fledged bloody war always convinced leaders to contain those disputes without resorting to armed clashes.

In the late 1990s, a thaw began in the cold bilateral relationship, as the two countries sought resolutions to the many problems between them. This warming of relations culminated in a sustained détente, which has progressed since 1999. A vast number of academic studies, offering a multitude of perspectives, examine the root causes of this rapprochement process. Some scholars have explained the winds of change as a product of 'disaster/earthquake diplomacy' (Siegl, 2002; Keridis, 1999; Ganapati et al., 2010), while others have focused on the impact of the EU's 1999 Helsinki Summit, where Turkey obtained candidacy status (Öniş and Yılmaz, 2008; Grigoriadis, 2011). In conjunction with the latter, the pursuit of Europeanisation through its blend of stipulations and incentives also contributed to changes in the foreign policies of both countries (Grigoriadis, 2003; Rumelili, 2003; Güvenç, 2004). The empowerment of civil society actors and NGOs favouring Turkish–Greek relations and cooperation acted to catalyse the rectification of the relationship (Rumelili, 2004; Evin, 2005). There is also a prevalent view that the role of third parties such as the United States bolstered the rapprochement process. However, the latest bout of reconciliation in Turkish–Greek relations started, more accurately, due to a chain of events rather than based on a simplistic view of natural disasters. In the words of

Öniş and Yılmaz (2001, 4), the 'Greek–Turkish rapprochement is a complex process with multiple layers and has been shaped by multiple critical domestic and international factors and actors'.

The bilateral rapprochement contributed significantly to the constructive atmosphere that culminated in the March 2016 migration deal between Greece and Turkey. The absence of any tangible changes in the core disputes between them is incontrovertible, yet both Greece and Turkey managed to establish a dialogue. Hampering this nearly twenty years of productive dialogue, however, are new disputes, including the extradition of eight military officers who had fled Turkey following the failed July 2016 coup attempt, fears of mounting tension in the Aegean and Eastern Mediterranean, the conversion of the Hagia Sophia into a mosque and the migrant-related crises between the two countries.

This enduring rivalry has attracted the interest of countless scholars; as a result, a substantial literature has emerged on almost every aspect of this bilateral relationship. Some scholars have focused on its political and historical aspects (Clogg, 1980; Nachmani, 1987; Constas, 1991; Bahçeli, 2001; Aksu, 2001; Keridis and Triantaphyllou, 2001; Tsakonas, 2001a, 2001b; Öniş, 2001; Fırat, 2002; Başeren, 2006; Rumelili, 2003, 2007; Moustakis, 2003; Aydın and Ifantis, 2004; Çarkoğlu and Rubin, 2005; Ker-Lindsay, 2007; Öniş and Yılmaz, 2008; Demirözü, 2008, 2017; Heraclides, 2010; Karakatsanis, 2014; Heraclides and Alioğlu Çakmak, 2019). Conversely, others have concentrated on economic, social, cultural and religious dimensions (Alexandris, 1992; Hirshon, 2004; Rumelili, 2004; Theodossopoulos, 2007; Özkırımlı and Sofos, 2008; Akgönül, 2008; Tsarouhas, 2009; Heraclides, 2012; Millas, 2016; Kutlay, 2019; Romain Örs, 2019). This book examines Turkish–Greek relations from a critical security perspective and analyses the issue around the central research questions of whether, how and to what extent Greece has constituted an issue of security for Turkey, by using the methodology and main concepts of the securitisation theory employed by the Copenhagen School. This book, first, intends to make an empirical contribution to the literature by analysing Turkish–Greek relations with a particular focus on the post-Cold War period, through the perspectives of securitisation and desecuritisation. Second, it puts emphasis on the political nature of securitisation in that it focuses on the making of Turkish foreign policy.

Securitisation and Desecuritisation: Theory, Concepts and Methodology

Securitisation theory has found its way into two perspectives of security studies – traditionalists and wideners – by offering an alternative and comprehensive framework for the field. Amidst the lively debate in security studies, which started with 'the rise of the economic and environmental agendas in international relations during the 1970s and 1980s', the scholars of the Copenhagen School presented a ground-breaking framework 'based on the wider agenda that will incorporate the traditionalists' position' (Buzan et al., 1998, 2–4). Buzan et al. (1998), in their co-authored book *Security: A New Framework for Analysis*, tried to demonstrate how the security studies agenda can be extended without destroying the field's intellectual coherence. As a result, they developed the securitisation theory to identify issues of security that transcend the traditional military and political arenas and combine them with the emergent realms of economics, society and environment (Nyman, 2013, 52). As Buzan et al. (1998, vii) have argued, they offered 'a constructivist operational method' to understand and analyse how, when and by whom issues become securitised.

In essence, securitisation is 'presenting an issue as an existential threat requiring emergency measures and justifying actions outside the normal bounds of political procedure' (Buzan et al., 1998, 23–24). Thus, security issues are not a guaranteed certainty but are constructed as result of intersubjective interaction (Buzan et al., 1998). In practice, an issue becomes one of security when it is presented as a threat, regardless of whether it reflects a threat that is 'real' or that even 'exists' (Buzan et al., 1998, 24). Wæver (1995, 54) has encapsulated the concept by saying that 'something is a security problem when the elites declare it to be so'. Therefore, the speech-acts of political elites have a primary role in this process. And, according to Buzan et al. (1998, 25), the way to examine securitisation is to 'study discourse and political constellations: When does an argument, with this particular rhetorical and semiotic structure, achieve sufficient effect to make an audience tolerate violations of rules that would otherwise have to be obeyed?' Accordingly, a researcher or analyst does not necessarily have to determine whether threats raised by securitising actors are legitimate. Instead, one must 'understand who securitises, on what issues (threats), for whom (referent objects), why, with what results, and, not least, under what conditions (i.e. when securitisation is successful)' (Buzan et al., 1998, 32). The constructivist perspective posits that issues may move between three realms: the private/non-politicised, the public/political and security. Accordingly, securitisation theory refers to the placement of issues in the security realm as securitisation and their removal as desecuritisation (Baysal and Dizdaroğlu, 2022).

Although the theory of securitisation has been criticised for different aspects (McDonald, 2008; Balzacq, 2005, 2010; Baysal, 2020), the critique by the scholars of the Paris School, also known as International Political Sociology, is particularly significant. The Paris School criticises the over-emphasis on discourses in securitisation theory, claiming that the practices of security professionals also play an important role in the securitisation of issues (Bigo, 2014; Baysal et al., 2019).

In contrast, desecuritisation denotes the inverse process – that is, 'the shifting of issues out of emergency mode and into the normal bargaining process of the political sphere' (Buzan et al., 1998, 4). The transformation from securitisation to desecuritisation is a difficult task considering that the latter is more abstract than the former. The Copenhagen School did not fully explore the methodology of desecuritisation in its initial works. However, Lene Hansen (2012, 539–45) has propounded four forms of desecuritisation to analyse the process.[6] This study also utilises Lene Hansen's four forms of desecuritisation, which she outlined in her article titled 'Reconstructing Desecuritisation: The Normative-Political in the Copenhagen School and Directions for How to Apply It'. These forms, as she listed them, provide a systematic framework for empirical studies:

> . . . change through stability (when an issue is cast in terms other than security, but where the larger conflict still looms), replacement (when an issue is removed from the securitised, while another securitisation takes its place), rearticulation (when an issue is moved from the securitised to the politicized due to a resolution of the threats and dangers), and silencing (when desecuritisation takes the form of a de-politicization, which marginalizes potentially insecure subjects). (Hansen, 2012, 529)

Securitisation theory has been used to analyse a vast number of issues, including terrorism (Buzan, 2006; Amicelle, 2007; Rychnovska, 2014), migration, human security and identity (Bigo, 2002; Boswell, 2007; Hayes, 2009;

Robinson, 2017; Grigoriadis and Dilek, 2019), the environment and climate (Warner and Boas, 2019), women's rights (Hansen, 2000) and specific regional or national problems or bilateral relations (Kaliber, 2005; Aras and Karakaya Polat, 2008; Balamir Coşkun, 2009; Balcı and Kardaş, 2012; Baysal, 2019; Adamides, 2020). There are also a multitude of studies researching the theoretical dimension of the Copenhagen School (McSweeney, 1998, 2004; Hansen, 2000, 2011, 2012; Bilgin, 2002, 2007; Stritzel, 2007, 2011, 2012; Wilkinson, 2007; Peoples and Vaughan-Williams, 2010; Akgül Açıkmeşe, 2011; Roe, 2012; Nyman, 2013; Howell and Richter-Montpetit, 2019; Wæver and Buzan, 2020). The theory has also found use in deciphering issues pertaining to Turkish foreign policy and security strategies. Alper Kaliber (2005), for instance, has used securitisation theory for the case of Cyprus to interpret the conventional Turkish rhetoric and its repercussions for political balances and power relations in domestic politics. In addition to Kaliber's work, Bilgin (2007) has explained the underlying reasons for the transformation in Turkish politics in the post-1999 period from the perspective of desecuritisation. Aras and Karakaya Polat (2008), using the theory, have analysed the transformation of Turkish-Iranian relations. Karakaya Polat (2009) has focused on the 2007 parliamentary elections and evaluated the securitisation and desecuritisation of political Islam and the Kurdish issue. Using the securitisation perspective, Balcı and Kardaş (2012) have explored Turkish-Israeli relations, while Akgül Açıkmeşe (2011) has focused on the security speech-acts on 'Kurdish separatism' and 'political Islam' to understand the EU's role as desecuritisation agent for Turkey.

Despite the vast number of studies on Turkish–Greek relations, the literature has notably lacked an analysis conducted from the securitisation perspective, of whether, how and to what extent Greece has represented a security issue for Turkey. Two rare and recent examples by Türkeş-Kılıç (2019) and Baysal and Dizdaroğlu (2022) have used the securitisation and desecuritisation framework to analyse the bilateral relations from the Turkish point of view. Thus, as already mentioned, this book aims to fill this gap with the help of the Copenhagen School's methodology and concepts in order to examine Turkey's securitisation and desecuritisation of Greece in foreign policy. Securitisation theory offers a way to understand the bilateral relationship from an altogether different and critical angle. The security issues that presently exist between the two countries provide a fruitful case-study.⁷ This book thus focuses on detailed accounts of the discourses amplified by securitising actors, in order to interpret the ways in which they handle problems and to comprehend how these problems impact the relationship. The *sui generis* characteristics of Turkish politics require a thorough explanation to illuminate the roles of these actors in decision-making processes.

As Buzan, Wæver and de Wilde (1998, 35–36) have stressed, it is imperative to draw a distinction between the units 'referent object' and 'securitising actors' to fully explain instances of securitisation. As this study's methodology is mainly based on a discourse analysis of official texts – collected from newspapers and the official websites of state institutions – as well as oral and written interviews, and statements and press releases of the relevant actors, it is important to ask who these actors are in the Turkish case. Firstly, security is about the survival of the referent object, something that is deemed to face existential threats and that has a legitimate claim to survival. Like the traditionalists, scholars of securitisation theory believe in the primary role of the state as referent object. In this analysis, the Turkish state will constitute the referent object, as its perception of Greece has always been one of a 'source of threat' or 'enemy' of Turkey's national security. Due to the mutual mistrust and misperceptions between the two countries, a lack of confidence in their respective national security has long plagued both nations. Turkey's perception of Greece is reflected in its foreign and security policy rhetoric. The traditional security discourse in Turkey has featured two major components, as Bilgin (2005, 183) has proposed: 'fear of abandonment and fear of loss of territory', as well as the assumption of 'geographical determinism'. The former component stems from the Treaty of Sèvres (1920), which was detrimental to the Ottoman Empire and destructive for its homeland, as it allowed Turks to keep only a small, desolate section of Central Anatolia (Aydın, 1999, 158; Bilgin, 2005, 183–84). Yet, the assumption of 'geographical determinism' refers to Turkey's geopolitical location, which has been used to legitimise caution and risk in the formulation of policies (Bilgin, 2005, 185–87). As Bilgin (2005, 187) has argued, these two components characterised the traditional security discourse that emerged in and dominated the Republican era.

The Turkish–Greek relationship has comprised a preat portion of this traditional discourse as well. For example, in a 1996 article entitled '2 ½ War Strategy', former Under-Secretary of the Ministry of Foreign Affairs Şükrü Elekdağ presented the reasons for Turkey's scepticism of its neighbours. In his (1996, 34) view, '[t]wo countries, namely Greece and Syria, who have claims on Turkey's vital interests, constitute an immediate threat for Turkey'. Greece's claims to extend its territorial waters in the Aegean, its financial and symbolic support to the PKK, its efforts to alter the balance of power in the Aegean with its naval and air forces, and its Enosis[8] plans with Cyprus have posed grave threats and challenges for the referent object's security and survival (Elekdağ, 1996, 33–43). To prevent these claims from encroaching on its vital interests, Turkey has implemented several preventative measures in its foreign and security policies. Turkey's policy of *casus belli* – meaning the treatment of any Greek initiative to extend its territorial waters in the Aegean beyond six miles as an act of war – is the most obvious example of its preventative policies and the continuation of its traditional security discourse.

Similarly, Turkey's perceptions of a persistent external threat from Greece are also evident in its Cyprus policy. For instance, during the Tripartite Conference between Turkey, Greece and the UK regarding the fate of the island in 1955, the Turkish delegation reminded the other parties of the island's vital importance for the protection of Turkey's southern coast, pointing out that, if the power that controlled Cyprus also controlled the Aegean islands (as did Greece), then Turkey would be surrounded (Armaoğlu, 1963). Turkey has always feared Greek policies that would limit its own maritime access, vital for its defence and survival. Accordingly, securitising actors have guided foreign and security policy in view of the survival of the referent object vis-à-vis Greece, the existential threat.

Although the referent object is apparent in analyses of Turkish–Greek relations, identifying the securitising actors is a more onerous task, due to the nature of the Turkish political system. Wæver (2000, 252–53) has noted that the speaker who performs the speech-act must have 'social capital' and 'be in a position of authority'. The dramatisation of an issue as an 'existential threat' and the accompanying calls for 'emergency action' before an audience require such a position of authority. Hence, political leaders, government representatives and elites may be considered actors who securitise issues through the performance of speech-acts. Although the complexity of the bureaucracy prevents a clear distinction between actors who contribute to decision-making processes, the senior-most figures in the relevant units most likely reflect the position of the collective unit. According to the Turkish constitution, the president and the prime minister, who also chairs the Council of Ministers, are thus designated as the primary figures in the decision-making process. However, influencing and advising these figures are other actors within the state configuration. According to the Law on the Organisation and Duties of the Ministry of Foreign Affairs (1994),[9] the Ministry is tasked with effecting the necessary preparation work and providing suggestions to determine the nation's foreign policy of the country, as well as coordinating and implementing this foreign policy in accordance with the goals and principles set by the government. Therefore, the president, prime minister and foreign minister together embody the main securitising actors in Turkey's foreign policy decision-making processes. It should be noted that a constitutional referendum on 16 April 2017 abolished the office of the prime minister and replaced the existing parliamentary government with a presidential system of government, in which executive power and functions are exercised and carried out by the president. Thus, until 2017, the prime minister's statements will be used for the analysis of events.

Due to the characteristics of the Turkish legislative process, other actors have also garnered decisive influence, depending on the relevant issues. In particular, military authorities are collectively acknowledged as a determinant actor in foreign and security policy-making. As Bilgin (2007, 563) has suggested, the military's active involvement in the formulation of the national security policy document, particularly in the post-1980 period, has influenced Turkey's security agenda, which is dominated by military voices. The responsibilities of the chief of the general staff, according to Article 117 of the Constitution,[10] are solely directed to the prime minister, thus granting him a status equal to that of the other members of the Council of Ministers (Özcan, 2001, 16). The chief of the general staff serves on the National Security Council (NSC), a body established in 1961 and whose members include (in addition to the chief of the general staff) the prime minister; the deputy prime ministers; ministers of foreign affairs, defence and interior; and the general commanders of the army, navy, air force and gendarmerie, with the president presiding as chair over the council. The military has wielded clear authority in the government with the presence of the High Command on the NSC (Heper and Güney, 2000, 637). The role of the NSC secretary-general, until 2004 filled by a high-ranking military official, is key to understanding the NSC's influence in the decision-making process. Although the NSC functions, in theory, as an advisory body, the government tends to closely follow its suggestions. The secretary-general has the authority to pursue, control, direct and coordinate the implementation of the NSC's decisions on behalf of the president, prime minister and the NSC itself (Uzgel, 2003, 191–92). Once Turkey gained candidate status for EU accession at the 1999 Helsinki Summit, attempts to diminish the privilege and primal role of the military and the NSC proliferated. Despite all changes, however, the military maintained political influence by issuing declarations until the mid-2000s (Karaosmanoğlu, 2011, 253). Because the Turkish military authorities have shouldered such a substantial and historical role in conducting foreign and security policy, this study regards the chief of general staff and the NSC as securitising actors, in addition to the president, prime minister and foreign minister.[11]

In the context of the legislative and decision-making processes for Turkish security and foreign policy, this book then analyses the official texts to understand the influence of securitising actors in Turkey. Focusing on the speech-acts of decision-makers, placing special importance on those pertaining to Greece, will present invaluable insights into Turkey's securitisation and desecuritisation of Greece. This study focuses only on official statements to understand the discursive influence that securitising actors in Turkey wield in regard to their understanding of Greece from a security perspective. It will also help readers in observing potential changes in the rhetoric surrounding Greece in Turkey's security perceptions. This study is based on a range of official texts, collected from newspapers and the official websites of state institutions; oral and written interviews; and statements and press releases by relevant actors. Since the targeted audience's approval, which constitutes the intersubjectivity of the process, is imperative to the completion of securitisation processes, all official documents that this study uses must be unclassified and have been publicised by the relevant actors during the implementation of the policies.[12]

According to Balzacq (2005, 184), the audience can be divided into two: 'the formal audience', which must be convinced to adopt extraordinary measures and whose support provides formal legitimacy; and the 'moral audience', which gives moral legitimacy to the actions to be performed. While the parliament can be considered as formal audience, a country's citizens can be identified as moral audience. As such, enough members of each group must be convinced about an issue for a successful securitisation to take place (O'Reilly 2008, 67).

The matter of the relevant audience's acceptance of the securitisation process represents a difficult task for interpretation. However, public surveys or polls may be employed to gauge public perceptions. This study accordingly uses open-access public surveys (along with those conducted by the author) as an input to measure the success of the government's policies as they relate to both specific issues and general trends. But it is important to remember that the democratic election of representatives already indicates that the public – that is, the moral audience – has approved of the government's actions and policies. Since the present study correlates securitising actors with the government's democratically elected representatives, the relevant audience's approval would, naturally, be implied. As Balzacq (2005, 185) has illustrated, a 'formal decision by an institution [. . .] mandates the government to adopt a specific policy'. Consequently, this study will consider the legitimacy of the government's policies as an implicit component of the audience's approval, based on the assumption that democratically elected officials and governments have the organic support of the majority of their citizens.

Overview of the Book

This book focuses broadly on the main issues of contention between Turkey and Greece, in particular on the post-Cold War era, within the framework of securitisation and desecuritisation. Its structure is developed around three main parts, through which it assesses trends in securitisation and desecuritisation. The introduction presents the rationale, summary and contributions of the study by highlighting the gaps in the existing theoretical and empirical literature. Following a brief history of Turkish–Greek relations to familiarise readers with the issues affecting the bilateral relationship, this section also includes a brief review of securitisation theory, which will help to offer a broader understanding of when, under what conditions and by what kind of actions processes of securitisation and desecuritisation succeed. This section also covers the methodology employed here, which is primarily based on a discourse analysis of official texts, oral and written interviews, and statements and press releases by the relevant actors in Turkish politics.

The first part addresses the post-Cold War era, specifically the period from 1991 to 1999, which represents the peak of securitisation in Turkish foreign policy due to the simmering contention between the two countries. Before analysing the issues in detail, this chapter introduces how the end of the Cold War influenced the reformulation of Turkey's foreign and security priorities in light of its nascent security needs. The sub-sections within this part will examine bilateral disputes – including disputes in the Aegean Sea, the Cyprus problem and terrorism. Its goal is to show the securitising discourses of Turkish decision-makers and to place special significance on these actors' statements, rather than to consider the bilateral relationship within the logic of diplomatic history. During this period, the Turkish elites securitised issues mainly through security speech-acts. A 'threatening' and 'hostile' tone became visible in the discourse of the Turkish elites regarding almost every matter of contention between the two countries, including issues of delimitation – territorial waters and the continental shelf – and sovereignty in the Aegean Sea – the status of the islands, islets and rocks, as well as the (de)militarisation of the islands. Also brimming with examples of such a tone are problems related to Cyprus and Greek ties to terrorist organisations. The strong and rough character of the security speech-acts suggests that Turkey was preparing to plunge into armed conflict with Greece.

The second part begins by briefly assessing Turkish–Greek relations between 1999 and 2016. Despite the failure of earlier attempts to ease the bilateral tension, enormous earthquakes in both Turkey and Greece, in August and September 1999, respectively, fostered empathy and solidarity between the citizens of the two nations. This part also provides a detailed account of the rapprochement process between Greece and Turkey. First conducting a review of the literature, it classifies research under four main categories: the impact of earthquakes and the empowerment of civil society, the Europeanisation process in both countries, the role of two solution-oriented foreign ministers, and the role of third parties such as the US. It then presents a novel approach, by utilising Lene Hansen's four forms of desecuritisation, and unravels the correlation between rapprochement and desecuritisation. While at that time the Turkish elites securitised issues related to Greece with an aggressive tone, the bilateral relations paradoxically evolved into almost cooperative behaviour after rapprochement ensued in 1999. The discourse of the elites changed drastically during this period, emphasising 'friendship' rather than focusing on existential threats, and decision-makers began to substitute their security rhetoric with a more positive and cautious tone. Accordingly, the objective of this part is to inquire whether the rapprochement process has culminated in desecuritisation and whether it is possible to explain the rapprochement within the framework of desecuritisation. Employing Hansen's four forms of desecuritisation, this part argues that reconciliation in Turkish–Greek relations fits the form of *change through stabilisation*.

The third part focuses on recently emerging crises, large and small, including the extradition of eight military officers who fled Turkey following the failed 15 July 2016 coup attempt, fears of mounting tension in the Aegean and Eastern Mediterranean, the conversion of the Hagia Sophia into a mosque and migration-related issues. All these disputes have slowed down further rapprochement, and the pattern in Turkish foreign policy once more reverted to its default securitisation setting, particularly after the 2016 coup attempt. Following an overview of the failed coup attempt and its repercussions on Turkish–Greek bilateral relations as well as Turkish politics, this part also examines the issue of the Eastern Mediterranean; the latter is quite crucial for investigating the successful securitisation of Turkish foreign policy, either through statements or through policy practices. There occurred subsequent crises in the year 2020 – an *'annus horribilis'*, in the words of Kirişci (2021a, 3) – which caused rising tensions in bilateral relations. Ranging from the humanitarian crisis triggered by Turkey threatening to 'open the borders' over the Hagia Sophia's conversion into a mosque to the brinkmanship policy of Turkey and Greece in the Eastern Mediterranean, several crises brought the two countries to the brink of conflict. All these problems in bilateral relations accompanied changes in Turkish domestic politics and precipitated adjustments in the rhetoric of Turkish decision-makers. In addition to the emerging crises of the period, Turkey's official statements, along with its naval deployments in the Eastern Mediterranean, have revealed securitising practices in its foreign policy. The analysis of the post-2016 period demonstrates a shift from desecuritisation to securitisation, but this time exclusively by civilian authorities rather than military bureaucrats.

Following this analysis of changing trends in Turkish foreign policy towards Greece in the three main parts, the conclusion briefly summarises the study and its contributions, as well as its limitations and future avenues for research. The summary analysis of each section highlights the changing trends in securitisation and desecuritisation within foreign policy and thus enables us to see their political nature. On both sides, the decision-makers' ways of handling issues continue to cause problems between the two countries. As argued in the respective parts, none of the decision-makers on either side want to take responsibility for conciliatory policies. However, there is a need for easing bilateral tensions and changing security-oriented discourses so as to pave the way for stability and cooperation between the two countries.

Notes

1. During that time, the Greeks created tension in their pursuit of the *Megali Idea*, as they were scattered throughout the southern Balkan peninsula – that is, Macedonia, Bulgaria, Albania, Serbia and Romania, as well as Cyprus and Crete. There also lived a large Greek population in the Ottoman Empire (Clogg, 1992, 55–69).
2. The Balkan Entente was established between Turkey, Greece, Yugoslavia and Romania in February 1934. The idea of cooperation between Balkan states in the interwar period originated as a reaction to revisionist powers, particularly Italy. The proposal of Italian fascist leader Benito A. Mussolini, in office from 1922 to 1943, of a Four-Power Pact aimed to initiate European cooperation between Italy, Britain, France and Germany to dictate the terms of European peace. It also forced Turkey and its Balkan neighbours to gravitate towards the entente (Barlas, 2005, 444). Turkey, as the driving force behind the cooperative relationship, sought to form a bloc of 'neutrality' in southeastern Europe by using its diplomatic influence on the Balkans (Barlas, 2005, 443–47).
3. For more information about the periods of cooperation in the Turkish–Greek relationship, see Tulça, 2003; Barlas, 2005; Demirözü, 2008.
4. After World War II, the US administration launched economic aid programmes for 'friendly regimes' under the auspices of the Truman Doctrine and the Marshall Plan. The Americans' 1947 decision to support Turkey and Greece with a policy named after President Harry S. Truman facilitated Turkey's inclusion in the Western bloc together with the US economic recovery programme in Europe, from which Turkey received aid after joining the Organisation for European Economic Cooperation (OEEC) in 1948 (Hale, 2002, 115–16).

5. On the emergence and evaluation of the Cyprus problem, see Volkan, 1979; Hannay, 2005; Kızılyürek, 2005; Palley, 2005; Hoffmeister, 2006; Dodd, 2010; Ker-Lindsay, 2011; Diez and Tocci, 2013.
6. The Copenhagen School began to develop with the collaboration between Ole Wæver and Barry Buzan under the Copenhagen Peace Research Institute (COPRI), which was established in 1985. The COPRI was institutionalised with the establishment of the Centre for Advanced Security Theory (CAST) in 2008, at the University of Copenhagen (Bilgin, 2010, 41). Today, the CAST comprises a group of core scholars and researchers of the Copenhagen School, including Ole Wæver, Barry Buzan, Jef Huysmans, Michael Williams and Lene Hansen. Hansen, with her contributions to securitisation theory, could also be identified as a representative of the Copenhagen School.
7. It should be noted that this study does not argue that the problems between Turkey and Greece are solely created by the Turkish elites – namely, securitising actors. Rather, the Turkish elites, like their Greek counterpart, have used (or securitised) the existing issues between Turkey and Greece, in line with the traditional security discourse in Turkey.
8. *Enosis* refers to the desire of Greek Cypriots to have Cyprus incorporated into Greece.
9. This law was superseded by Law No 6004, which went into effect on 7 July 2010. Sub-clauses 2(a) and 2(b), which regulate ministerial duties, remained unchanged.
10. According to Article 117 of the Constitution, '[t]he Chief of the General Staff shall be appointed by the President of the Republic following the proposal of the Council of Ministers. His/her duties and powers shall be regulated by law. The Chief of the General Staff shall be responsible to the Prime Minister in the exercise of his/her duties and powers' (Constitution of the Republic of Turkey, 1982).
11. It is important to highlight the characteristics of securitising actors, who can be classified in two groups: hawks, who advocate for an aggressive foreign policy stance in international politics, and doves, who prefer to create dialogue rather than aggression and to resolve issues without the threat of force. However, these categories may change over time. For instance, Mümtaz Soysal, a diplomatic hawk who briefly served as foreign minister between 27 July and 28 November 1994, tried to escalate tensions between Turkey and Greece during his tenure. By contrast, İsmail Cem, a dove, worked to foster dialogue between the two countries. The positions and supported discourses of both ministers are apparent in the major issues between Turkey and Greece, as discussed here.

12. Due to the strict confidentiality of National Security Council meetings, the only information available is that featured in the institution's press releases. These statements, going back to 2003, are accessible on the NSC website, but the researcher had to apply to the NSC to access earlier press memos. The tone of these press releases from the past twenty years is more general in nature. One example included the following statement: 'The NSC has reviewed the public order and security throughout the country as well as the domestic and external developments that influence them'. Such an abstract emphasis on the 'external developments' – that is, threats – and their ramifications on national security do not guide the researcher to a deeper analysis.

Part 1

TURKEY'S SECURITISATION OF GREECE (1991–99)

PART 1 INTRODUCTION

During the Cold War, the differences between Turkey and Greece on several issues brought the two countries to the brink of war and threatened the stability and security of the Western Bloc. However, the potential burden of assuming responsibility for war persuaded leaders on both sides to avoid escalation, and all crises were ultimately diffused with the support of the US and the EU within the alliance system. The demise of the East-West competition following the collapse of the Soviet Union and the beginning of a US-dominated unipolar system – with its unrivalled economic and military capabilities – created a completely different environment in international politics. In the post-Cold War era, the security agenda widened to include new issues such as environmental threats, human and drug trafficking, migration and cross-border crime. The new system also heralded an era of inter- and intra-state rivalries as result of the Soviet Union's disintegration. As Coufadakis (1996, 41) has stressed, . . .

> During the Cold War, the Soviet threat provided a convenient heuristic device to explain events, to assess emerging threats, and to formulate foreign and defense policies, even though many times such simplistic explanations only distorted the interpretation of events. The post-Cold War era created great uncertainty as to the role of states and their institutions.

Foreign and security policy-making therefore became much more complicated in the new atmosphere of the post-Cold War era. This new period inevitably also impacted Turkey and Greece. Both countries, like so many others, had to reformulate their foreign and security policies in order to address nascent security concerns. Primarily, the absence of a common enemy and changes in the nature of security threats led to this policy re-evaluation. Although Greece's security policy considerations did not change entirely, since Turkey had already represented one of its main security threats apart from the Soviet Union, the new security environment heightened Greece's perception of Turkey as a threat.[1] During the Cold War, Greece felt that it could depend on the West to prevent any attack from Turkey (Nachmani 2001, 72; Moustakis and Sheehan 2002, 82). Even reliance on the Western alliance – mainly the US and NATO – proved ineffective as a means of protection for Greece, as the Turkish intervention in Cyprus demonstrated that Greece lacked offensive capacity and deterrence against external attacks (Platias 1991, 97–98; Tsakonas and Dokos 2004, 106). The Balkan crisis in the post-Cold War period added another layer of insecurity for Greece, in addition to the existing threat from Turkey. Turkey, however, felt isolated due to the rocky start to its relationship with the EU, which had rejected its membership application in December 1989. Moreover, Turkey and Greece both felt a notable decline in their significance for their Western partners due to the disappearance of the Soviet threat in international politics. Change in the post-Cold War period became unavoidable, as numerous borders shifted and new states were founded in the vicinity of Turkey and Greece. Those changes and Turkey's security perceptions were reflected in the words of Turkish Foreign Minister Hikmet Çetin:

> Because its geopolitical and geostrategic location places Turkey in the neighbourhood of the most unstable, uncertain and unpredictable region of the world, it has turned into a frontline state faced with multiple fronts. It is at all times possible for the crises and conflicts in these regions to spread and engulf Turkey. (Sezer, 1994, 25)

Soon afterwards, the Gulf War once again highlighted Turkey's strategic importance. Turkish President Turgut Özal decided to support the US efforts in the First Gulf War in 1991 by granting access to İncirlik Air Base, shutting down its pipelines and cutting off Iraqi oil exports, thus renewing cooperation between Turkey and the United States (Türkmen, 2009, 113). This was a departure from Turkey's traditional policy, which previously had emphasised caution, non-interference and support for the status quo, as opposed to a more active foreign policy that some scholars described as 'daring' (Müfti, 1998, 48; Makovsky, 2000, 92; Türkmen, 2009, 119). Likewise, Greek foreign policy gradually began to adopt a more pragmatic character in the late 1990s, due to its diplomatic isolation following the fragmentation of Yugoslavia (Larrabee, 2005, 405–10). At the beginning of the Yugoslavia crisis, Greece was at odds with the US, unable to agree on a settlement. But the new Greek foreign policy direction largely coincided with that of the US and gained momentum with the solution-oriented Greek Prime Minister Kostas Simitis (Larrabee, 2005, 416).

In the new, unstable environment of the 1990s, the two countries stumbled into a range of crises: Greece's intentions to extend its territorial waters in the Aegean Sea, Turkey's *casus belli* decision in response to Greek desires for this expansion, the Kardak/Imia incident, the S-300 missiles crisis and the capture of the leader of the terrorist organisation PKK, Abdullah Öcalan, at the Greek Embassy in Kenya. The two countries also began to compete over issues of regional stability and balance on the Balkans. The post-Cold War tension between the two countries – key components of the Western security system – remained one of the most dangerous breaking points in Europe. As Anastasakis (2004, 45) has pointed out, the US in particular 'feared that Greece and Turkey would become part of the Balkan problem and that any new war in the region might ignite a conflict between those two countries'.

The following sections explore a range of challenges between the two countries to illustrate whether, how, by whom and to what extent Turkish decision-makers securitised issues related to Greece. This process of securitisation is defined as a speech-act 'through which an intersubjective understanding is constructed within a political community to treat something as an existential threat to a valued referent object, and to enable a call for urgent and exceptional measures to deal with the threat' (Buzan and Wæver, 2003, 491). This political process 'marks a decision, a 'breaking free of rules and the suspension of normal politics' (Williams, 2003, 518). In other words, through securitisation, 'an issue becomes a security issue not because something constitutes an objective threat to the state, but rather because an actor has defined something as existential threat to some object's survival' (Buzan and Wæver, 2003). Bilgin (2007, 559) has correspondingly emphasised the political character of the act, which 'involves making choices about how an issue would be handled: ordinary or extraordinary'. According to Wæver (2000, 251), '[i]t is always a choice to treat something as security issue'. Security is therefore defined as a political process, which can be analysed by drawing on the 'speech-act'.

Within this framework, the meaning of security becomes secondary to 'the essential quality of security in general' (Buzan et al., 1998, 26), considering it a sort of action. As Buzan et al. have argued (1998, 26), . . .

> That quality is the staging of existential issues in politics to lift them above politics. In security discourse, an issue is dramatized and presented as an issue of supreme priority; thus, by labeling it as security, an agent claims a need for and a right to treat it by extraordinary means. For the analyst to grasp this act, the task is not to assess some objective threats that 'really' endanger some object to be defended or secured; rather, it is to understand the processes of constructing a shared understanding of what is to be considered and collectively responded to as a threat.

The main aim of securitisation is, therefore, to break conventional norms and remove issues from the sphere of typical politics in order to combat threats.[2] By doing so, securitising actors use extraordinary means of 'secrecy, levying taxes or conscripts, and limitations on otherwise inviolable rights' (Wæver, 1996, 106). Buzan et al. (1998, 26) have identified the main two components of successful securitisation as 'existential threat' and 'emergency action'. Securitisation theory outlines a process that starts with evaluating a certain issue as existential threat and highlighting the issue as an emergency situation for a referent object.

However, security issues cannot be reduced merely to a subjective process. Although an issue may be dramatised as a 'supreme priority', it also requires approval, because 'whether an issue is a security issue is not something individuals decide alone' (Buzan et al., 1998, 31). The success of an attempt mainly depends on the existence of – and, to some extent, acceptance by – a relevant audience, which closely relates to the third component of securitisation: 'intersubjectivity' (Buzan et al. 1998, 26–31; Peoples and Vaughan-Williams, 2010, 78). Roe (2004, 281) has defined this intersubjective dimension of securitisation as a 'call and response' process in which 'an actor makes a call that something is a matter of "security", and the audience must then respond with their acceptance of it as such'. Without approval by the audience, the process is neither complete nor successful; it is no more than an attempt. Wæver believes that politics should be done consensually and through dialogue and deliberation, as opposed to a top-down process (Floyd, 2010, 50). This refers to the intersubjectivity of successful securitisation. Wæver (2003, 14) has described this characteristic of the process as such: '[I]n order to avoid simply moving from objective to subjective – it should be stressed that securitisation is never decided by one sovereign subject but in a constellation of decisions it is ultimately inter-subjective'.

Without the audience's acceptance, the attempt remains incomplete and is designated a 'securitizing move' rather than 'securitisation'.[3] In other words, securitising actors must convince their audience of the suspension of normal rules in this emergency situation. Thus, the approval by the relevant audience is considered a *sine qua non* for the securitisation process. A passage from the book *Security: A New Framework for Analysis* illustrates this further:

> Successful securitisation is not decided by the securitizer but by the audience of the security speech act: Does the audience accept that something is an existential threat to a shared value? Thus, security (as with all politics) ultimately rests neither with the objects nor with the subjects but *among* the subjects. (Buzan et al., 1998, 31, emphasis in original)

Buzan et al. (1998) have suggested that the security agenda could be broadened to different sectors under certain circumstances: military, political, economic, societal and environmental. In doing so, they provide a way to specify security within these five sectors and avoid over-expanding the scope of the security agenda, which wideners are inclined to do. But one could also argue that securitisation theory contributes to debates regarding the limitation of the security agenda to these five sectors. According to a study co-authored by Buzan, Wæver and de Wilde (1998, 35–36), analysing a security issue requires a clear distinction between three types of units:

'referent objects', 'securitising actors' and 'functional actors'. The referent object is something that is perceived as facing an existential threat and that has a legitimate claim to survival. As mentioned above, the Turkish state will constitute the referent object in the framework of securitisation theory as employed in this analysis. Although the state has traditionally retained its primary role as the referent object, this can vary according to the different sectors where the threat is located. In other words, the referent object is closely linked to the rhetoric used by the securitising actor; this, in turn, raises the issue of the qualifications of the speaker.

The speaker, as Wæver (2000, 252–53) has argued, must have 'social capital' and 'be in a position of authority'. Securitisation is a process that is structured, in practice, by the differential capacity of actors to make socially effective claims about threats (Williams, 2003, 514). In general, political leaders, bureaucrats or government elites fill this role, but it is still difficult to identify the securitising actor due to a variety of issues. As Buzan et al. (1998, 40) have argued, there exists a level-of-analysis problem in identifying actors, since 'the same event can be attributed to different levels (individual, bureaucracy, or state, for instance)'. These actors may consist of entities such as political elites, a government or interest groups who securitise issues by performing speech-acts. The president, prime minister, foreign minister, chief of staff and the NSC together embody the main securitising actors in Turkey's foreign policy decision-making processes. However, functional actors differ from securitising actors, since they help securitising actors identify the relevant issues due to the significant influence that they wield in decision-making processes. Yet, the influence of functional actors is limited, and they never become securitising actors.

This part of the book argues that the Turkish elites' discursive tone regarding Greece was 'threatening' and 'hostile'; notwithstanding the lack of direct war between the two countries since the foundation of the Republic of Turkey, the speech-acts of the securitising actors indicate the extent to which Turkey is prepared to engage in armed conflict with Greece. Thus, the following subsections focus on the securitising discourse that Turkish decision-makers have pushed, giving special importance to those actors' statements rather than the bilateral relations within traditional diplomacy. Accordingly, the main issues of contention between Turkey and Greece will be analysed within the framework of securitisation theory, in order to examine the speech-acts of Turkish elites.

After providing a brief background on the disputes, each section will discuss specific cases from the post-Cold War era, starting with the Turkish Grand National Assembly's (TGNA) *casus belli* declaration, as this constituted the peak of securitisation in Turkish–Greek relations. The post-Cold War disagreements between the two countries can be classified in three groups: the disputes over territorial waters in the Agean and the Kardak sovereignty issue; the Cyprus issue, specifically regarding the S-300 missile crisis; and Greece's support to terrorist organisations. The analysis of these three issues will demonstrates that the decision-makers define these issues as a matter of successful securitisation. This will suffice to illustrate the general securitisation dynamics in the 1990s.

The securitised pattern in the rhetoric of Turkish decision-makers was apparent in the reactions to Greece's ratification of the UNCLOS in its parliament, the Kardak incident, the S-300 missile crises and the revelation of Greek politicians' support for the PKK. All these cases contained the necessary components of successful securitisation: 'emergency action', 'existential threats' and the 'approval of the relevant audience'. Through securitisation, 'an issue becomes a security issue not because something constitutes an objective threat to the state, but rather because an actor has defined something as existential threat to some object's survival' (Buzan and Wæver, 2003). Bilgin (2007, 559) has correspondingly emphasised the political character of the act od securitisation, which 'involves making choices about how an issue would be handled: ordinary or extraordinary'. According to Wæver (2000, 251), '[i]t is always a choice to treat something as security issue'. Security is therefore defined as a political process, which can be analysed based on 'speech-acts'. This part of the book argues that the deterioration of bilateral relations due to a variety of crises has paved the way for securitisation policies in Turkish foreign policy. Turkey's weak coalition governments during this period understood the positive impact that securitisation policies had on the consolidation of nationalist votes, and this also influenced the country's relationship with Greece.

Notes

1. Greek sentiments towards Turkey stemmed from three historical traumas, according to Nachmani (2001, 72): the fall of Constantinople (1453), the loss of Asia Minor (1922) and the partition of Cyprus (1974).

2. Buzan et al. (1998, 25) have noted in their Pentagon example that rule-breaking can take various forms: 'Pentagon designated hackers as "a catastrophic treat" and "a serious threat to national security" that could possibly lead to actions within the computer field but with no cascading effects on other security issues'.
3. T. Balzacq (2005) has defined securitisation as an 'audience-centred' process, even though securitisation theory has no clear definition of the concept of an 'audience'. Critiques of this vagueness will be discussed below.

2

THE DISPUTES IN THE AEGEAN SEA

The semi-enclosed[1] Aegean Sea is located between the Greek and Turkish mainlands; it is connected to the fully enclosed Marmara Sea and Black Sea in the north and to the open Mediterranean Sea in the south. The Aegean Sea covers about 214,000 square kilometres between the geographic coordinates 41° to 35° North and 23° to 27°/28° East. It contains more than 1,800 islands, islets and rocks, although only about a hundred of these are inhabited, with the rest being uninhabitable due to unsuitable conditions (Başeren, 2006, 5–7; İnan and Acer, 2004, 1). As a passage between the closed-off bodies of water to the north and the open Mediterranean Sea, the Aegean Sea is vital to both Turkey and the littoral states of the Black Sea.

As the two littoral states, Turkey and Greece have been at odds for decades over disputes in the Aegean Sea. The main sources of this contention relate to sovereignty rights over the islands, islets and rocks in the Aegean Sea, the delimitation of maritime boundaries and the continental shelf, the breadth of territorial waters, control over the airspace and the demilitarised status of the East Aegean islands. However, the two countries are unable to define even the exact number of conflict areas; in fact, Greece has only endorsed the continental shelf issue among all other prevailing challenges. In either way, in essence, 'conflict is not the territory itself, but mainly about control over the vital area of the Aegean Sea' (Siegl, 2002, 41).

In the eyes of Turkish decision-makers, Greece's claims over territorial waters and airspace in the Aegean would effectively turn it into a 'Greek lake', and Turkey would be locked out of the Aegean Sea (Bölükbaşı, 1992, 38). Turkey's insistent perception of an existential security threat emanating from Greece and reference to the survival of the referent object is regularly visible in the statements of the Turkish elites. For instance, Ambassador Şükrü Elekdağ, a former under-secretary to the minister of foreign affairs, has argued: 'The military equipment trends of Greece between 1989 and 1995 as well as the defence expenditures showed its intention to change the balance of air and naval power in the Aegean in its favour, which are detrimental to the vital interests of Turkey' (Elekdağ, 1996, 35–37). Likewise, Deputy Chief of General Staff General Ahmet Çörekçi also stated: 'It is observed that Greece is simultaneously preparing to seize sovereignty over the Aegean and to annex Northern Cyprus. A miscalculation would make war inevitable. The Turkish Armed Forces are prepared to protect the country's interests and to neutralise the threat' (*Milliyet*, 1 July 1995).

Turkish decision-makers, or securitising actors, have usually feared that Greek policies would sever Turkey's free access to open waters – which is vital for the country – through the Aegean Sea. This was a continuation of the traditional security discourse. As clearly seen in Elekdağ's statement, any changes in the regional balance of power were perceived as an existential threat and would be, in his words, 'detrimental to the vital interests of Turkey'. While his statement did not incorporate an 'emergency action' in the face of this threat, this emphasis does appear in the statement of the deputy chief of general staff. In addition to the significance that General Ahmet Çörekçi assigned to an existential threat – as he perceived Greek preparations to threaten the 'country's interests' – he also dramatised the issue by stressing the inevitability of war as result of Greece's actions. Çörekçi proposed emergency actions to neutralise the threat that Greece allegedly posed.

The developments of the 1990s were not independent from the major issues unfolding in the Aegean. Although this book focuses specifically on post-Cold War attempts at securitisation, it is worth to analyse the main disputes between the two countries within the framework of securitisation theory to understand the problems also in a broader context. In doing so, this book will untangle the root causes of the tensions between Turkey and

Greece to determine whether the statements of Turkish decision-makers are consistent. The following pages will examine the historical background to the contentious issues between the two countries in two categories: delimitation and sovereignty rights. The first category includes issues such as the breadth of territorial waters as well as of the continental shelf, while the second category covers the matter of sovereignty over islands and islets and the fortification of islands in the Aegean Sea.

Issues of Delimitation in the Aegean Sea

The Question of the Continental Shelf: The Background

New developments in international law regarding the definition of 'continental shelf', which the Geneva Convention on the Continental Shelf defined in 1958 and implemented in 1964, added a new dimension to the existing disputes between Turkey and Greece. The continental shelf issue mainly stems from the absence of a delimitation agreement between Turkey and Greece, due to their disagreements around the topic. The Geneva Convention on the Continental Shelf (United Nations Treaty Series, 1964, 311–21) has defined the continental shelf as follows:

> (a) to the seabed and subsoil of the submarine areas adjacent to the coast but outside the area of the territorial sea, to a depth of 200 meters or, beyond that limit, to where the depth of the superjacent waters admits of the exploitation of the natural resources of the said areas; (b) to the seabed and subsoil of similar submarine areas adjacent to the coasts of islands.

The differences over the convention initially did not cause problems in the Turkish–Greek bilateral relations; however, the desire to explore natural resources paved the way for a new dispute between the two countries. As a signatory to the Geneva Convention, Greece claimed exclusive off-shore mineral rights to about two-thirds of the Aegean Sea and issued a number of exploration licenses to petroleum companies during the 1960s, when oil reserves were discovered near the Greek island of Thassos (Hale, 2002, 159; İnan and Acer, 2004, 29; Ker-Lindsay, 2007, 19–20). In response, Turkey, which had refused to be a party to the convention due to concerns over the Aegean islands, conducted its first seismic research activity in 1968. But with the intensification of Greek activities in the Aegean Sea, it also granted exploration permits to the state-owned Turkish Petroleum Company (TPAO) in 1973, for twenty-seven locations across the Aegean Sea – along several in the Sea of Marmara – that did not exceed the median line between the Turkish and Greek mainlands (Bölükbaşı, 2004, 239–40; Hamilton and Salmon, 2012, 41).

While the two countries had not negotiated any delimitation agreements in the Aegean, both have maintained contradictory claims over the continental shelf. Traditionally, Greece has argued that this is a legal issue and should be resolved with the adjudication of the International Court of Justice (ICJ), in accordance with the 1958 Geneva Convention and the 1982 United Nations Convention on the Law of Sea. Greece has argued that it rightfully owns most of the continental shelf, because 'Greece is a state consisting of mainland and its islands', therefore requiring a review of the territorial integrity and indivisibility of the state in accordance with international law (Fırat, 2010, 457). Moreover, Greece recognises only the continental shelf issue as a legitimate dispute and rejects Turkish claims on other issues. In contrast, Turkey has preferred bilateral negotiations regarding the continental shelf and other interrelated issues in the Aegean, rather than ICJ mediation, as it has perceived the issue in a political – rather than legal – context. Turkey has argued that much of the continental shelf is a geological extension of the Anatolian mainland, and that the islands located on the natural prolongation of Anatolia cannot have a continental shelf (Aydın, 1997, 118; Athanassopoulou, 1997, 77; Fırat, 2010, 457). Accordingly, the Turkish government believes that delimitation should be on an equal basis considering the special circumstances of this semi-enclosed sea.

A conflict erupted in May 1974 when a Turkish survey ship, the *Çandarlı*, conducted seismic research in areas previously granted to the TPAO, but developments in Cyprus later that year temporarily pushed the tension in the Aegean Sea to the background (Hale, 2002, 160; Bölükbaşı, 2004, 240). Nevertheless, the two countries exchanged a number of diplomatic notes during this period. On 28 January 1975, the Karamanlis administration in Greece proposed that the two countries appeal to the ICJ to resolve this disagreement, prompting a reply from the Turks on 6 February 1975: 'In principle, [the Turkish government] favourably considers the Greek government's proposal to refer the dispute of delimitation of the Aegean continental shelf jointly to the ICJ' (Bölükbaşı, 2004, 242; Heraclides, 2010, 83).

Subsequent meetings between the foreign and prime ministers culminated in a joint communique that then Turkish Prime Minister Süleyman Demirel and Greek Prime Minister Constantine Karamanlis issued on 31 May 1975. Both sides agreed to resolve outstanding problems through negotiations and to elevate the continental shelf issue to the ICJ. According to the Brussels Communique (1975, paras 94–108), '[t]hey [the two prime ministers] had decided that those problems should be resolved peacefully by means of negotiations and as regards the continental shelf of the Aegean Sea by the ICJ at the Hague'. However, Demirel later back-tracked under domestic pressure; on 30 November 1975, he declared that substantial negotiations should first be held and that the ICJ option, if necessary, should only be considered as a last resort (Heraclides, 2010, 86). Disputes around potential oil reserves in the Aegean Sea have persisted as a source of threat between Turkey and Greece. Issues related to the continental shelf caused relations to worsen and tensions to escalate at various points in time, for instance, in 1976 and 1987.

Meetings between Turkey and Greece started in Berne at the end of January 1976. Two meetings between experts – between 31 January and 2 February and, later, between 19 and 20 June 1976 – proved fruitless, with both sides insisting on their traditional arguments. A potential crisis between Turkey and Greece flared up in the summer of 1976 when Turkey deployed a seismic research ship, the *Hora* (or *Sismik I*), accompanied by warships, to conduct scientific research in the disputed regions west of Lesbos *(Midilli)* between 6 and 8 August 1976. The Greek armed forces went on full alert, with some leaders proposing extreme measures. Pan-Hellenic Socialist Party (PASOK) leader Andreas Papandreou, for instance, called for the sinking of the *Hora*, an act that undoubtedly would have resulted in war. Karamanlis, on his part, reacted calmly and opted for recourse to both the UNSC and the ICJ (Clogg, 1992, 176; Heraclides, 2010, 88). As Bölükbaşı (2004, 260) has written, this was the only instance of appeal to the UNSC throughout the long history of Turkish–Greek disputes in the Aegean.

On 10 August 1976, George Papoulias, the permanent Greek ambassador to the UN, issued a letter to the UNSC president, requesting an urgent meeting on the grounds that, 'following recent repeated flagrant violations by Turkey of the sovereign rights of Greece on its continental shelf in the Aegean, a dangerous situation has been created threatening international peace and security' (UNSC, 1976). In response, the UNSC adopted Resolution 395 on 25 August 1976, calling upon the parties 'to resume direct negotiations' leading to a 'mutually acceptable solution', and invited Turkey and Greece to continue 'appropriate judicial means, in particular the ICJ, [which] are qualified to make the settlement of any remaining legal differences' (UNSC, 1976).

A unilateral appeal that Greece filed with the ICJ on 10 August 1976 requested the institution's services for 'interim provisional measures of protection in order to preserve the respective right of the parties' and 'to call both Greece and Turkey to refrain from any exploration activity or any scientific research' without the consent of their counterparts and the final judgement of the ICJ. On 11 September 1976, the ICJ rejected the Greek request on both counts. While the ICJ denied the Greek request for interim measures in its 11 September 1976 decision, on the grounds that there was not sufficient risk of irreparable damage to Greece's rights, it later decided, by a vote of twelve to two, on 19 December 1978, that it had no judicial authority to entertain the Greek appeal regarding disputes between Turkey and Greece over the continental shelf (İnan and Acer, 2004, 31; Bölükbaşı, 2004, 267–68; Fırat, 2010, 456).

Following UNSC Resolution 395(1976), both sides decided to resume bilateral dialogue, ultimately leading to the Berne Agreement on the Continental Shelf on 11 November 1976. After a series of meetings, the parties compromised on a ten-point agreement, which contained principles for negotiations that would resume in secrecy to 'reach an agreement based on mutual consent regarding the delimitation of the continental shelf'. Moreover, the sixth and seventh articles of the Berne Agreement (1976) stipulated that both parties would refrain from any initiative or action concerning the continental shelf:

6. Both parties undertake to abstain from any initiative or act relating to the Continental Shelf of the Aegean Sea which might prejudice the negotiations.
7. Both parties undertake, as far as their bilateral relations are concerned, to abstain from any initiative or act which would tend to discredit the other party.

The naming of the document already caused problems. The document is known as the 'Berne Communique' in Greece in order to downgrade its importance, whereas Turkey called it the 'Berne Declaration' in an attempt to elevate its significance (Heraclides, 2010, 90). The agreement is still valid and binding for the two countries.

In the vein of this positive atmosphere was a summit between Prime Minister Bülent Ecevit, who had recently assumed leadership from Süleyman Demirel, and his Greek counterpart, Constantine Karamanlis. The two leaders met in Montreux on 11–12 March 1978 to build trust between the two countries. As Heraclides (2010, 96) has written, 'Montreux is unique and of considerable value, for it was the first and in fact the last time that the leaders of two countries discussed, at length and in detail, the Aegean dispute as a whole'. The two countries resumed *ad referendum* talks at different levels – between experts, secretaries-general and foreign ministers – for three and a half years. However, the spirit of Montreux, which had sparked hope for the normalisation of relations and the resolution of disputes, collapsed dramatically in late 1981. Several factors fundamentally altered the trajectory of long-term bilateral relations, including the victory of Andreas Papandreou, who regularly criticised the resumption of talks with Turkey, PASOK's performance in the general elections on 18 October 1981 and Greece's accession to the European Economic Community (EEC) as its tenth member-state on 1 January 1981.

Meanwhile, Turkey declared Greece to be the primary threat in its updated National Defence Concept Paper after the dialogues over the Aegean Sea disputes had failed (Fırat, 2010, 457). Likewise, the Papandreou government announced, in December 1984, that Greece's new defence doctrine would regard Turkey as the country's main external threat following an incident on 8 March 1984, when five Turkish warships fired on a Greek destroyer patrolling the Aegean Sea (Ker-Lindsay, 2007, 23). Despite the fragility of the relationship between Turkey and Greece and the Greek government's reservations regarding Turkey, Turgut Özal, the new prime minister of Turkey, showed his willingness to initiate channels of dialogue between the two countries. Özal's approach to foreign policy was mainly driven by economic interests rather than focusing on existing problems. This compelled him to extend an 'olive branch' to the Greek government with a slew of overtures – lifting the visa requirement for Greek citizens visiting Turkey, calling for a cooperation agreement to enhance trade between the two countries and granting some concessions to Turkey's Greek minority (Ker-Lindsay, 2007, 23–24; Heraclides, 2010, 118). Despite all his efforts to put aside the problems and to instigate dialogue between Turkey and Greece, Papandreou persisted in his hard-line stance.

Another crisis erupted in the Aegean Sea in March 1987, following a series of misunderstandings regarding oil exploration. When Greece announced its purchase of shares of the Canadian-led North Aegean Petroleum Company, which on 18 February had received permission to actively drill in the Aegean Sea in order to conduct oil exploration operations outside of Greece's territorial waters – in areas adjacent to Thassos Island – Turkey proceeded to issue a license on 25 March to the state-owned TPAO for exploration in the disputed areas (Aydın, 1997, 118; Ker-Lindsay, 2007, 24–25; Heraclides, 2010, 120–21). Turkey viewed Greece's actions as violations of the Berne Agreement. In a statement, Turkish Ministry of Foreign Affairs Spokesperson Yalım Eralp articulated the Turkish government's opposition to Greece's initiatives:

> Greece's oil exploration activities beyond its continental shelf, until the signing of a delimitation agreement between the two countries on the continental shelf, is a violation of the Bern Agreement of 1976, which prescribed abstention from such behaviours. So far, Turkey has followed the Bern Agreement with maximum sensitivity and abstained from any initiatives relating to the continental shelf. In this context, Greece must immediately stop its violations. Otherwise, Turkey will take all necessary precautions in order to protect its rights and interests in the Aegean Sea. (*The Directorate General of Press and Information*, 5 March 1987)

Following Greece's oil exploration activities outside its own territorial waters, the Turkish Ministry of Foreign Affairs, through its spokesperson, warned Greek officials of their breach of the Berne Agreement, stressing 'Turkey's rights and interests in the Aegean Sea'. As Eralp's statement has highlighted, Greece's activities negatively impacted Turkey's rights and interests in the context of the continental shelf issue, and Turkey called for an 'immediate' stop to Greek activities. Eralp cautioned that the Turkish government would adopt 'all necessary precautions' if Greece persisted. This statement mentioned an existential threat and referenced emergency measures, thus embodying a successful securitisation of the issue.

The tension between the two countries came to a boiling point shortly after Turkey had sent its vessel, the *Piri Reis*, to conduct seismic research off the coasts of the Greek islands of Lemnos (*Limni*), Lesbos (*Midilli*) and Samothrace (*Semadirek*), which Greece considers to be on its own continental shelf (Aydın, 1997, 118; Ker-Lindsay, 2007, 25). This constituted one of the most serious instances of tension between the two countries since 1974. The crisis was also important in terms of the balance of power between the hawks and the doves in the Turkish decision-making mechanisms. As reflected in the Turkish media several years after the crisis, the tension was created by Minister of State Hasan Celal Güzel in 1987, in the absence of both Turkish Prime Minister Turgut Özal, who had left the country to receive heart surgery, and Turkish Minister of Foreign Affairs Vahit Halefoğlu, who was abroad for a meeting. Turkish Minister of State Hasan Celal Güzel unveiled his strategy during the crisis of 1987 in an interview:

> [Turkey] missed a historical opportunity when Turgut Özal stepped in. If we [Turkey] could have put more pressure, Greece would never sail in the Aegean Sea anymore. The U-turn on this issue was against Turkey's national interest. But, unfortunately, Turgut Özal run counter it and destroyed our plans. (*Cumhuriyet*, 9 July 1994)

In response to Turkey's research in the region, Greek Prime Minister Papandreou issued a harsh warning and threatened to use military force in order to halt the vessel, an action deemed unacceptable in the eyes of Turkish officials, who responded accordingly (Ker-Lindsay, 2007, 25; Heraclides, 2010, 120). General Güven Ergenç, the secretary-general of the Turkish chief of staff, outlined Turkey's stance on the issue in a statement he gave during the crisis: 'The air force, navy and army are in a state of alert. [. . .] If there is an attack it is clear what has to be done. An attack on a warship is a cause for war' (*The New York Times*, 28 March 1987).

Likewise, Turkish Prime Minister Özal, in an interview with BBC Two on 27 March 1987, declared:

> If [the Greeks] take action for oil exploration in the international seas, it would be our natural right to sail to the international seas, even if not the same place, and perform research activities as well. But if they touch our ship by arguing that 'The international sea is under our control', it would be a *casus belli*. (*The Directorate General of Press and Information*, 28 March 1987)

Although the statements by Ergenç and Özal did not contain all the necessary components of securitisation, they are remarkable examples of the security grammar that political figures utilised to emphasise a *casus belli* regarding Greek interference with Turkish ships exploring for oil in international waters.

The controversy between the two countries was once again defused upon the encouragement of the US and the NATO. On 28 March 1987, Özal guaranteed that Turkish ships would avoid any exploratory activities outside of Turkish territorial waters so long as Greece did not enter the disputed waters (*The New York Times*, 29 March 1987). Soon afterwards, Özal and Andreas Papandreou met at the World Economic Forum in Davos in January 1988, seeking to establish a mechanism of dialogue between the two countries so as to prevent future crises. The Davos Process, which was a clear attempt to defuse tension and build confidence between Turkey and Greece, was a significant deviation from Papandreou's traditional 'no-dialogue policy' with Turkey (Aydın, 1997, 121; Tsakonas, 2010, 46–47). Within the framework of the Davos Process, the two countries also signed a Memorandum of Understanding on 27 May 1988 and Guidelines for the Prevention of Accidents and Incidents on the High Seas and Airspace on 8 September 1988, with the goal to foster mutual trust in the bilateral relationship.

Following the crises over the continental shelf, first in 1976 and later in 1987, the leaders of the two countries effectively sought resolution by using channels of dialogue. Although several scholars interpret the Davos Process as the third rapprochement process and 'the fore-runner of the more recent rapprochement between two countries' (Öniş and Yılmaz, 2001, 2; Kutlay, 2009), the Davos Process was a short-term cooperation initiative engineered by Turgut Özal, which quickly crumbled by the end of 1989. Some progress was made in developing a set of confidence-building measures to prevent accidents in international Aegean waters, but the uncooperative public opinion and media attitudes, swelling domestic pressure and challenges from the political opposition quickly disrupted the momentum of the 'Davos spirit' (Aydın, 1997, 121; Rumelili, 2004, 5). Even the Greek–Turkish Business Council, which had been founded to deepen economic ties in the spirit of cooperation that the Davos Meetings had engendered, remained inactive (Liargovas, 2003, 133; Oğuzlu, 2004, 95; Heraclides, 2010, 151). According to Tsarouhas (2009, 44), '[b]usiness attempts at cooperation were kept in the shadow of the complex political agenda'.

The dispute between Turkey and Greece over the continental shelf remains politically and legally unresolved. As with other problems in the Aegean, both parties have pursued compromise rather than consensus on the issues (Aksu, 2002, 111). These fundamental problems fester in their relationship and drive both countries further into conflict.

The Breadth of Territorial Waters: The Background

It was the Treaty of Lausanne in 1923 that outlined the principles regarding the breadth of territorial waters, granting littoral states a limit of three nautical miles. In 1936, Greece unilaterally extended this from three to six nautical miles, at a time when the relationship with Turkey was generally cordial. At the time, Turkey did not perceive Greece's expansion as an act of hostility, but it did also extend its own territorial waters to six nautical miles on 15 May 1964, when relations between the two countries had soured because of the Cyprus problem.

The countries maintained amicable relations as late as the 1960s, since both countries upheld similar ideals around the expanse of territorial waters. Until 1958, during the first UN Conference on Law of the Sea (UNCLOS I), both Greece and Turkey supported the three-mile limit, even though Greece had already extended the limit of its territorial waters to six nautical miles. Even at the UNCLOS II, held from 17 March to 26 April 1960, Greece opposed a limit of twelve nautical miles and favoured the six-mile limit, arguing that such an extension would not be in the best interest of the international community, as it would close seas to international navigation, hinder trade and cause friction (Bölükbaşı, 2004, 129–30; Heraclides, 2010, 181–82).

However, Greece drastically altered its position on territorial waters in 1974, instead favouring the twelve-mile limit. This abrupt reversal coincided with the emergence of the Cyprus problem and the increased tensions that accompanied it. During that time, an early signal of Turkey's securitisation of the issue appeared: a letter that Turkish Foreign Minister İhsan Sabri Çağlayangil sent to US Secretary of State Henry Kissinger on 15 April 1976. In the letter, Çağlayangil, as one of the Turkish securitising actors, declared:

It is obvious that the Greek government's fundamental aim is to create a *fait accompli* by extending its territorial waters to 12 miles, and by doing so, gaining a political victory over Turkey. Such a move might cause the Aegean Sea to be transformed into a Greek lake, and as a result it would de facto abolish Turkey's inherent and traditional rights in [the Aegean Sea]. This situation will give Turkey no choice but to consider this development a *casus belli*. (*Milliyet*, 11 February 1996)

Following the changes in Greece's position on maritime borders, Çağlayangil cautioned Kissinger about the threat that the Greek policy posed, mentioning its negative implications on Turkey's rights and interests in the Aegean. Any Greek political victory in the Aegean would sever Turkey's access to the high seas – an existential threat to its national security. Çağlayangil also dramatised the territorial intentions of the Greek government, prominently employing the term 'Greek lake'. In his letter, Çağlayangil warned Kissinger about the emergency measures that the Turkish government would be forced to take and noted that the government considered the Greek policy a *casus belli*. The letter included a direct and explicit call for emergency measures, overstepping the established rules and eclipsing normal politics by emphasising that the government had 'no choice' but to adopt the necessary measures. The letter's tone clearly demonstrates the change in the securitising actors' rhetoric, parallel to the changes in the Greek government's policies. This letter exemplified successful securitisation, having been penned by the Turkish foreign minister, a representative of a democratically elected government that naturally garners the approval of the relevant audience – approval being an essential component of securitisation. The earliest changes regarding the territorial waters would become more explicit in the discourse of securitising actors in the 1990s.

The issue continued to exist without any serious crisis, because both sides refrained from confrontation until the approval of the UN Convention on Law of the Sea (UNCLOS) on 10 December 1982. The convention introduced a new dimension to the ongoing dispute, with Article 3 confirming that 'every state has the right to establish the breadth of its territorial sea up to a limit not exceeding 12 nautical miles, measured from baselines determined in accordance with this Convention' (UNCLOS, 1982). The two countries maintained divergent positions on the topic of territorial waters. Greece, as a signatory to the convention, supported the idea that every state has the right to establish a maritime territory extending twelve miles from its coast, as Article 3 of the UNCLOS confirmed. It was the UNCLOS that determined the expanse of territorial waters for both the Greek mainland and the Greek islands, ensuring that this limit could not be restricted (Aydın, 1997, 116; Fırat, 2010, 454). In contrast, the Turkish government claimed that the UNCLOS-defined limits constituted a maximum, not an automatic and universal designation, particularly in enclosed or semi-closed bodies of water – a category that included the Aegean Sea (Heraclides, 2010, 182–84; Fırat, 2010, 453–54). Because the semi-enclosed Aegean Sea contains a great number of Greek islands and has unique geographic features, such a unilateral expansion would adversely affect Turkish rights and interests regarding navigational freedoms and sovereignty (Bölükbaşı, 2004, 186; Fırat, 2010, 454; Heraclides, 2010, 184). Under the previous six-mile limit, Greece and Turkey controlled approximately 43.5 percent and 7.5 percent of the Aegean Sea, respectively, designating the rest as international waters. If the twelve-mile limit were applied to the Aegean Sea, Greek territorial waters would leap to a share of 71.5 percent, while Turkey's share would increase slightly to 8.8 percent, and only 19.7 percent of the sea would be considered international waters (Wilson, 1979/1980, 36–37). This would drastically limit the ability of Turkish vessels to access the high seas, and Turkey would become land-locked, since all Turkish vessels would be forced to pass through Greek territorial waters to reach the Mediterranean.

Starting in 1982, the Greek government issued several statements claiming its right to adopt the provisions of the UNCLOS. The Turkish government, in response, consistently reiterated its objections to Greece's unilateral extension – an alleged violation of international law – also considering it an act of provocation. After the most recent crisis over the continental shelf in 1987, tensions once again escalated when the UNCLOS went into effect on 16 November 1994. Fears that Greece would extend its territorial waters to twelve nautical miles immediately after the UNCLOS went into effect appeared in the statements of Turkish decision-makers. Foreign Minister Mümtaz Soysal, for instance, in an interview answered a question about who would benefit from a potential conflict between Turkey and Greece:

> In case of a conflict, we know who will have the greater advantage. But we do not think that such a benefit befits us. We can defeat Greece. But this

means war – people would die. It is not right to ask for it, so we do not want it either. [. . .] We want to provide peace by saying we will fight to defend our rights. An extension beyond six miles is a *casus belli*. (*Cumhuriyet*, 15 November 1994)

Soysal's statement was a continuation of the official Turkish position on any Greek attempts at expansion. His statement collectively included both defiant and prudent tones. While he cautioned Greece about Turkey's ability to emerge victorious from an armed conflict waged to defend its own rights, he emphasised peace as well as Turkey's hesitancy to be drawn into a conflict.

Ironically, a day before the UNCLOS went into effect, Turks and Greeks conducted simultaneous air and naval exercises in the Aegean, code-named *Denizkurdu 2–94* (Sea Wolf 2–94) and *Niriis-94*, respectively. The two countries' exercises entailed overlapping plans, but the exercises concluded without any incident (*Cumhuriyet*, 15 November 1994). However, Turkey's traditional security perception became prominent once more when the Greek parliament ratified the UNCLOS on 31 May 1995, granting Greece the right to extend its territorial waters (Athanassopoulou, 1997, 76; Müfti, 1998, 34; Ker-Lindsay, 2007, 29; Grigoriadis, 2011, 129). The Greek government viewed limiting territorial waters to six nautical miles a threat to its territorial continuity in the Eastern Aegean and, because of the geographically dispersed nature of the Greek islands, to the links between the islands and the Greek mainland (Siegl, 2002, 41). In contrast, Turkey, which had refused to sign the convention and proclaimed itself a 'persistent objector', contended that Greece's territorial demands would virtually sever Turkey's maritime connection to the high seas and enclose Turkey (Aydın, 1997, 116; Siegl, 2002, 41). A verbal declaration that the Turkish parliament adopted in June 1995 embodied Turkey's official position on the unilateral extension, which it declared to be a *casus belli*.

Upon receiving early signals that the Greek parliament had ratified the UNCLOS, Turkish decision-makers issued relatively calm statements in response. Turkish Foreign Minister Murat Karayalçın, for instance, had previously stated: 'We are closely monitoring Greece's attempts, but the current situation does not necessitate any concrete reactions yet' (*Milliyet*, 1 January 1995). However, after Greece ratified the UNCLOS, Turkey – which was not a signatory to the UNCLOS – changed its stance considerably. In response to Greece's attempt, the TGNA unanimously agreed on the declaration on 8 June 1995. The official announcement of the resolution by the TGNA (1995) stated the following:

> While [the TGNA] hopes that the government of Greece will not decide to expand its territorial waters in the Aegean beyond six miles in a fashion which will disrupt the balance established in [the Treaty of] Lausanne. [The TGNA] has decided to grant to the Turkish government all powers, including those that would be deemed militarily necessary, in order to safeguard and defend the vital interests of our country in such a case, and to announce this to the Greeks and the global public with friendly sentiments.

With this declaration, the TGNA granted the government the right to take all necessary measures and declare a *casus belli*. The TGNA's official statement is highly relevant since it includes all the components of successful securitisation. The governing body acknowledged Greek attempts at territorial expansion as existential threats to Turkey's vital interests. By disrupting the system that the Treaty of Lausanne had established, Greece was trying to change the status quo in the Aegean Sea, thus constituting a direct threat against Turkey's sovereignty and security. The wording of the statement shifted the context of the issue away from a normal bargaining process and granted the Turkish government the authority to adopt emergency measures, including military action, to ensure the defence of the country and its interests abroad. Despite the emphasis on 'friendly sentiments', the warning about the necessary actions to respond to the Greeks was a direct result of the TGNA's securitised discourse. The relevant audience's natural approval of the TGNA's decisions is also assumed to be present, as the legislative body comprises democratically elected representatives and members of the Council of Ministers.

The securitising actors continued their statements in a similar tone, even after the TGNA's declaration. For instance, a representative of the Turkish Armed Forces reiterated the mention of emergency measures to counter threats in a press briefing: 'Any situation that breaks the status quo in the Aegean Sea would make a potential war unavoidable' (*Milliyet*, 23 July 1995). Likewise, Turkish Foreign Minister Erdal İnönü declared that 'Turkey would see Greek enforcement of the treaty as a hostile act', after saying that he did 'not expect Greece to extend its waters' and was 'hoping to hold talks on the topic' (*The New York Times*, 2 June 1995). The Permanent Turkish Representative to the UN İnal Batu, in response to Greek accusations, sent a letter to UN Secretary-General Boutros Ghali on 22 June 1995 in order to share Turkey's concerns about Greece's intentions in the Aegean Sea and to emphasise his country's determination not to allow border violations in territorial waters: 'Turkey would not hesitate to take necessary precautions based on the developments, and it is determined to protect its rights and interests, including the protection of the status-quo in the Aegean Sea from attempts at *fait accompli*' (*The Directorate General of Press and Information*, 23 June 1995).

The points argued in the letter were a continuation of the previous discourse of the securitising actors. As a high-ranking representative of Turkey in the UN, Ambassador İnal Batu's statement clearly reflected the official position of the Turkish government and the Turkish Ministry of Foreign Affairs. Ambassador İnal Batu once again articulated the existential threat – Greek 'attempts at *fait accompli*' and territorial expansion – in order to reiterate that the government would adopt measures in response. The letter also noted the existential threat against the referent object's rights and interests. The letter's discourse clearly demonstrated the securitisation rhetoric, which had previously been explicit with the Turkish parliament's declaration of a *casus belli*.

In addition to the declaration and statements, the Turkish Armed Forces conducted the military exercises *Efes*-95 and *Denizkurdu*-1/95 in the Aegean Sea immediately after the Greek parliament had ratified the UNCLOS. These military exercises turned the decision-makers' speech-acts into security professionals' practice – something that the authors of the Paris School, also known as International Political Sociology, consider significant (Baysal et al., 2019). In response, Greek officials accused Turkey of exacerbating tensions in the Aegean Sea as an act of retaliation. But Turkish Armed Forces officials denied the Greek allegations and emphasised that the exercises had been scheduled well in advance, as reflected in the following statement: 'The exercise is a scheduled one which has been advised to all countries concerned long before. There is nothing about it to escalate tension' (*The New York Times*, 2 June 1995).

The contention over the breadth of territorial waters and the status of the islands, islets and rocks in the Aegean Sea brought Turkey and Greece to the brink of direct confrontation over subsequent years. A Turkish ship, the *Figen Akat*, sparked one particular crisis on 25 December 1995, when it ran aground while travelling through the Aegean Sea. This crisis constitutes another significant case-study to highlight the continued securitisation in Turkey. It is worth examining the context, causes and aftermath of this crisis in a different section, after focusing on two further disputes between Turkey and Greece in the Aegean Sea: airspace and the militarisation – as well as demilitarisation – of islands.

Sovereignty and Fortification in the Aegean Sea

Because of the Ottoman Empire's sovereignty over the Aegean islands,[2] islets and rocks – dating back to its conquest of Constantinople in 1453 – developments concerning these formations have had ramifications on their contemporary sovereignty. Several diplomatic and international agreements have laid out the status of the Aegean islands, islets and rocks, including the Treaty of Lausanne (1923), the Montreux Straits Convention (1936) and the Paris Peace Treaty (1947). However, changes in the sovereignty rights between Italy, the Ottoman Empire and Greece, especially in the past century, resulted in serious contention. While Italy occupied the Twelve Islands during the 1911–12 Tripolitania-Benghazi War, which Italy fought with the Ottoman Empire, Greece occupied the Strait Region Islands and the Saruhan Islands during the 1912–13 Balkan Wars. The Twelve Islands remained under Italy's control after the Treaty of Lausanne had been signed in 1923, and Greece occupied the other group of islands, except for Imbros (*Gökçeada*), Tenedos (*Bozcaada*) and Rabbit Island (*Tavşan Adası*).

Articles 6, 12 and 15 of the Treaty of Lausanne clearly regulated the sovereignty over the islands in the Aegean Sea. Article 6 states that 'islands and islets lying within three miles of the coast are included within the frontier of the coastal state', while Article 12 outlines sovereignty rights for Greece and Turkey:

> [R]egarding the sovereignty of Greece over the islands of the Eastern Mediterranean, other than the islands of Imbros, Tenedos and Rabbit Islands, particularly the islands of Lemnos, Samothrace, Mytilene, Chios, Samos and Nikaria, is confirmed, subject to the provisions of the present Treaty respecting the

islands placed under the sovereignty of Italy which form the subject of Article 15. Except where a provision to the contrary is contained in the present Treaty, the islands situated at less than three miles from the Asiatic coast remain under Turkish sovereignty.

Although Article 15 set forth the sovereignty over the Twelve Islands, their status was finally settled in the Paris Peace Treaty of 1947. According to Article 14 of the Paris Peace Treaty, Italy transferred the sovereignty of the Dodecanese Islands (Twelve Islands) and the adjacent islands to Greece.

Turkey and Greece interpret the provisions of these treaties differently. Greece argues that all the islands lying beyond three miles – except for Gökçeada, Bozcaada and the Tavşan Islands – belong to Greece, whereas Turkey claims that only the islands mentioned explicitly in the treaty were left to Greece. Turkey also asserted that 'islands beyond three miles distance but not mentioned in name should be regarded as inherited by Turkey as the successor of the Ottoman Empire' (İnan and Acer, 2004, 7). Additionally, Turkey declared its intention to determine, through bilateral negotiations with Greece, the sovereignty over the islands outside of this three-mile boundary, which were not explicitly left to Greece (İnan and Acer, 2004, 7). According to Başeren (2006, 49), there are approximately 150 islands, islets and rocks in the Aegean Sea whose sovereignty status has not yet been determined.

Apart from the sovereignty rights over the islands, islets and rocks, Turkey and Greece have long been at odds with each other over the fortification and militarisation of the Eastern Aegean islands. Both Turkey and Greece have variously interpreted the legal effects of the several treaties regarding the status of the islands; thus, the two countries have not been able to reach any agreement about this issue. The first disagreement pertains to the Greek islands of Lemnos (*Limni*) and Samothrace (*Semadirek*), and the Turkish islands of Imbros (*Gökçeada*), Tenedos (*Bozcaada*) and Rabbit Island (*Tavşan Adası*), which are collectively known as the Strait Region Islands. While Article 4 of the Convention on the Regime of the Straits annexed to the Treaty of Lausanne regulated the demilitarised status of the islands, Article 6 of the convention offered details about the types of military units and equipment in these demilitarised zones. For instance, it only allowed police and gendarmerie forces to occupy the demilitarised zones and to be armed only with revolvers, swords, rifles and four Lewis guns for every hundred men.

In 1936, Turkey requested that the Convention on the Turkish Straits be revised in order to adapt to new developments in international politics. On 20 July 1936, the status of the islands was changed, and the 1936 Montreux Straits Convention granted Turkey the right to 'remilitarise the zone of the Straits'. Greece claimed that the Lausanne Convention had replaced the Montreux Straits Convention and, as such, given Greece the right to militarise Lemnos and Samothrace, which had ben demilitarised along with both shores of the straits under the Treaty of Lausanne. Although there was no explicit mention of these two islands, Greece presented a speech that Turkish Foreign Minister Affairs Tevfik Rüştü Aras had given in the TGNA on 31 July 1936 to legitimise its militarisation of the two islands. Conversely, Turkey argued that the provisions of the Lausanne Convention remained valid, as the Montreux Convention regulated only the status of the Turkish islands. A protocol addendum to the Montreux Convention explicitly stated that 'Turkey may immediately remilitarise the zone of the Straits as defined in the Preamble to the said Convention' but contained no mention of Greece. Turkey acknowledged Aras' statement about the issue but claimed that it had no legal validity, as Turkey continuously sent notes to Greece to communicate its unease about Greece's actions (Fırat, 2010, 459).

The partial demilitarisation of a second group of islands – known as the Saruhan Islands and including Mytilene, Chios (*Sakız*), Samos (*Sisam*) and Nikaria (*Nikarya*) – was stipulated by Article 13 of the Treaty of Lausanne. Accordingly, there would be no naval base and fortification on these islands, flying over the Anatolian coast and these islands would be forbidden to both parties and, finally, military forces would be limited to the normal contingent called for military service as well as a force of gendarmerie and police.

Since the foundation of the Turkish Republic, its security and foreign policy regarding the fortification of the Aegean islands has been consistent, although it has proposed some revisions in line with developments in international politics. The Aegean islands surrounding Anatolia encapsulate an extremely sensitive issue for the security of Turkey – the referent object. As Aksu has pointed out (2002, 109), Turkey's concerns regarding its security appeared during the Lausanne Conference. İsmet İnönü, who served as the Turkish delegation's chief negotiator at Lausanne and later as minister of foreign affairs, illustrated the Turkish position on the islands in two parts: (1) Imbros (*Gözçeada*), Tenedos

(*Bozcaada*) and Samothrace (*Semadirek*) as well as small and close-by islands should be given to Turkey; (2) the remaining islands should be demilitarised and become neutral and autonomous. He continued as follows:

> The Mediterranean and Aegean islands are geographically a part of Anatolia, and they are extremely important for Anatolia's security. The islands are near the coast and are small and big in size. For this reason, those within the territorial water limits should be placed under the sovereignty of Turkey. [. . .] The decisions regarding these islands are to be taken by the Big States [Great Powers]; these decisions should be taken with respect to the security of both countries. The present decision does not satisfy Turkey. Greece's globally recognised ambitions regarding Anatolia – the artificial ambition the Greek government instilled in its country to construct another Greece in Anatolia – has shown how dangerous Greece's possession of these islands is for Turkey. (Bilsel, 1998, 243–44)

İnönü's statement clearly outlines an existential threat against the safety and security of the country – the referent object. Greece's ambitions for Anatolia, the continuation of a long-desired goal to unite all Greeks under a single flag and country, posed a serious danger for Turkey's security, both economically and politically. It is for this reason that he articulated how 'extremely' and 'vitally' important the islands were for Turkey. All the islands were considered geographical extensions of Anatolia. Turkey also criticised the decisions regarding the fate of the islands that the 'great powers' had made without considering the security arrangements of either Turkey or Greece. Although there was no emphasis on measures, especially considering the Ottoman Empire's situation immediately before the modern Turkish Republic's establishment and given that concerns over the country's security were a salient issue, the points made by the foreign minister, who later became modern Turkey's prime minister, reflected the country's official security position. Assessing the issues of the militarisation and demilitarisation of the Aegean Islands through the lens of security reveals that İnönü's statements did not include an 'existential threat' and 'emergency action' – that is, the necessary components dictated by the securitisation theory. However, securitisation attempts in the early Republican Era would eventually become successful securitisation, as the statements by securitising actors in subsequent crises clearly demonstrate.

The last group of islands in the southeastern Aegean Sea – the Dodecanese Islands, also known as the Twelve Islands – were handed over to Greece under Article 14 of the Paris Peace Treaty of 10 February 1947. The related article put emphasis on the 'dimilitarised' status of these islands as well.

Turkey's official position regarding Greece's acquisition of the islands is clearly visible in an interview that then Foreign Minister Feridun Cemal Erkin gave to the Greek newspaper *Elefteria* in 1964. Erkin had served as under-secretary in the Ministry of Foreign Affairs between 1945 and 1947, and in the interview, he stated:

> I was working as the undersecretary in the Ministry of Foreign Affairs in 1946. When I learned of the decisions of the Great Powers about the Twelve Islands, I immediately summoned the ambassadors of the US and the UK to Ankara to explain the risks that the implementation of these decisions posed for the future of the relationship between [Turkey and Greece]. I drew their attention to the disruption of balance in the Aegean Sea against Turkey. The outcome of these decisions would be grave. It is impossible to predict the repercussions in [Turkey's] relations with Greece. [. . .] At the very least, half of the Twelve Islands, which are close to Turkey, should be given to Turkey. (*Cumhuriyet*, 25 May 1964)

These statements perpetuated the securitised perception dating back to the early Republican Era. In his interview, Erkin stressed that Turkey perceived Greece's acquisition of the islands as a direct threat to the security of the referent object and to its bilateral relations with Greece. Similar to the securitisation attempts during the early Republican Era, as evident in İsmet İnönü's statements during the Lausanne Conference, Feridun Cemal Erkin also sustained the same discourse twenty-five years later.

Although Greece respected the regulations in the treaties, it began remilitarising the islands starting in the mid-1960s. It claimed that the islands faced a real threat and that the provisions for the demilitarisation of the islands no longer applied, since Greece had the right to defend its territory against Turkey (Heraclides, 2010, 203; Fırat, 2010, 459). Turkey, however, protested Greece's actions on 29 June 1964 due to its militarisation of the islands for the first time (Başeren, 2006, 75–76). In tandem with developments in Cyprus in the mid-1970s, both countries took significant steps to defend themselves.

Specifically, Greece argued that it had a legitimate right to self-defence considering the aggressive stance that Turkey adopted in 1974 and that it began its acts of militarisation accordingly (Bölükbaşı, 2004, 722; Aksu 2002, 121; Başeren, 2006, 106; Heraclides, 2010, 204). Turkey claimed that no threats to the islands emanated from itself and that, therefore, Greece could not interpret the right to extensive self-defence and the remilitarisation of the islands on such grounds (Fırat, 2010, 459). Turkey also voiced its concerns in a letter sent to the UN Secretary-General on 8 April 1975:

> The government of Turkey considers those unlawful and unilateral actions by Greece as tending to compromise the balance in the Aegean Sea, thus constituting a threat to the security of Turkey and increasing the tension in the region. [. . .] It is the earnest hope of the Turkish government that the Greek government will realise its obligations under international treaties and recognise its duties to return the island to their demilitarised status. (Bölükbaşı, 2004, 730)

This letter, sent by the Turkish Ministry of Foreign Affairs, clearly emphasised the existential threat against Turkey's security. Similar to previous statements by securitising actors, the Ministry of Foreign Affairs viewed Greece's attempts to alter the balance of power in the Aegean Sea as direct threats to Turkey's security. The letter especially emphasised Greece's 'unlawful' and 'unilateral' fortification of islands in the Aegean Sea. Although the text of the letter continued in this vein, it made no mention of 'emergency action' to counter Greece's conduct. Accordingly, this statement does not represent an example of successful securitisation. Rather, it may be considered an attempt at securitisation, as it corresponds to some of the arguments presented in securitisation theory.[3]

While Greece continued to remilitarise the islands in the Aegean Sea, Turkey established its Fourth Army (the Aegean Army), which had been formed in 1975 and is headquartered in Izmir, to address issues of national security. Turkey continued to submit the issue to the agenda of the UN at every opportunity. Tension increased between the two countries in the summer of 1976, due to Turkey's seismic research at the disputed Aegean islands. In a debate at the UN General Assembly on 13 August 1976, stemming from Greek complaints over Turkey's violations of its continental shelf, Turkish

Minister of Foreign Affairs İhsan Sabri Çağlayangil reiterated Turkey's concerns about the demilitarised status of the islands:

> Since 1963, a grave situation has existed in the region because of the very dangerous path Greece has set for itself. Simultaneously with the effort to annex the independent island of Cyprus – in utter defiance of international treaties governing the status of Greek islands along the coast of Turkey – the Greeks have heavily armed and militarised those very islands, thus creating a serious threat to the security of Turkey. Greece assumed the solemn international commitment of respecting the status of all these islands, and yet practically all these islands are, at present, heavily militarised. [. . .] Since 1964, Turkey has repeatedly alerted the Greek government of these flagrant violations and the grim consequences that could follow. [. . .] The Turkish government believes that the unlawful militarisation of the island constitutes a serious threat to peace and security in the region. (Bölükbaşı, 2004, 731–32)

Turkish Foreign Minister Çağlayangil's statement at the UN Security Council was a clear extension of Turkey's securitised perception of the issue. He emphasised Turkey's concerns about its security before the members of the UN Security Council. Viewed within the framework of securitisation theory, there was an explicit emphasis on the existential threat (namely, Greece's militarisation of the islands near the Turkish coast and its efforts to annex Cyprus) to the security of the referent object (that is, Turkey). He dramatised the issue by stressing Greece's 'course of actions in a frenzy of warlike activities', 'utter defiance of international treaties', as well as years of 'flagrant violations' by fortifying the islands close to the Turkish coast. Çağlayangil also stressed the danger to regional peace and security. He hinted at the 'grim consequences that could follow' the Greek violations, appealing to the UN Security Council to consider measures necessary to prevent Greece from taking further action. Both his emphasis on the 'grim consequences' and his appeal to the UN Security Council may embody the emergency measures that securitisation theory stipulates. The Turkish prime minister's statement, parallel to the discussion at the UN Security Council, closely followed behind emergency measures requested at the international level. Collectively and simultaneously assessing these securitising actors' statements allows for their interpretation as a successful instance of securitisation.

In this regard, Turkish Prime Minister Süleyman Demirel's statement on the militarisation of the islands, which he considered a Greek attempt to escalate the situation, constituted further emergency action: 'Don't forget, the islands cannot remain armed. If the [Greeks] continues to violate our rights, we know how to protect ourselves'. Similar to the minister of foreign affairs, Demirel also emphasised the existential threat to the rights and interests of the referent object and the emergency measures that would become necessary to secure these rights and interests. Aksu (2002, 124) has evaluated the situation in the Aegean Sea as follows: 'The problems at hand which could not be solved through peaceful, just and permanent means not only increased the lack of trust, but also sharpened the belief that the only way to an expedient solution would be through war'. Despite Turkey's objections and the exchange of various notes between Turkey and Greece, the issue remains unresolved, making military preparations inevitable while endangering the national security of both nations.

The ambiguity over the islands, islets and rocks which the treaties did not explicitly mention has been a source of dispute between Turkey and Greece. Liksewise, the demilitirased status of these islands has been a cause of tension between the two countries. Despite the burden of these disagreements, both have managed to avoid any serious provocation in the Aegean Sea. Yet, the two came came close to conflict in the Aegean Sea over a series of tiny, uninhabited islets called Kardak (known in Greek as Imia) in the eastern part of the Aegean before the effect of the earlier tensions had dissipated.

The Kardak (Imia) Crisis

The crisis – the worst of its kind – erupted when a Turkish ship, the *Figen Akat*, ran aground on 25 December 1995, on an islet approximately 3.8 nautical miles off the Turkish coast in the Eastern Aegean Sea.[4] At the time, nobody could have predicted that this simple incident would trigger a domino effect that would once again bring the two countries to the brink of war and threaten peace and stability throughout the Aegean Sea (Aydın, 2003, 224; Larrabee, 2012, 477). Immediately after the accident, Greek naval forces offered to conduct a rescue mission, but the captain of the *Figen Akat* refused, claiming that the ship was still in Turkish waters. This dispute was, in essence, a continuation of the disagreements over territorial waters and the possession of the islands, islets and rocks that were located more than three nautical miles off-shore.

Prior to the media's involvement in the issue, the incident remained within the bounds of diplomacy, and both countries exchanged diplomatic notes claiming ownership over the islets. While rescue operations were still ongoing, on 25 December 1996, Greece sent to Turkey a note calling for the suspension of its rescue mission and claiming that the ship was in Greek territorial waters. On the same day, Turkey sent a response denying Greece's claims (Başeren, 2006, 46). However, the media's involvement in both countries unexpectedly escalated the crisis. The nationalist and offensive language that peppered news reports polarised the two nations, increased the pressure on decision-makers and further cemented each country's stubbornness. As Evin (2005, 398) has noted, '[p]ublic opinion remains potentially volatile on both sides of the Aegean, and any event that is misunderstood, misrepresented or exaggerated by the media could rekindle old doubts and hostilities in public opinion'. At the time, decision-makers used the media, intentionally or unintentionally, as a tool of manipulation because of its influence on public opinion. Heraclides (2010, 134) has outlined the role of the media: 'Routine events got out of hand due to the irresponsible stance of the media and press, in what could have been the first media-triggered war in history'. Nevertheless, the Kardak crisis constitutes an important case-study to understand how the media shaped public perception and galvanised decision-makers to barrel towards war just one month after the crisis had begun.

The incident was leaked to the Greek magazine *Gramma* on 20 January 1996, a day after Kostas Simitis had been called to form the new Greek government after Prime Minister and PASOK Chairman Andreas Papandreou had resigned due to health issues (Aydın, 1997, 109; Ker-Lindsay, 2007, 29; Bayar and Kotelis, 2014, 248). Soon after the incident had become public, a group of Greek civilians, accompanied by the mayor of the island of Kalymnos and a local TV channel, travelled to Kardak on 26 January 1996 to raise a Greek flag. While the Turkish media broadly covered this scene on 27 January, journalists from the Turkish newspaper *Hürriyet* visited the islet to replace the Greek flag with a Turkish one. The images broadcast in Turkey and Greece from this flag-hoisting competition aroused an intense reaction from the public. Moreover, retaliatory actions continued, as the

Greek government sent its navy to the islet to once more hoist and protect the Greek flag, a move the Turkish government considered 'an act of aggression and armed hostility against Turkish sovereignty' (Aydın, 1997, 110). Responding to Greece's mobilisation of its naval and air forces on 29 and 30 January, the Turkish government, under immense pressure from the media and the public, deployed assault boats around the islet.

With the exchange of notes between Turkey and Greece (Turkey's note dated 29 January 1996 and Greece's note dated 16 February 1996), the questions of sovereignty over the islands, islets and rocks became an official issue between the two countries (Kurumahmut, 1998, 14; Başeren, 2006, 47–48). The political and legal implications of the Kardak crisis thereafter marked a turning point in Turkey and Greece's bilateral relations, especially considering the uncertainty surrounding the 150 islands, islets and rocks in the Aegean Sea.

Throughout the crisis, the newspaper *Hürriyet* played a central role in energising the Turkish public into displaying a belligerent frenzy, an aspect that appeared in the statements of securitising actors (Çarkoğlu and Kirişci, 2004, 117). Turkish Foreign Minister Deniz Baykal shared his government's official position regarding the islets in a meeting with Greek Ambassador to Turkey Dimitrios Nezeritis on 29 January 1996:

> Attempts by Greece to inhabit the small islands, islets and rocks in question, in an artificial and demonstrative fashion can, in no way create any legal consequences in regard to their status.
>
> The Government of Turkey is prepared to enter into negotiations with Greece with a view to determine the possession of small islands, islets and rocks in the Aegean Sea. After such negotiations, the issue of the delimitation of territorial waters could also be discussed and finalised. In the meantime, the Ministry would like to suggest that the Parties should refrain from any unilateral act that would aggravate the situation in the region.
>
> In this context, Turkey requests that the unacceptable deployment of Greek troops to the rocks of Kardak be terminated and all indications of sovereignty be removed without delay. (Bölükbaşı, 2004, 827)

According to the press release, Baykal delivered a stern warning to the Greek ambassador: 'Turkey would not accept Greece's *fait accompli* in the

Aegean, it is beside the point. We know how to protect our rights' (*The Directorate General of Press and Information*, 29 January 1996).

Baykal's subsequent statement is instrumental for understanding how problems were handled when faced with a threat. Even Baykal was prudent and wished to continue the dialogue between the two countries. In his first statement, he labelled Greek activity on the Kardak rocks as 'unacceptable' and underlined the issue of 'sovereignty', which he correlated with the act of raising a flag. His next statement made it clear that Turkish decision-makers considered Greek activities on the rocks an existential threat to Turkey's rights in the Aegean Sea. Accordingly, he emphasised implicit emergency action in the face of 'Greece's *fait accompli*', while warning the Greek ambassador that 'we know how to protect our rights'. Baykal's statements highlight the 'existential threat' and 'emergency measure' – an instance of successful securitisation.

During the crisis, it was Turkish Prime Minister Tansu Çiller who adopted the most aggressively securitised language. After the NSC's emergency meeting on 29 January 2016, she made a promise at a press conference: 'Kardak is Turkish territory. We cannot accept a *fait accompli*. That flag will be removed. Those troops will leave'. She continued: 'I say we must act in a peaceful manner, but it is not possible for us to accept any *fait accompli* on the island' (*Milliyet*, 30 January 1996). In another statement that same day, she remained adamant that Greek forces should be withdrawn: 'This is our legacy: we do not give away territory. We do not concede even an inch of territory or a pebble. We can sacrifice lives, but not pebbles. The Turkish state is right, and it will do what is necessary' (*BBC*, 30 January 1996).

She thus defined the Kardak islets as Turkish soil and painted Greece's actions as *fait accompli*. Her assessment of the sovereignty over the islets stemmed from the Turkish government's official position on the ambiguity of the relevant articles in the Treaty of Lausanne, in which the status of some islets in the same region are not explicitly defined. In line with the official position, Greece's initiatives in the region were considered an existential threat to Turkish sovereignty. As she reiterated the violation of Turkish territorial rights, she also dramatised the issue, emphasising the word 'pebble'. As she pointed out, the government was prepared to enact the measures necessary to protect its rights and interests in the Aegean Sea – or, in Çiller's dramatised words: 'We can sacrifice lives, but not pebbles'. These measures also became apparent in the subsequent statements of other securitising actors. Security grammar, dramatisation and the components of successful securitisation – 'existential threat', 'emergency measure' and 'approval by the relevant audience' – are certainly present in Çiller's statements during the crisis. She had secured the tacit approval of the Turkish public by merit of being the representative of a democratically elected government.

Following the Turkish prime minister's statements, Chief of General Staff İsmail Hakkı Karadayı suggested deploying troops to the other islet near Kardak, an idea presented by Ambassador İnal Batu, the deputy undersecretary at the Ministry of Foreign Affairs. During an interview with Cansu Çamlıbel on TRT Türk in August 2009, Batu explained how that critical night transpired:

> If we deploy our troops to the second islets to raise our flag, using the cover of night, that will allow the US and EU to get involved, which will equalise our position with Greece. Within 24 hours, either [Greece] or [Turkey] will withdraw, and the crisis would be over, and the issue of Kardak will fade away. [. . .] Suddenly, Güven Erkaya, the commander of the Turkish Naval Forces, said 'Dear Batu's formula is important', stood up and turned to the Turkish prime minister and asked, 'If you would excuse me, can we evaluate dear Batu's formula?'

The tense security meeting made its way into the memoirs of Turkish Naval Forces Commander Admiral Güven Erkaya. Reading Admiral Erkaya's comments alongside Prime Minister Çiller's statements provides insight into the emergency measures that would have been necessary to prevent a Greek *fait accompli* in the Aegean Sea. In his memoirs, he wrote:

> While I was on my way to the meeting, they told me that Prime Minister Çiller was on the phone. The prime minister asked for a briefing and my personal opinion on the Kardak issue. I said to her, 'The chief of general staff would give you the relevant information in detail. But if you asked my opinion, I can tell you that Kardak is a Turkish island, thus all political preparations and initiatives should be made and implemented accordingly'. [. . .] In the meeting, I made the announcement for any military operation on Kardak, in line with the order from the government. The political decision may rest on

two alternatives. The first was to give up everything, saying, 'The island does not belong to us', and the other was to defend the island in full force and to remove the Greek troops there, saying 'The island belongs to us'. (Erkaya and Baytok 2001, 192)

The alternatives offered to Turkey during this crisis also appeared in the memoirs of other Turkish securitising actors. As Admiral Erkaya concluded, 'Kardak is a Turkish island'. Therefore, it was important to protect the sovereignty of the Turkish state vis-à-vis Greek threats. Greece sought to claim sovereignty by raising its flag on the island. He stressed both political and military measures – including a military operation on Kardak – in his conversation with Prime Minister Çiller. As seen in his statement, he dramatised the issue while offering, as an alternative, to 'defend the island in full force' in order to remove the Greek troops from the island. The statements by Admiral Erkaya include both an 'existential threat' and 'emergency action', thus satisfying the criteria for a successful instance of securitisation.

The monologue statements of the securitising actors – the prime minister, foreign minister and high-ranking military officers – demonstrate how these actors employed security grammar while evaluating sources of threat and how they determined what was at stake for Turkey – in this case the violation of sovereignty of the referent object.

The determination and intervention of Turkish President Süleyman Demirel conceivably prevented further crises from igniting between the two countries, as he emphasised during his interview regarding that night:

> The ships surrounded the islets [. . .] The prime minister came and said, 'Let's deploy our troops to the islets and raise a flag'. The military officials advised her, then visited me. [. . .] I asked if there was another way to solve the crisis. I said explicitly [. . .] You, as the chief of general staff, cannot carry the burden of this! You, as prime minister, cannot either. You, as minister of foreign affairs, cannot assume this responsibility [. . .] No one can bear it. Find alternatives. You can always intervene, but it must be as a last resort. (Batur, 2004, 51–52)

Consequently, Ambassador İnal Batu's idea about landing marines and instructing them to hoist the Turkish flag on the next-smallest islet of Kardak eased tension and precluded further escalation (Aydın, 1997,

110). International concern over the mounting tensions between Greece and Turkey had been growing since the beginning of the crisis. Along with statements from the NATO and the UN, the US played a significant role in the aversion of military clashes between its two allies. In addition to efforts by US President Bill Clinton, senior members of his administration launched an intense campaign of telephone diplomacy between Ankara and Athens to defuse tension and secure an agreement (Ker-Linday 2007, 30). During these diplomatic exchanges, US Special Envoy Richard Holbrooke issued a stern warning to Turkey and Greece: 'The first party to fire would be responsible for the consequences and get into serious trouble with the US' (Bayar and Kotelis, 2014, 252). In the end, diplomatic pressure on both governments doused the flames in the Aegean Sea. Under US supervision, both countries on 1 February 1996 withdrew their troops and lowered their flags without any incident.

At the beginning of the crisis, Turkish and Greek officials had attempted to resolve the issue peacefully through prudent negotiations. But the swelling domestic pressure that followed the involvement of the media altered the tone and the way in which decision-makers in Turkey handled problems. As Bayar and Kotelis (2014, 253) have pointed out, . . .

> Democratic actors, namely the media, opposition parties, opinion-makers, and activists, pushed their governments to win the conflict, rather than to seek a common ground through dialog and mutual respect, and the democratically elected governments had clear 'red lines' for which they risked war.
>
> Officials from both sides adopted a hard-line approach as, on the one hand, if handled successfully, the crisis offered them a chance to strengthen their political position, but, on the other hand, the political cost would be great had they been perceived as the party that yielded to the threats of the other side. (Bayar and Kotelis, 2014, 248)

Prime Minister Çiller exploited the crisis and the subsequent securitised discourse as a political manoeuvre after the elections. She even adopted a tougher stance than the other securitising actors, since she was trying to instrumentalise the Kardak crisis to boost her own popularity (Athanassopoulou, 1997, 86; Bağcı, 1997, 160–61; Ker-Lindsay, 2007, 30; Heraclides, 2010, 135).

Even after tensions had dissipated, Prime Minister Çiller continued her securitised discourse using the same security grammar. On a TV programme, for instance, she said: 'We had a promise. We do not have a pebble to give. We will not give a rock away at all. We said that the flag will be lowered and that soldiers will depart. The flag was lowered, and the troops have departed' (*Milliyet*, 1 February 1996).

In another interview, she reiterated the possibility of an existential threat against the referent object, and the emergency actions necessary to address it:

> If [the Greeks] bring soldiers to Kardak and hoist a flag once again, the same thing will happen. [The Turkish government is] saying, 'Do not create a de facto situation by opening up the place for settlement. [Turkey] will not allow this. [Turkey] would regard this as a genuine provocation and a cause for war.' (interview with Mehmet Ali Birand, Show TV, 13 February 1996, cited by Kesgin 2012, 43)

Similar to Çiller's previous securitised discourse, her interview also reflected all the necessary components of successful securitisation. She stressed that any Greek endeavours on the Kardak islets or any other islands, islets or rocks of indeterminate sovereignty status, or any Greek attempts to establish settlements would be considered a 'provocation' and 'cause for war'. In response to the existential threat endangering Turkish sovereignty, she reminded the public that 'the same thing would happen', meaning the emergency actions that had been proposed in previous situations. As seen during the Kardak crisis, the Turkish government implemented the necessary measures, by deploying troops to the islets and considering additional, decisive actions to prevent threats against the sovereignty of the referent object. Çiller's statement was another example of successful securitisation.

The crises in the Aegean Sea reflect how securitising actors in Turkey handled issues through normal bargaining processes and how they securitised issues by using speech-acts. The statements by securitising actors during the Kardak crisis clearly reflect a successful securitisation of sovereignty rights in the Aegean Sea. These statements present and dramatise the existential threat that Greece's claims posed against the territorial integrity, sovereignty and national security of the referent object. In response, the Turkish government instituted emergency measures such as the deployment of troops in order to protect its rights and interests. Assessing the Kardak crisis, Siegl (2002, 43) has concluded: 'It was not about the real control of these islets, but about preventing the opposite side from capturing them and asserting the "right" in the Aegean'. This clearly mirrors the stance of securitising actors in Turkey. Whenever a crisis erupted in the Aegean Sea, Turkish securitising actors considered that crisis an 'existential threat' to Turkey's security and sovereignty and maintained their traditional views of the issue.

The Kardak crisis introduced an additional layer to the growing heap of issues between Turkey and Greece and once again caused the international spotlight to shine on their bilateral relationship. In the immediate aftermath of the crisis, the US initiative to act as an intermediary between Turkey and Greece, a decision that the leaders of both countries accepted, was a novel occurrence, since they had previously opposed the idea of third-party involvement (Athanassopoulou, 1997, 77). Turkish Prime Minister Mesut Yılmaz on 24 March 1996 called upon Greece to 'enter into a procedure of peaceful settlement, which will not exclude from the outset any method of settlement including third-part arbitration' (Heraclides, 2010, 137). As a result, Greek Prime Minister Kostas Simitis and Turkish President Süleyman Demirel met against the backdrop of the NATO summit in Madrid on 8 July 1997 and expressed their mutual commitment to peace, respect for each other's sovereignty, the principles of international law and agreements, and each other's legitimate, vital interests and concerns in the Aegean Sea (The Madrid Joint Declaration, 1997). They also expressed their willingness to avoid conflicts and vowed to settle disputes peacefully and without the use of force or threats of unilateral action. The crux of this declaration was the suspension of Greece's unilateral initiatives in the Aegean Sea and Turkey's *casus belli* decision.

The Madrid declaration, as an expression of goodwill, played a significant role in dousing the flames raging between the two countries over the Aegean. Both countries had agreed to suspend their policies – a *casus belli* for the Turks and unilateral actions for the Greeks – but they did not renounce their claims. The declaration has, without a doubt, become an ideal reference point to initiate subsequent bilateral dialogue. Turkish Foreign Minister İsmail Cem proposed a meeting with his counterpart to resolve the disputes in the Aegean Sea on 12 February and 11 March 1998, since he viewed the Madrid declaration as a mutually beneficial outcome (Cem, 2009, 86–92).

Despite several attempts to ease the tension between the two, particularly the Madrid Joint Statement of July 1997, there was little movement towards change. The relations between Turkey and Greece continued to be strained due to issues including Cyprus, the EU and Greek support for the leader of a terrorist organisation. The following section will focus on one major dispute, a decade-long issue of contention between Turkey and Greece – that is, Cyprus.

Notes

1. Enclosed and semi-enclosed seas are defined in Articles 122 and 123 of the United Nations Convention on the Law of the Sea (UNCLOS, 1982) as 'a gulf, basin or sea surrounded by two or more States and connected to another sea or the ocean by a narrow outlet or consisting entirely or primarily of the territorial seas and exclusive economic zones (EEZ) of two or more coastal States'. Although Turkey is not a signatory to the UNCLOS, it used the term 'semi-enclosed' for the first time to describe the Aegean Sea in its note to Greece on 27 February 1974 and continues to do so (Başeren, 2006, 10).
2. The islands in the Aegean Sea can be grouped according to their geographical locations as follows: the North Sporades, the Cyclades, the Strait Region Islands, the *Saruhan* Islands and the Dodacanese (Twelve) Islands. The last three groups of islands are also called the 'Eastern Aegean Islands' (Kurumahmut, 1998, 4; İnan and Acer, 2004, 1; Başeren, 2006, 7).
3. Securitisation theory also acknowledges attempts at securitisation in the absence of the audience's approval, the third component of securitisation. According to securitisation theory, the process remains incomplete without the approval of the related audience. However, this book will use the word 'attempt' for cases that do not contain all three components.
4. The Kardak islets are composed of two geographical features located 385 metres apart, in the Dodacanese (Twelve) Islands. The east Kardak islet covers about 19,730 square metres, while the west Kardak islet covers 16,680 square metres. The two islets are 3.6 and 3.9 nautical miles, respectively, off the Turkish coast.

3

THE CYPRUS PROBLEM

The Cyprus problem has been the most serious and challenging dispute between Turkey and Greece since the mid-1950s. This book does not offer a chronological account of the Cyprus events; rather, it provides a brief background to the issue by examining significant turning points such as the foundation of the Republic of Cyprus (RoC), the 1964 and 1967 crises, as well as the Turkish military's intervention on the island in 1974 and its impact on bilateral relations. This background information will familiarise readers with both countries' official positions regarding the Cyprus problem. However, the primary focus of this chapter will be on the S-300 crisis, another instance of securitisation during the 1990s.

The Cyprus Problem and its Impact on Turkish–Greek Relations

The island of Cyprus was under Ottoman rule from its conquest in 1571 until 1878, when the Ottomans handed over its administration to Britain in exchange for an alliance against Russia. Temporary British rule became permanent with the British annexation in the wake of World War I, and this was confirmed during the Treaty of Lausanne. Although the strategic location of Cyprus at the centre of maritime trade routes in the Eastern Mediterranean was of vital importance for Turkey's security, the peaceful foreign policy adopted by the founders of the Turkish Republic as well as the international balances of power at the time ensured the formal acceptance of this outcome

(Kaliber, 2003, 143; Elekdağ, 2006, 34). While the Turkish delegation relinquished its rights over the island, the Turkish delegation raised the newly founded Republic of Turkey's concerns with a particular emphasis on the 'vital importance' of the island for the protection of Turkey's southern coast (Dodd, 2010, 3). A quote from Mustafa Kemal Atatürk, the founder of the Turkish Republic, illustrates the importance of the island: 'If Cyprus was in the hands of a hostile country, all supply routes to Anatolia would be cut off, and Turkey's security would be threatened' (Manizade, 1975, 17, quoted from Elekdağ, 1996, 43).

The period of British control over the island saw no conflict between Turkey and Greece, but the emergence of the Cyprus issue in the mid-1950s pulled the two countries into a diplomatic conflict, and much of the goodwill that had developed between the two governments quickly evaporated (Ker-Lindsay, 2000, 216). Hence, one may argue that the Cyprus issue ended three decades of amicable relations between Athens and Ankara. Turkey in fact considered all issues related to Cyprus as the UK's domestic politics and did not attempt any involvement, as long as the UK maintained its rule. Turkish Minister of Foreign Affairs Necmettin Sadak clearly expressed this sentiment in an interview he gave on 25 January 1950: 'There is no such issue as the Cyprus problem. I clearly told that to the journalists a long time ago. Cyprus today is under the British sovereignty and rule [. . .]' (*Yeni İstanbul*, 24 January 1950).

However, the eruption and intensification of inter-communal troubles in Cyprus due to the attacks of the National Organisation of Cyprus Fighters (*Ethniki Organosis Kyprion Agoniston*, EOKA) in April 1955 and the reaction within Turkey brought the issue to the forefront of Turkish foreign policy, particularly in its relations with Greece. The initial signs of change in the Turkish position on the Cyprus issue appeared in the government's discourse. The acting government, formed by Prime Minister Adnan Menderes, began to gradually pursue a more active policy and altered its previous position of maintaining the status quo in Cyprus. Prime Minister Adnan Menderes raised Turkey's security concerns by stating: 'Cyprus is the continuation of Anatolia and constitutes one of the pivotal elements for its security' (cited from Ayın Tarihi, 1955, 170). Thus, Turkey supported returning the island to Turkey if there was any change in the island's status. The then prime minister's statement can be considered a turning point in Turkey's formal recognition of the issue. It should also be noted that the British administration's encouragement and invitation to the tripartite conference in London drew Turkish politicians' attention.

Between 1955 and 1959, a series of conferences were held at Britain's initiative and with the support of Turkey and the US. It is worth noting that, at the time, the US had no strategic interest in Cyprus and considered the issue a potential source of enmity between Turkey and Greece. Thus, the main concern of the US was the prevention of any dispute that might destabilise the NATO's southeastern flank. While Britain organised a conference attended by Turkish and Greek delegates in London to discuss political and security issues in the Eastern Mediterranean – especially Cyprus – major riots erupted against the non-Muslim communities, particularly the Greeks, of Turkey between 6 and 7 September 1955 and pushed relations between two countries to the breaking point. The 6–7 September riots were a reaction to a story that circulated in the Turkish press, in a state radio news bulletin at 4 pm on 6 September, which was repeated in the pro-government afternoon daily paper *İstanbul Ekspres*. The story claimed that 'the birthplace of Mustafa Kemal Atatürk [the founder of the Republic of Turkey] in Thessaloniki had been bombed' (Alexandris, 1992, 256). The demonstration in Istanbul morphed into widespread riots against the property of the city's Greek population. According to Fırat (2010, 359), the 6–7 September events had two important consequences. First, whenever Ankara began to feel intensifying pressure concerning the Cyprus issue, it responded by exerting pressure on the Greek minorities living in Turkey. And second, the events created another layer of mistrust in Turkish–Greek relations. More generally, each subsequent issue relating to Cyprus has, in some way, adversely impacted Turkish–Greek relations.

When the inter-communal violence intensified in 1958, the NATO powers encouraged Turkey and Greece to negotiate the issue in order to prevent any instability within the Western alliance. Following the Zurich and London conferences in 1959, the Republic of Cyprus was established in 1960 under the auspices of Greece, Turkey and the UK in their capacity as guarantor powers to maintain the territorial integrity, independence and sovereignty of the emergent state. The Treaty of Guarantee, particularly, paved the way for the further involvement of both Greece and Turkey in the Cyprus problem.

Whenever there occurred problems between the Greek and Turkish Cypriot communities, as seen during the crises of 1964, 1967 and 1974, Turkey and Greece as motherlands played active roles. In other words, the Cyprus problem became a decisive factor in Turkish foreign policy (Kazan, 2002, 59).

The logic behind the foundation of the RoC was predicated on binational independence and political equality, as well as the administrative partnership of the two communities (Müftüler-Baç and Güney, 2005, 282). Although Cyprus became an independent state in 1960, no one believed that the independence would last long. As Camp (1980, 46) has pointed out, '[t]he Zurich-London Accords in July 1960 ended the first phase of EOKA's struggle by Greek Cypriot nationalists to establish an independent Cyprus', but it was a step towards their 'maximum demand of union with Greece' – a notion dubbed *Enosis*. Disputes immediately after the RoC's establishment, over (among other issues) tax collection and access to public services, ushered in a new phase. The thirteen constitutional amendments proposed by RoC President Archbishop Makarios on 30 November 1963 sparked fierce tension between the two Cypriot communities as well as between Turkey and Greece. The thirteen amendments proposed by RoC President Archbishop Makarios included the abolition of majorities in the legislative process, the elimination of separate governments in the five major municipalities and the elimination of the veto power of the vice president, a Turkish Cypriot. In short, these amendments were intended to end the current system and establish Greek Cypriot dominance on the island (Fırat, 1997, 123–24; Camp, 1980, 49–50; Ker-Lindsay, 2007, 17). Turkey promptly rejected all amendments, triggering the eruption of violence on the island. A subsequent announcement by Archbishop Makarios, on 1 January 1964, outlined his intentions to abrogate the accords, eliciting a vehement reaction from Turkey and almost causing the Turks to intervene (Camp, 1980, 50).

The tension that the Cyprus issue produced in Turkish–Greek relations was exacerbated by the election of George Papandreou, who wholeheartedly supported *Enosis*, as prime minister of Greece in February 1964 (Fırat, 1997, 139–40; Ker-Lindsay, 2007, 17). A letter that Papandreou sent to Archbishop Makarios on 25 February, on his ninth day in office, to highlight the full support of the Greek government for Makarios' position negatively affected the relationship between Turkey and Greece (Fırat, 1997, 140). In response to Prime Minister Papandreou's support for Archbishop Makarios,

Turkish Prime Minister İsmet İnönü on 13 March 1964 announced the abrogation of the Treaty of Neutrality, Conciliation and Arbitration, which had been signed in the 1930s during a time of cordial relations between the two countries, and he began expelling Greek minorities living in Istanbul (Fırat, 1997, 152–53; Kaliber, 2019; Oran, 2019). This decision by the Turkish government precipitated a mass migration among the Greek community that also caused imbalances between Turkey and Greece in terms of minorities living in the two countries (Oran, 1991, 298–99). Culminating in the 6–7 September incidents, the expulsion of Greek minorities after the abrogation of the treaty further damaged the bilateral relationship.

When intercommunal violence peaked in Cyprus and when the Turkish government, on 2 June 1964, 'decided to land forces in Cyprus to establish a political and military beachhead' (Bölükbaşı, 1993, 516), the US took action: US President Johnson wrote a letter to Turkish President İsmet İnönü on 5 June 1964. The letter had serious consequences for Turkey's position on Cyprus, persuading Turkey not to intervene in Cyprus and forcing changes in Turkey's overall foreign policy. Notwithstanding the US pressure on Turkey, the Turkish Armed Forces were ill-prepared to undertake a naval or aerial intervention in Cyprus at that time. The US mediation restored the *status quo ante* but failed to resolve either the underlying conflict on the island or the tensions between Turkey and Greece.

After a military coup d'état on 21 April 1967, a new government espousing an *Enosis*-based Cyprus policy seized power in Greece. Turkish Prime Minister Süleyman Demirel and new Greek Prime Minister Constantine Kollias met on 9–10 September 1967 in Keşan and Alexandroupoli (*Dedeağaç*), towns on the Turkish–Greek border (*Milliyet*, 5 September 1967). Demirel presented four conditions in response to the Greek government's proposal for unconditional *Enosis*:

> First, Cyprus should not be annexed unilaterally by either Greece or Turkey; secondly, neither Cypriot community should dominate the other; thirdly, the 1959 Cyprus Treaties should not be revised unilaterally; and finally, the balance of power established by the Treaty of Lausanne (1923) in the Mediterranean between Turkey and Greece should be preserved. (Göktepe, 2005, 435)

The meetings between the two prime ministers ended in failure. Turkey's feelings regarding these meetings were clearly reflected in the words of Turkish President Cevdet Sunay during his visit with British Prime Minister Harold Wilson on 6 November 1967, as well as the statement of Turkish Minister of Foreign Affairs İhsan Sabri Çağlayangil:

> The meetings in September between the Turkish and Greek prime ministers were beneficial in helping each government to learn the senior-level views. The Turkish government sincerely desired a peaceful solution to the Cyprus problem, in accordance with the previously outlined principles. But the Greek Government seemed uncompromising in their insistence on *Enosis*. In fact, the agreements still in effect precluded both the proposals for *Enosis*, which the Greek government had previously advanced, and those for partition, which the Turkish Government had advanced. [. . .] Turkey's interest in a peaceful solution and willingness to talk did not mean that her patience would be endless. Provocation, efforts to create a *fait accompli* and inhumane pressures all created difficulties for Turkey. (Göktepe, 2005, 437)

Two months after the negotiations between the Turkish and Greek prime ministers, the infiltration of some 10,000 fighters from the Greek mainland and a fresh outbreak of fighting provoked another crisis in November 1967 (Müfti, 2009, 44; Özdamar and Erciyas, 2020). Although the Turkish Parliament had authorised the government to intervene in Cyprus, the Turkish army's inability to successfully deploy its forces caused delays. Instead, on 17 November 1967, Çağlayangil sent a note to the Greek ambassador to Turkey, communicating a range of Turkish demands that included the expulsion of General Grival Grivas, the withdrawal of Greek troops stationed in Cyprus in defiance of the agreements, compensation for damages caused by the latest developments and the reinforcement of the UN Peacekeeping Force in Cyprus (UNFIYCP), which had been established and deployed to the island according to the UNSC Resolution 186 (1964) (Fırat, 1997, 224).

In the midst of the crisis, UN Secretary-General U Thant on 22 November 1967 urged the prime ministers of Turkey and Greece along with RoC President Makarios to do what they could to avoid the danger of war over Cyprus. Moreover, the US played a role as mediator, appointing Cyrus Vance as US President Johnson's special envoy and, as a result, preventing the crisis from escalating. On 30 November, both sides reached an agreement, in which Athens withdrew its fighters from the island and accepted most of Turkey's demands under pressure from the US, thus avoiding further trouble with Turkey comparable to the 1964 dispute (Müfti, 2009, 44). In the aftermath of the crisis, Turkish Cypriots took advantage of the circumstances and established the Provisional Turkish Administration of Cyprus on 28 December 1967.

Although Cyprus is but a small island in the Eastern Mediterranean, its crises had serious ramifications for its own communities as well as for Turkish–Greek relations and regional and international politics. However, another dispute erupted on the island when the Greek junta administration orchestrated a coup d'état against President Archbishop Makarios on 15 July 1974, communicating its intention to implement its long-desired *Enosis* by installing Nicos Sampson, an anti-Turkish supporter of *Enosis*, to replace Makarios. The Turkish National Security Council issued a statement in response: 'This is a Greek intervention. The constitutional order on the island has been overturned and an illegal military administration established. Turkey considers this to be a violation of the treaties and guarantees' (Sarıca, Teziç and Eskiyurt, 1975, 180).

As the TGNA resolution that authorised the government to intervene in Cyprus was valid, Turkish Prime Minister Bülent Ecevit ordered the Turkish Armed Forces to prepare for military action in Cyprus following consultation with the British government (Fırat, 2010, 447–48). As Dodd (2010, 112) reported through the British House of Commons Select Committee on Cyprus, 'Britain could have intervened either alone or in conjunction with Turkey, a fellow guarantor power, to have overthrown the Sampson regime'; however, 'she [Britain] did not intervene for reasons the Government refuses to give'. Soon afterwards, on 20 July 1974, Turkey launched its military operation, known as 'Peace Operation', to prevent a *fait accompli* by Greece, and Turkish troops landed in Cyprus.

The NSC declaration evaluated the Greek coup d'état in Cyprus as an intervention, which reversed the constitutional order by establishing a military administration on the island. It was deemed a violation of the treaties and guarantees that required emergency action in the form of an intervention in Cyprus in order to prevent Greek attempts at *fait accompli* fuelled by pro-*Enosis* sentiments. From the viewpoint of traditional Cyprus policy, which is considered a heavily securitised issue in Turkey, the identification of the island as a 'national cause', 'babyland' or 'floating military base' are all in line with the traditional discourse on security (Bilgin, 2005; Kaliber, 2005). Thus, due to 'the inseparability of the security of Turkey and TRNC', Greece's actions on the island constituted an existential threat to the referent object (Kaliber, 2003, 183). The NSC's declaration, together with the statement by Turkish Prime Minister Bülent Ecevit, represent an example of successful securitisation in Turkish foreign policy:

> [The Turkish troops] are in Cyprus for peace, not war. They are there not to invade Cyprus but to put an end to the invasion. This latest Greek action on the island is not simply a coup; it is intended to destroy the independence of the Cypriot state and to undermine the international agreements on which the Cyprus Republic was founded.

Ecevit's justification of the Turkish operation clearly emphasised the external threat that Greece posed to Cyprus' independence and to the international agreements to which Turkey was also a signatory. He deemed Greece's efforts to replace the administration on the island an invasion seeking to destroy an independent state located in a geographically strategic position for Turkey's security. The Turkish military had already been conducting the emergency action raised by the NSC declaration before the statement had been released. This means that Turkish securitising actors removed the issue from normal political procedures in response to Greek attempts in order to change the regime on the island and implemented the emergency measures after a successful securitisation.

With the justification of the Turkish government to intervene in Cyprus in 1974, based on the 1960 Treaty of Guarantee, which gave any one of the guarantor powers – either unilaterally or jointly – to intervene in order to maintain independence, territorial integrity and sovereignty, the international atmosphere coalesced in Turkey's favour. As Hale (2002, 159) has noted, Turkey had enjoyed broad international support at the time of the initial military landing in Cyprus, as the Greek junta administration threatened the island nation's independence. The Greek junta administration, conversely, was not received warmly among the international actors.

On the same day, the UNSC adopted Resolution 353 (1974, 7), which called on the relevant parties to agree to a ceasefire, to exercise the utmost restraint and to immediately end the foreign military intervention in Cyprus (UNSC, 1974, 7). Following the UNSC's call for a ceasefire, the Ministries of Foreign Affairs of Turkey, Greece and Britain, along with representatives from the US, the UN and the Soviet Union, gathered in Geneva between 25 and 30 July and then again between 8 and 14 August 1974. Following the collapse of the tripartite talks in Geneva concerning the future of Cyprus, Turkey launched its second military operation in Cyprus on 14 August 1974. Although Turkey's initial operation was considered justified as a reaction to the junta coup to overthrow Makarios, its subsequent action was internationally regarded as an illegitimate 'occupation'.

This was also reflected in Resolution 3212, which the UN General Assembly passed during its 2,275th meeting on 1 November 1974. The resolution called on 'all states to respect sovereignty, independence, territorial integrity and non-alignment of the RoC and to refrain from all acts and interventions directed against it', and it 'urged the speedy withdrawal of all foreign armed forces and foreign military presence [. . .] and the cessation of all foreign interference in its affairs' (UN General Assembly Resolution, 3212, 1 November 1974).

After Turkey's military operation, the UN attempted to start negotiations between the parties. In this atmosphere, Turkish Cypriots unilaterally formed and declared the Turkish Federated State of Cyprus on 13 February 1975 to gain equal footing during the negotiations. According to Rauf R. Denktaş (Denktash, 1988, 80), the first leader of the federated state and later president of the TRNC until 2005, 'the Turkish Cypriots' action was merely to establish the Turkish wing of the envisaged Federal Republic of Cyprus', which had been accepted ahead of the negotiations. This was an act over which the UNSC expressed its regret in Resolution 367 (1975) on 12 March, in which the UNSC implored the parties to resume talks under the auspices of the UN secretary-general. Inter-communal talks did resume, although they failed to negotiate a solution due to the political turmoil and polarity on the island.

The Turks' intervention had far-reaching consequences for Cyprus, Greece and Turkey, among others. One impact for Greece was the replacement of the Greek junta with a civilian government, meaning that the

Turkish intervention in Cyprus had influenced Greece's domestic politics and resulted in its transition to democracy. On 24 July 1974, Constantine Karamanlis returned to Greece to lead the new civilian government (Ker-Lindsay, 2007, 18). Glafkos Clerides replaced the Sampson regime in Cyprus on 25 July 1974. Another positive impact of Turkey's intervention in Cyprus was that it pushed Greece into a closer union with the EU, seeking a source of security in the face of the Turkish threat (Öniş, 2001, 34). As Öniş (2001, 34) has pointed out, political (democratic consolidation) and security considerations rather than purely economic concerns were instrumental in Greece's decision. Although the initial reactions to Greece's application were negative, its accession bid was ultimately successful, and the country became a member of the EU in early 1981.

Cyprus has persisted as a central issue in Turkish–Greek relations ever since the problem first emerged in the mid-1950s. Furthermore, the intensifying animosity between two countries has managed to strain the relations of both countries with the US. After the US failed to prevent Turkey from intervening in Cyprus, Greece withdrew from the military wing of the NATO under an overwhelming wave of domestic pressure on Prime Minister Constantine Karamanlis (Larrabee, 2012, 472).[1] Similarly, Turkish relations with the US deteriorated after an intense pressure campaign by the Greek lobby in the US compelled Congress to impose an arms embargo on Turkey in 1975 (Larrabee, 2012, 472).[2]

Starting in the mid-1970s, the issues in the Aegean Sea, along with a host of other developments in the domestic and foreign policies of Turkey and Greece, replaced the Cyprus problem as primary point of tension between the two countries. As Greece dealt with the consolidation of its democracy and preparations for full membership in the EU, Turkey was engrossed in a range of internal political disputes and foreign policy crises, including the US arms embargo. Regarding the Cyprus problem, the inter-communal negotiations – which aim to produce a federal state based on a bi-communal and bi-zonal federation arrangement, a tenet of the 1977 and 1979 Summit Agreements and, subsequently, the main UN parameter for a comprehensive settlement – have continued (Sözen, 2017). Amid the deadlock on the principles of a federal system, the Turkish Cypriot administration unilaterally declared the formation of the Turkish Republic of Northern Cyprus (TRNC) on 15 November 1983. The newly established TRNC is considered 'legally invalid' by the UN Security Council, based on Resolution 541 (1983).

Although negotiations between the island's two communities continued throughout the 1980s, various challenges preventing a resolution were not only confined to the island but also had repercussions on Turkish–Greek relations. The crises that appeared in the 1990s, particularly the S-300 missile crisis, hindered the improvement of relations. The following sub-section focuses on one of these crises as a case-study to demonstrate how the Turkish elites used speech-acts to securitise the issues over which Greece and Turkey fought in Cyprus.

The Case of the S-300 Crisis

As mentioned above, Turkey and Greece have been at odds for almost half of a century since the emergence of the Cyprus problem in the mid-1950s. The problem itself also dominated Turkish foreign policy in various aspects during 1990s. The early indicators of the existence of the Cyprus problem began to appear in Turkish-EU relations when the RoC applied for membership of the European Union on 4 July 1990 and when the European Commission recommended to the Council to start accession negotiations with the RoC on 30 June 1993. Likewise, nineteen years after the Turks had conducted military operations on the island, a Joint Defence Doctrine, which once again strained the bilateral relationship, was signed in November 1993 between the Greek government and the Greek Cypriot administration. With the defence doctrine, Cyprus would be included in Greece's defence area; Greece would consider a Turkish attack on Southern Cyprus to be an attack on itself and a *casus belli*; Greece and the Greek Cypriot government would jointly formulate and implement their defence plans; and Greece would construct a new joint air base in Paphos, in Southern Cyprus (Fırat, 2010, 802; Liaropoulos, 2008, 27; Dodd, 2010, 181). Greece's plans were considered a direct threat to Turkish national security and, consequently, drove the Turkish government to create the same support structures for the Turkish Cypriots.

Greek Cypriot Foreign Minister Alekos Michaelides exacerbated tensions on 5 January 1997 when he announced that the Greek Cypriot administration had decided to acquire a Russian medium-range S-300 surface-to-air missile defence system. Despite the UNSC Resolution 1092 on 23 December 1996

(UNSC, 1996) regarding 'grave concerns about excessive levels of military forces and armaments in the RoC', as well as 'the rate at the introduction of sophisticated weaponry', the Greek Cypriot administration followed through with the purchase of the Russian missile defence system. The risks of increased tension both on the island and in the region were raised by the UNSC, along with the US, which warned that the purchase of S-300 systems 'would complicate efforts to frame a settlement for the divided Mediterranean island' (*Washington Post*, 7 January 1997). Likewise, Turkey strongly objected to the deployment of the new system; with the ability to intercept and destroy aircraft at ranges up to 150 km, it far exceeded the security needs of the RoC.

While the Greek Cypriot administration claimed that the system merely served defensive purposes, Turkey viewed it as an expansion of offensive capabilities, because its range meant that it could reach the Turkish mainland (Nachmani, 2001, 77). Turkey therefore argued that the new system would pose an existential threat to its security, and this sentiment appeared in the statements of securitising actors. Turkish officials quickly warned Greece and the RoC that it would take any action it deemed necessary, including conducting military strikes against the missiles, in order to prevent the missile defence system from being deployed in Cyprus. Foreign Minister and Deputy Prime Minister Tansu Çiller assessed the RoC's attempt to acquire S-300 missiles:

> The pursuit by Greece, which is a NATO member, of a hostile policy towards Turkey by manipulating the Greek Cypriots, and its endeavour to threaten Turkey's southern region through the Greek Cypriot sector, are the product of an extremely dangerous and irresponsible policy [. . .] Turkey cannot be a spectator as Greece encircles the country from the south and alters the balance between the two countries or turns Cyprus into a festering wound in the Eastern Mediterranean. (*Turkish Ministry of Foreign Affairs*, 10 January 1997)

An analysis of Çiller's statement reveals another clear instance of securitisation in Turkish foreign policy. In discussing the Greek Cypriots' acquisition of the Russian S-300 missiles, she portrayed the purchase as an act of provocation on the part of Greece rather than of the RoC, threatening and surrounding Turkey's southern region. She dramatised the existential threat against the security of the referent object by placing special emphasis on Greece's 'extremely dangerous' and 'irresponsible policy'. In addition to emphasising the survival of the referent object, she continued to dramatise the issue by focusing on the region in a broader context and claiming that such an attempt that would turn the island into a 'festering wound'. Although she did not explicitly outline emergency measures, her statement that 'Turkey cannot become a spectator to Greece' may be considered an implicit declaration of action. However, in another statement in which she addressed the issue, Çiller plainly warned both Greece and the RoC against purchasing Russian missiles and proposed emergency measures to be adopted, if the sale were to be finalised:

> Without a doubt, Greece is the country that encourages Greek Cypriots to take this path, directing and supporting them, and it is this country which carries the greatest responsibility for this aggressive policy [. . .] These offensive weapons will not be deployed to southern Cyprus. [. . .] If deployed, Turkey will do whatever is necessary. If this includes striking at them, this will be done, too. (*Milliyet*, 11 January 1997)

Her statement contains an explicit condemnation of Greece, blaming the country for the RoC's initiative to acquire missiles. She also stressed that 'Turkey would do whatever is necessary', including using military action to target the missiles if deployed to the RoC. Chief of General Staff İsmail Hakkı Karadayı also supported the emergency measures that Çiller referenced, in a statement he gave during a visit to the TRNC:

> A weapon which has a range of 150–160 kilometres and can deeply penetrate the airspaces of neighbouring countries cannot be portrayed as defensive. No one can expect us to be onlookers to the use of these weapons against Turkey and the TRNC [. . .] the political authority commands, and we strike. The Turkish Armed Forces are prepared to neutralise all threats. (*Cumhuriyet*, 11 and 14 January 1997)

Furthermore, Turkey's resolute stance on the missiles was also evident in a written statement issued by the NSC secretary-general after its monthly meeting on 27 January 1997:

> Emphasis was placed on the measures that have been and will be taken in order to protect the rights and interests of Turkey and the TRNC, particularly against

Greece's recent attempts to disrupt the peace in the Aegean Sea, Cyprus and Eastern Mediterranean. In tandem with those measures, [the NSC] decided that such measures will be definitively implemented in accordance with our national policies.[3]

These statements by senior Turkish officials contain all the necessary components of effective securitisation: an 'existential threat', 'emergency measures' and 'the approval of the relevant audience'. As stated above, the decisions made by the TGNA can be interpreted as the tacit approval of the audience. When Chief of General Staff Karadayı provided specific information about the range of missiles, he argued that the offensive nature of such weaponry would pose an existential threat, not just to neighbouring countries, but also to Turkey and the TRNC. He reiterated the proposed emergency measures, including strikes against missile sites, in order to 'neutralise all threats' rather than to monitor developments as an 'onlooker'. A similarly securitised tone was adopted in the NSC meeting, during which Turkish officials considered a range of measures that they would implement resolutely so as to protect the rights and interests of the referent object.

Likewise, various discursive elements of other securitising actors regarding the issue at hand were consistent with the foreign minister's speech-acts. Representatives of Turkish decision-makers interpreted the deployment of S-300 missiles to the island as an existential threat to Turkey's security. Ayman (2002, 9–10) has suggested that the attempt to deploy the missiles was considered a 'significant step of the grand Greek strategy aimed at enclaving Turkey with a strategic belt from the Ionian Sea to the Gulf of Iskenderun and closing all the naval routes of transportation of Anatolia'. Several other statements by Turkish securitising actors emphasised the 'existential threat' against the security and survival of the referent object and reiterated the 'emergency measures' that were necessary to mitigate this threat. Turkish Prime Minister Mesut Yılmaz, for instance, echoed these considerations as well as the policy to address the existential threat: 'Greece has demonstrated aggressive intentions with missiles and by deploying its air force to southern Cyprus. Turkey cannot remain passive in the face of this. What is important to us is the neutralisation of the threat toward the TRNC and Turkey. And this will be done' (*Milliyet*, 19 June 1998).

Yılmaz in his statement made explicit references to Greek activities on the island, and he determined that the acquisition of missiles or the deployment of air forces constituted an imminent threat to Turkey and the TRNC. In the face of such a threat, he declared, the 'neutralisation of the threat' without hesitation constituted the most suitable response, as 'Turkey cannot remain passive'. Although Greek Cypriot authorities intended to deploy the missiles to the island, Turkish securitising actors considered any existential threat to the TRNC as a direct assault on the survival and security of the referent object, the Turkish state. Such an assessment was also depicted in a statement by Foreign Minister İsmail Cem in 1998:

> With its arms and armaments, air assault fields, Russian military experts and S-300s, the Greek Cypriot administration has attempted to threaten not only the TRNC but Turkey as well. The security of the TRNC is directly the same as the security of Turkey. Any threat, provocation or aggression against the existence of the TRNC will be treated as the direct targeting of Turkey. (*Turkish Ministry of Foreign Affairs*, 30 March 1998)

As Cyprus has been considered as an integral part of Turkey's security, in his statement, the foreign minister restated the existential threat that the actions of the Greek Cypriot administration represented for the security of the TRNC and Turkey, mentioning 'armaments' and 'air assault fields'. In another example, Cem communicated the risks of acquiring missiles to his Greek counterpart during a UN General Assembly meeting in New York: 'We oppose the deployment of the S-300 missiles to the Greek side. Indeed, we do not desire the creation of another front in the Eastern Mediterranean. Everything would change with the arrival of missiles on the island. Cyprus could become the new Bosnia' (*Milliyet*, 24 July 1997).

In this statement, Cem emphasised potential similarities between Cyprus and Bosnia, should the RoC acquire the S-300 missiles. His dramatisation of the issue in this context mainly stemmed from the humanitarian crisis – especially the massacre of thousands of Bosnian Muslims in Srebrenica in July 1995 – among the Serbian, Croatian and Muslim ethnic groups during the Bosnian War (1992–95). The altered balance of military power on the ground as well as between the Cypriot communities would precipitate further conflicts on the island. Cem stressed the importance of maintaining the status quo in the Eastern Mediterranean in order to preserve regional stability.

The securitised discourse of Turkish decision-makers continued in a similar pattern on several occasion. Turkish President Süleyman Demirel assessed the situation in his opening speech before the TGNA in October 1998:

> The armament campaign of the Greeks and Cypriot Greeks, and their attempts at increasing the tension threaten peace and security on the island and in the Eastern Mediterranean. We will continue to take the necessary measures to ensure our territorial security and that of the TRNC. (*Milliyet*, 2 October 1998)

After identifying the imminent threat posed by the Greek and Greek Cypriot administrations against the referent object's survival and security, the Turkish president alluded to the emergency measures that would be necessary to address this threat. As the representatives of a democratically elected government and as appointed members of the decision-making process, these actors, as well as their statements, inherently received the approval of the public. As such, all relevant statements by Turkish actors included components of successful securitisation.

It is also important to highlight the underlying motivations behind the RoC's decision to deploy a sophisticated weapons system to the island in order to understand the securitised rhetoric that Turkish officials adopted. As Ayman (2002, 8) and Ker-Lindsay (2007, 30–31) have concluded, the Greek Cypriot administration potentially had two interrelated goals: one that was focused on the military, and another that was political, with the latter being more heavily emphasised. However, in either case, the Turkish officials' reactions in the form of a securitised discourse were quite understandable, as Ayman (2002, 5) has suggested, because 'the state that employs brinkmanship policy is forcing his adversary to make a difficult choice between backing away from his commitment and/or to fight or start a war'. Faced with this situation, Turkish securitising actors openly warned that it would allow no attempts by Greece or the RoC to counter-balance Turkey's power and that Turkey 'would respond to all attempts by adopting a response either matching or exceeding the Greek provocations', in order to ensure that the missiles would not be deployed to the island (Ayman, 2002, 16). Turkey was hesitant to permit any form of change to its superiority on the island.

This crisis exacerbated relations between Turkey and Greece and resulted in third-party intervention to find a solution. At the time, in addition to US President Bill Clinton and UK Prime Minister Tony Blair, the EU also cautioned the Greek Cypriot government about its decision. Following internal debates regarding the cost of the deployment of missiles to the island, given the challenges associated with defending the island in the event of a Turkish incursion and the potential repercussions for Greece and the RoC's relations with the EU, Greek Prime Minister Kostas Simitis offered to place the missiles on the Greek island of Crete instead of Cyprus (Ker-Lindsay, 2000, 218).

Although the decision to relocate the planned missile defence system to Crete eased the simmering tensions, the discourse wielded by Turkish securitising actors during the crisis encapsulated the Turkish decision-makers' doubts and threat perceptions concerning Greece. Their statements reflected how Greek Cypriot policies – with the encouragement of the Greek government – posed an existential threat to the security and interests of the referent object by altering the military balance in the region. Turkey's determination to prevent the deployment of the missiles to the island and to maintain the regional status quo, even through the use of military force, represents a clear example of the securitisation process. An emergency action against an existential threat and the influence of securitising actors compelled the decision-makers to prioritise the issue. This becomes particularly obvious when comparing the statements by the same securitising actors on different foreign policy issues. Whenever the Cyprus problem caused problems in Turkish-EU relations, for instance, the statements encapsulated tones of criticism rather than securitised speech-acts. Different from previous examples, the Greek government's use of its veto right to obstruct the improvement of relations between Turkey and the EU was not considered an imminent or existential threat to Turkey's security. On the contrary, the securitising actors evaluated Greece's use of veto rights as a 'hostile' approach that targeted Turkey's interests in international politics. But rather than securitising the issue, they opted to address it within the scope of normal political processes.

Notes

1. Greece pulled out of the NATO's military wing in August 1974 to protest the failure of the US to prevent Turkish operations in Cyprus. However, Greece

returned in October 1980, when Turkey lifted its veto against Greece's re-entering the military wing. The Rogers Plan, which brought Greece back into the NATO, was prepared by and named after Supreme Allied Commander General Bernard Rogers on 18 October 1980.
2. The relationship between Turkey and the US further deteriorated due to the 'opium crisis'. The US administration applied serious pressure on the Turkish government to coerce it into discontinuing its cultivation of opium in the 1970s. This issue also played a significant role in the US arms embargo. For further details, see Aydın and Erhan, 2003.
3. According to the National Policy, as identified in the book *The Concept of Scope of the State*, published by the NSC in 1997, '[n]ational policy includes desires coming from history and matching the interests of a nation, as well as it is about the existence of a nation' (*Milliyet*, 28 January 1997).

4

THE ISSUE OF TERRORISM AND THE CAPTURE OF ÖCALAN

Another highly contentious issue that has plagued the relationship between Turkey and Greece consists of terrorism. The issue of terrorism became a serious challenge in Turkish–Greek relations particularly in the mid-1980s. Turkish authorities argued that the Greek government supported the terrorist organisation known as the Kurdish Workers' Party (*Partiya Karkerên Kurdistanê*, PKK), while Greek authorities responded by stressing Turkey's human rights violations against the Kurdish community. Allegations of Greek support to the PKK were prominently reflected in the statements of Turkish securitising actors. In particular, the bilateral relationship reached its 'lowest ebb' following the capture of Abdullah Öcalan, the leader of the PKK, at the residence of the Greek Ambassador to Kenya Georgios Costoulas in 1999. Despite all denials by Greek officials, this crisis revealed Greece's involvement in the issue. This chapter supports the assessment that Turkish actors securitised the link between the PKK and Greece by employing security rhetoric in their statements.

The Roots of PKK Terrorism in Turkey

For almost forty years, the Turkish military has been engaged in direct conflict with the PKK, a terrorist organisation active primarily in the country's southeastern region. The organisation has been an important political actor also in neighbouring countries, such as Syria, Iran and Iraq. This is partly related to the PKK's success in mobilising masses and becoming a social movement with mass appeal in the diaspora (Baser, 2015). The armed terrorist organisation first appeared in Turkey in 1984, under the leadership of Abdullah Öcalan; the subsequent conflict has claimed more than 40,000 lives. In fact, the roots of the PKK can be traced back to the early 1970s, a time when Öcalan studied theories of revolutionary activity and clandestinely organised a party that aimed at starting a communist revolution by means of guerrilla warfare and establishing a separate Kurdish state (Criss, 1995, 18). The organisation was built on a Marxist-Leninist ideology and benefitted from the liberal atmosphere of the 1961 Constitution, which offered opportunities for diversity. To achieve its main objective of establishing an 'Independent, United and Democratic Kurdistan', the PKK has maintained its armed struggle not solely against the Turkish state, but also against its own kin (Criss, 1995, 19; Özcan, 1999, 64). As Criss (1995, 19) has argued, the logic behind murdering Kurds has been threefold: (1) to demonstrate its power in order to convince people to join the rebellion; (2) to prevent people from remaining passive in this struggle; and (3) to stop the Kurdish village guards' collaboration with the state. The Turkish governments did not take into account the local support for the organisation and long held the assumption that the PKK operated through safe havens outside the country.

The ultimate goal of establishing a separate Kurdish state predates the foundation of the Republic of Turkey, when European powers divided the Ottoman Empire into several parts and promised the Kurds (along with the Armenians) the establishment of their own independent states through the Treaty of Sevres in 1920. The establishment of the Republic of Turkey in 1923 officially ended the conditions of the Treaty of Sevres and dashed the Kurds' aspirations. This caused the emergence of the 'Kurdish question' which for many decades has occupied both domestic and foreign policy in Turkey, to varying degrees (Aydınlı, 2002, 223; Yavuz and Özcan, 2006, 102).

A myriad of factors – including the power vacuum in northern Iraq following the Gulf War in 1990–91, the lack of a coherent strategy by the Turkish governments due to its under-estimating the PKK and heavy criticism against Turkey regarding human rights – paved the way for the PKK's ascendancy in the 1990s. Using this opportunity, the PKK terrorist organisation considerably increased its guerrilla attacks, causing a rapid rise in the fatalities for which it was responsible. The number of casualties virtually tripled between 1991 and 1993, when compared with the period between 1984 and 1990 (İlhan 2002, 306–7). Especially the safe havens abroad provided the terrorist organisation a comfortable living space, where it could carry out armed and political activities (Kayhan Pusane, 2015, 729). The terrorist organisation's annual income – derived from criminal activities including drug trafficking, arms smuggling, robbery, extortion and money laundering – was estimated at 86 million US dollars at its peak in the 1990s (Roth and Sever 2007, 906). The PKK even began to collect illegal taxes from the region's residents. From 1993 onwards, Turkey followed a determined counter-insurgency campaign against the PKK within its own borders and in neighbouring countries; this weakened the terrorist organisation considerably and disrupted its pipeline of foreign support. Through the combined military and political pressure, according to the Turkish NSC, the PKK's terrorist acts by 1997 had been reduced to a controllable degree (Kayhan Pusane, 2015, 729), and the Turkish government increased its pressure on foreign countries to stop their support to the PKK.

The conflict has had serious repercussions for Turkish domestic as well as foreign policies. In domestic politics, the conflict has transformed the demographic structure of the country due to large-scale population movements, particularly the willing and forced departure of millions of Kurds from their homes in southeastern Turkey to major cities in western Anatolia (Yavuz and Özcan, 2006, 103). The PKK used a strategy of murdering Kurds to demonstrate its strength and to convince people to 'side [with the PKK] and rise up in rebellion against the Turkish state'; otherwise, the PKK would consider those remaining passive as being on the enemy's side and punish them (Criss, 1995, 19). Thus, the Turkish government has used a wide range of political means to prevent the communalisation of the conflict between Turks and Kurds and has sought to differentiate the PKK from broader Kurdish issues (Yavuz and Özcan, 2006, 103). Turkey's determined counter-terrorism strategy against the PKK did not receive any meaningful understanding and support from the international community; instead, it has been harshly criticised (Çaycı, 2008, 98). Apart from its political impact, the PKK's terrorism has had serious economic repercussions due to uncertainty causing downturns in both business and tourism trends, the shift of resources from other sectors to the defence industry, an increase in military expenditures and so on. In their research, Bilgel and Karahasan (2017, 2) deduced that the emergence of terrorism caused an average decline of 6.6 percent of the real per capita GDP in eastern and southeastern Anatolia between 1988 and 2001. Moreover, PKK terrorism for many years halted development investments in the region.

In foreign policy, external moral, financial, logistical and military support to the terrorist organisation created serious crises between Turkey and various other countries, including neighbouring Iraq, Iran, Syria, Bulgaria, Greece, as well as further Middle Eastern and European countries. As Elekdağ (1996, 33–56) has argued, 'two countries among these neighbours, namely Greece and Syria, had claims on Turkey's vital interests' and 'have been providing every possible aid to the PKK in order to bring Turkey to heel'. This foreign support has created safe havens for PKK guerrilla fighters, allowing them to sustain their armed struggle against Turkey. Furthermore, the activities of PKK guerrillas, particularly near resorts and in areas reliant on tourism, have damaged not only Turkey's capacity to earn revenue from the exchange of foreign currency, but also its international reputation (Ker-Lindsay, 2007, 34). These dire circumstances have resulted in terrorism taking center-stage on the agenda and in the sensitive nature of the issue in Turkish foreign policy, especially in its relations with neighbouring countries. By late 1998, the Turkish government had decided to act in order to stop foreign countries' support to the PKK. Turkish-Syrian relations hit rock-bottom when Turkey threatened Syria with the use of force in October 1998 by deploying troops close to the border (Benli Altunışık, 2010, 152). Syria was an important country for the PKK since the Syrian administration provided support for the organisation and allowed it to operate from its territory. After the signing of the Adana Agreement on 20 October 1998, the bilateral relations between Syria and Turkey began to improve, following a near-war crisis (Aydın and Dizdaroğlu, 2018, 93). In accordance with the Adana Agreement, the Syrian government committed to end its support for the PKK, to recognise the PKK as a terrorist organisation and to deport Abdullah Öcalan from Syria. Following his expulsion from Syria, Öcalan became a fugitive in several European countries, which were 'faced with acute diplomatic dilemmas over the fate of the Kurdish rebel leader' (*BBC*, 16 February 1999).

The PKK leader Abdullah Öcalan first illegally sheltered in Russia before he was arrested and jailed in Italy on 12 November 1998. Despite Turkey's formal request for his extradition, the Italian government refused, on the grounds that a Turkish court could sentence him to death, believing that he should be given political asylum (*BBC*, 16 February 1999; Ker-Lindsay, 2007, 35). The diplomatic cost of providing him political asylum as well as mass protests over the Italian stance on terrorism convinced Italy to reject Öcalan's request for asylum. He was forced to leave Italy in January 1999. Öcalan attempted to find shelter in several other European countries (including the Netherlands, Switzerland and Greece), before he was captured at the Greek Embassy in Kenya. When Öcalan left the embassy on 15 February 1999, a team of the Turkish intelligence unit, with the support of the CIA, finally captured and brought him to Turkey. Öcalan was tried in a Turkish court and sentenced to death for treason and separatism on 26 June 1999. Since Turkey had abolished the death penalty as part of the reforms necessary to start accession negotiations with the EU, Öcalan's sentence was commuted to life imprisonment, and he was imprisoned on İmralı, an island in the Marmara Sea. The following sub-section focuses on the impact of Öcalan's capture at the Greek Embassy on bilateral relations.

The Repercussions of Terrorism on Turkish–Greek Relations

In the context of Turkish–Greek relations, the question of terrorism became a serious challenge in the mid-1980s. Turkish authorities continuously claimed that the Greek government supported the PKK in its brutal attacks against Turkey, while Greek authorities responded by highlighting Turkey's human rights violations against the Kurdish community (Ker-Lindsay, 2000, 218). Various statements by Turkish securitising actors reflect these allegations of Greek support to the PKK. In his well-known article '2 ½ War Strategy', Ambassador Şükrü Elekdağ, the former under-secretary of the Ministry of Foreign Affairs, has argued:

> The Athens government is providing heavy financial support to the PKK's campaign of terror in Turkey. The fact that Athens has sent to Turkey PKK terrorists whom it allowed to reside on its own territory to conduct acts of sabotage against the Turkish tourism industry demonstrates the magnitude of

the 'national paranoia' and hysterical hostility in which Greece has submerged itself against Turkey. (Elekdağ, 1996, 34–35)

Likewise, the Turkish chief of general staff also raised the issue in a statement illustrating the military's concerns over foreign threats emanating from Greece and Syria:

> During the 1980s, Greece allowed separatist terrorist elements to take refuge in the Lavrion camp by granting them status as political refugees. It is remarkable that the PKK and its front organisations have concentrated their efforts in Greece after Andreas Papandreu took office as prime minister. (*Milliyet*, 1 July 1995)

These statements clearly emphasised the threat emanating from Greece against the survival and unity of the referent object. Ambassador Şükrü Elekdağ described the Greek administration's support to the terrorist organisation as a result of 'hysterical hostility' and 'national paranoia' against Turkey. Moreover, he claimed that Greece sought to undermine Turkey's security by using the terrorist organisation, through the direct threats it posed to the unity of the referent object. Turkish Deputy Prime Minister Hikmet Çetin highlighted Greece's link with the terrorist organisation by referring to Greece's 'assistance of a terrorist organisation that aims to separate a country, that is by no means acceptable' (*Cumhuriyet*, 5 July 1995). These statements represent the sentiments that Greece's support to the PKK in the form of funding and of the hosting of terrorist camps on its territory were existential threats to Turkey.

The respective reactions and discourses of Turkish securitising actors were understandable, as the actions of Greek politicians made visible the link between Greece and the PKK. For instance, when Andreas Papandreou came to power in Greece after the 1993 parliamentary elections, Turkey was alarmed due to 'the PASOK's sympathy for the Kurds, and not least for the lethal PKK' (Heraclides, 2010, 133). Likewise, a public meeting in June 1995 between Panayottis Sgurides – the second speaker of the Greek Parliament – and Abdullah Öcalan, along with five other Greek members of parliament, fed Turkish decision-makers' suspicions about Greece's intentions (*Sabah*, 22 June 1995). The attitude of Greek politicians triggered a new series of confrontations between the two countries. In the immediate aftermath of the meeting, Prime Minister Tansu Çiller's rhetoric reached new heights of intensity when compared to her previous statements. As Müfti (1998, 34) has argued, she described the Greeks as 'dishonourable' and reminded them of their expulsion from Anatolia in 1922:

> History has shown the fate of those who attempt to dig a grave for the Turks. Dishonour is not fitting for a human. But dishonour for an entire nation is the worst of its kind.
>
> I call out to the Greek public. You should also warn your administration officials who have put on their blinders. I call out to the friends in the East and the West: Believe in our friendship but fear our enmity. (*Cumhuriyet*, 5 July 1995)

Despite concrete evidence, the Greek government denied all allegations that it provided support to the PKK. Greek Ambassador to Turkey Dimitrios Nezeretis was summoned to the Turkish Ministry of Foreign Affairs twice following the news that Öcalan had come to Athens. However, Ambassador Nezeretis denied all allegations and assured the Turkish diplomats: 'We have earlier said that Öcalan will not be given permission to come to Greece. If we say something, we keep our word' (*Anadolu Agency*, 1 February 1999). But Turkish–Greek relations suffered perhaps the worst crisis when Öcalan was captured at the Greek Embassy in Kenya.

After Öcalan had been driven from Syria, he sought refuge in several countries, including Italy and Russia, which were unwilling to offer him asylum, as well as Greece, which became the final destination for him and his two female aides on 29 January 1999 (Bonner, 2005, 60; Varouhakis, 2009, 2). Even the private plane that facilitated the escape of Öcalan and his aides was hired by a retired Greek navy officer, a long-time friend of Öcalan's (Varouhakis, 2009, 2). Athens sought to avoid the regional and international repercussions that would emerge if it became public that it was harbouring Turkey's most wanted fugitive and decided to fly Öcalan and his aides to Kenya, where they remained in the Greek Ambassador Georgios Costoulas' residence, hoping to negotiate an arrangement for asylum (Bonner, 2005, 60; Varouhakis, 2009, 2). As rumours about the whereabouts of the terrorist leader continued, Turkish Prime Minister

Bülent Ecevit organised a press conference and shared Turkey's position on the issue, saying the following:

> ... the important thing is that Öcalan encounters difficulties in finding a shelter for himself. He is wandering from one country to another, but he cannot find a country that will admit him on its territories. Everyone has realised the fact that sheltering Öcalan means to become an accomplice of his crimes against humanity. (*Anadolu Agency*, 1 February 1999)

On 15 February 1999, Abdullah Öcalan was arrested in a joint operation by the US Central Intelligence Agency (CIA), the Turkish National Intelligence Agency (MIT) and the Israeli Institute for Intelligence and Special Task Agency (Mossad) (Roth and Sever 2007, 905). He was placed on a plane where Turkish intelligence agents awaited him.

With the revelation of Greece's support to the PKK and its role in Öcalan's escape and hiding, Turkish–Greek relations reached their 'lowest ebb' (Alpogan, 2005, 165; Evin, 2005, 396). Öcalan's confessions during his interrogation regarding the role of Greece – along with Iran and the RoC – in procuring most of the group's heavy weaponry and providing training facilities at a refugee camp in Lavrion confirmed Turkey's fears about its security (Bonner, 2005, 61; Ker-Lindsay, 2007, 38). Öcalan was holding a false passport under the name Lazaros Mavros (a Greek-Cypriot journalist), which had been issued by the Greek Cypriot administration, and he claimed that the PKK had even received funds from the Greek-Orthodox Church (Ker-Lindsay, 2007, 38; Varouhakis, 2009, 2). In response, Turkey's securitising actors issued a harsh criticism of Greece's support to the PKK. Hüseyin Kıvrıkoğlu, the chief of general staff, reiterated the involvement of Greece: 'It was already known that Greece has been supporting the PKK. [The Greeks] have nothing to say, no place to escape to. The whole world has seen what they have done. They were caught red-handed' (*Sabah*, 23 February 1999; *BBC*, 22 February 1999).

Likewise, Turkish President Süleyman Demirel labelled Greece an 'outlaw state that sponsored terrorism' and said: 'Turkey reserves its right to take the necessary precautions for its self-defence arising from international law, if Greece continues its irresponsible behaviour' (*Milliyet*, 27 February 1999). In a similar tone, Turkish Prime Minister Bülent Ecevit emphasised: 'Greece was caught red-handed on the issue of terror, now Greece has paid the price for helping the PKK. It should be a lesson to any country that supports terrorism' (*BBC*, 19 February 1999; *Milliyet*, 19 February 1999).

Through the lens of securitisation theory, these statements demonstrate how Greece represented a threat for Turkey. The support for a terrorist organisation that sought to establish an 'independent, united and democratic' state on Turkish territory through its struggle against the Turkish state constituted nothing less than an imminent and existential threat against the referent object. The Turkish president's emphasis on self-defence in the face of such a threat mainly stemmed from a direct attack against its territorial integrity by a terrorist organisation that was 'sponsored' by neighbouring Greece. Despite the denials by Greek officials, this crisis revealed the extent of Greece's involvement, and Turkish officials asserted that Greece 'was caught red-handed' and engaging in 'irresponsible behaviour'. Turkish President Süleyman Demirel also underscored the emergency measures, stressing that 'Turkey reserved its right to take necessary precautions'. This rhetoric supports the conclusion that Turkish actors securitised the link between Greece and the PKK by using a security grammar.

Greek politicians' involvement in Öcalan's escape generated tension not just between the two governments, but also between long-standing collaborative initiatives. As Özel (2004, 255) has pointed out, following the Öcalan crisis the Turkish–Greek Business Council's meeting was cancelled upon Turkey's unilateral decision. The council, which had been established in 1988 in the spirit of the Davos Meeting, was an important initiative in order to create alternative dialogue channels among individuals in favour of friendly relations. However, the post-Öcalan climate caused the council to halt its activities.

The involvement of several Greek politicians in PKK leader Abdullah Öcalan's escape also led to domestic turbulence in Greece. Greek Prime Minister Kostas Simitis, faced with this political debacle, ordered the resignation of the involved ministers after heavy criticism from his own party and MPs. Accordingly, three members of the Greek cabinet – including Theodoros Pangalos (Minister of Foreign Affairs), Alekos Papadopoulos (Interior Minister) and Philipos Petsalnikos (Public Order Minister) – were forced to resign over their involvement in harbouring Öcalan. Greek Minister of Foreign Affairs Theodors Pangalos had been tasked with hiding Öcalan at the Greek ambassador's residence in Nairobi and finding him political asylum, whereas Interior Minister Alekos Papadopoulos had orchestrated the Greek National Intelligence Agency's (EYP) involvement in the operation, and Public Order Minister Philipos Petsalnikos had been in charge of the security forces that failed to prevent Öcalan from being smuggled into Greece. Moreover, the head of the EYP also resigned soon after Öcalan's seizure. Greek Prime Minister Simitis contained the scandal by replacing the involved ministers, which helped him change the balance of power in his cabinet in favour of moderates. As Verney (1997, 200) has pointed out, Simitis' major weakness in this period stemmed from 'his limited power base within his own party'. In a twist of fate, maybe one of the most unfortunate foreign policy issues for Greece – the involvement of several Greek politicians in PKK leader Abdullah Öcalan's escape – caused the removal of the hard-liners in the government. This fundamental change within the ruling PASOK party paved the way for an adjustment of Greek foreign policy, with a special focus on relations with Turkey and the EU.

The capture of Abdullah Öcalan and the revelation of Greek officials' involvement in his escape would likely have resulted in increasing distrust towards Greece from the Turkish side, as well as potential acts of retaliation. Ker-Lindsay (2007, 36–37) has written that 'the incident had become Greece's most humiliating post-war diplomatic fiasco' and that it culminated in a crisis between the two countries. However, the atmosphere within the bilateral relations changed dramatically, and the capture of the PKK leader ultimately became conducive to dialogue rather than retaliation (Nachmani, 2001, 87). Still, the issue created great sensitivity among Turkish decision-makers, and whenever similar problems have arisen between Greece and Turkey (as seen in the post-2016 period), the past has reared its head in their statements.

As will be discussed in the third part of this book, the escape of eight putschist soldiers to Greece following the 15 July 2016 coup attempt in Turkey, as well as the growing number of Turkish citizens seeking political asylum in Greece, awakened bitter memories. In the post-2016 period, Turkish decision-makers in their statements have regularly used similar rhetoric, either blaming Greece for or warning Greece not to become a 'harbour of FETO' and 'safe haven for terrorists'. It is even possible to discern an emphasis on the name Öcalan in various statements by the Turkish Ministry of Foreign Affairs:

> This reveals once again that the traditional sentiments of the Greek political power against Turkey have not changed. Greece, which provided a shelter to PKK Leader Öcalan in the past, today grants asylum to criminals wanted by Turkey and easily ignores the court judgements regarding their extradition [. . .] (*Turkish Ministry of Foreign Affairs*, 5 August 2018)

These kinds of crises have increased the sensitivity on both sides and caused a surge of nationalist sentiments, which in turn have caused further deterioration in relations. Since the public in both countries has considered each other as threat, the crises have had a snowball effect on relations. Even though the Turkish decision-makers' rhetoric has been quite accusatory towards Greece, the atmosphere in the post-Öcalan crisis somewhat changed under the initiative of the Turkish Ministry of Foreign Affairs, which focused on one of the critical junctures in Turkey's quest for EU membership, the Helsinki Summit. Thus, it is possible to argue that Turkish decision-makers did not want to retaliate against and antagonise Greece due to this critical juncture. Moreover, as Ayman (2002, 233) has argued, the Simitis government acted quickly to clean the debris of the Öcalan affair by forcing three ministers to resign, while Turkey was still debating how Greek support for the PKK could be brought up in international platforms.

Just a few short months after the capture of Abdullah Öcalan and the revelation of Greek politicians' involvement in sheltering him in the Greek Embassy in Kenya, on 24 May 1999, İsmail Cem, the Turkish Minister of Foreign Affairs, sent a letter to his Greek counterpart, George Papandreou. In his letter, İsmail Cem proposed that the two countries should discuss the terrorism problem and that the two ministers examine ways to initiate a plan of reconciliation between their countries (Ker-Lindsay, 2000, 220; Evin, 2004, 397; Alpogan, 2005, 166–67). Even though the connection between the three Greek politicians and PKK leader Abdullah Öcalan had been securitised by decision-makers in Turkey, İsmail Cem's letter triggered a change in discourse, followed by political engagement between the two countries. Nevertheless, İsmail Cem's letter was a diplomatic manoeuvre, as he implicitly asked the Greek administration to admit its connections with the PKK. In his letter, Cem (2009, 129) proposed cooperation against international terrorism and amelioration of relations as follows:

> Our initial step should be to address the problem of what is perceived in Turkey as links that exist in Greece with terrorist organisations and their systematic encouragement. This is a matter of crucial importance for us, and recent events have made it imperative that this issue be handled in an explicit manner and at the bilateral level between our two countries.
>
> I, therefore, suggest that Turkey and Greece conclude an agreement to combat terrorism. Resolution of this issue would permit us to approach our known differences with greater confidence. The substance of this agreement may be inspired by accords we have already signed with some of our other neighbours, but is should also be specific to the nature of the problem as it affects our relations. [. . .] I further suggest that parallel to the signing and implementation of such an agreement, we could also initiate a plan for reconciliation.

In his late response on 25 June 1999, George Papandreou sent his congratulations about Cem's re-appointment as Minister of Foreign Affairs and suggested to extend the cooperation in a number of areas:

> In parallel, we could also envisage resuming dialogue on issues, many of which we have attempted to deal with in the past. Cooperation in several fields of mutual interest such as culture, tourism, environment, crime, economic cooperation and ecological problems should be amongst the topics of our talks. (Cem, 2009, 131)

The reason behind the late response as well as Papandreou's suggestion to extend the areas of cooperation were related to concerns regarding the implications of ties between Greece and terrorist activities. As Heraclides (2010, 145) has stressed, Cem's 'letter was loaded with dynamite, for it implied that Greece had to admit, however indirectly, that it had condoned the activities of the PKK'. In his own account, İsmail Cem (2009, 129) has also admitted that he saw the Greek government's acknowledgement of the above-mentioned fact as a precondition for an amelioration of relations. Even though Cem (2009, 131–34) evaluated Papandreou's response as a political manoeuvre to turn the terrorism issue into an ordinary cooperation area between the two countries in order to prevent any criticism in domestic politics, he welcomed the approach of the Greek minister of foreign affairs, which would advance bilateral relations. Thus, it would not be wrong to argue that two solution-oriented foreign ministers planted the seeds of a slow but sure rapprochement process, at a time when relations experienced the peak point of securitisation due to subsequent crises.

Despite the various attempts to ease tensions – for instance, with the Madrid Joint Statement of July 1997 – there was little movement towards change. This underscores the importance of investigating the underlying reasons for the rapprochement between Turkey and Greece and how it was possible for Turkey to alter the trajectory of its relations with Greece following years of enmity and hostility. In this context, the next part of the book is dedicated to the rapprochement process between the two countries, which started with a letter that broke the orthodox securitised discourse on Greece. Hence, the letter of İsmail Cem, the Turkish Minister of Foreign Affairs, to his Greek counterpart, George Papandreou, on 24 May 1999 constitutes a milestone in the relationship between Turkey and Greece. Investigating the root causes of this rapprochement will assist us in better understanding the dynamics that contributed to the transformation of bilateral relations and to determine whether rapprochement has led to desecuritisation. The following analysis will employ Hansen's forms of desecuritisation to conclude whether desecuritisation adequately explains the rapprochement process.

Part 2

DESECURITISATION IN TURKISH FOREIGN POLICY: THE RAPPROCHEMENT BETWEEN TURKEY AND GREECE (1999–2016)

PART 2 INTRODUCTION

After 1999, Turkish–Greek relations entered a promising process of rapprochement, also referred to as détente, which lasted until 2016. The terms 'détente' and 'rapprochement' can be used interchangeably, as their definitions are quite similar. While 'détente' defines an improvement in the relationship between two countries that in the past were not friendly towards and did not trust each other, 'rapprochement' refers to the development of friendlier relations between countries or groups of people who have been enemies (Oxford Dictionary, 2006). Although all early attempts at easing the tension between Turkey and Greece had failed, earthquakes in both Turkey and Greece, in August and September 1999, respectively, created empathy and solidarity among Turks and Greeks and provided fertile ground for decision-makers to implement their already launched initiatives towards dialogue. The process started with 'low politics' – including economy, trade, energy, tourism and so on – rather than the traditional 'high politics' since there existed great suspicion due to core issues such as the Aegean and Cyprus (Lesser, 2001, 5; Öniş, 2001, 42; Liaropoulos, 2008, 28–29). However, both sides believed that it would be much more meaningful to focus on the core issues if the current dialogue- and confidence-building measures were consolidated and extended. With the initiation of the rapprochement process, Turkey and Greece have made serious progress in fields such as energy, economy and minority rights.

The rapprochement period has found overwhelming support on both sides, with 89 percent of the Turkish elites in favour, in contrast to 63.5 percent of their Greek counterparts, according to elite surveys jointly conducted by Triantaphyllou, Ifantis and Dizdaroğlu in both Greece and Turkey in 2015 and 2016, respectively. This support is quite valuable considering that the level of trust towards each other is relatively low. According to the surveys, only 28 percent of the Turkish elites think that Turkey can trust Greece, while the level of trust towards Turkey is much lower (11.4 percent) among the Greek elites. Despite their lack of trust, both countries' elites are in favour of the rapprochement. The focus on elites rather than public opinion is crucial since 'the competition among elites not only shapes public opinion but helps to formulate policy as well' (Triantaphyllou, 2017).

It is possible to classify the existing literature based on explanations regarding the root causes of the current rapprochement process, ranging from its being a product of 'disaster/earthquake diplomacy', over the impact of the Europeanisation process in both countries' foreign policies with a special focus on the EU's Helsinki Summit, to the role of civil society actors in both countries; from the role of the ministers of foreign affairs in both Turkey and Greece, to the role of third parties such as the US. First and foremost, the subsequent earthquakes in both Turkey and Greece in August and September of 1999, respectively, played a significant role in the growing mutual empathy in both communities. In such an atmosphere, the increase in interactions among citizens as well as civil societies allowed decision-makers on both sides to change the course of the relationship. Still, the common denominator in both countries' foreign policies (namely, 'Europeanisation') has triggered transformation in bilateral relations through changes in domestic and security policies. With the 1999 Helsinki Summit, a new era in bilateral relations began within the framework of the EU. While Greece started to 'reinterpret its national interests' within the EU, Turkey's quest for EU membership has played a catalyst role in terms of promoting policies that prioritise cooperation between the two (Grigoriadis, 2003; Rumelili, 2005). It would be naïve to think of all these developments as independent from the role of the two solution-oriented foreign ministers on both sides of the Aegean. Turkish Minister of Foreign Affairs İsmail Cem and his Greek counterpart, George Papandreou, played a crucial part in this transformation; thus, it is possible to identify both foreign ministers as the architects of the rapprochement process. Likewise, third parties, such as the US, played substantial roles in terms of eliminating potential tensions in the relationship between Turkey and Greece and providing a suitable atmosphere for the rapprochement. Moreover, this part of the book aims to provide a novel approach that will fill a gap in the literature by analysing the rapprochement process from the perspective of desecuritisation.

This book argues that, while it is possible to explain this rapprochement process based on the framework of forms of desecuritisation, this explanation must be closely interrelated with the above-mentioned explanations rather than contradicting them. Accordingly, the present argument posits that the case of Turkish–Greek rapprochement very well fits a form of desecuritisation termed *change through stabilisation*, which refers to a process of moving any issues out of the security discourse, even though the larger conflict still looms in the background. The rapprochement process was an exceptional period in bilateral relations, with the two countries focusing on cooperation and dialogue, even though there were no tangible changes in the core disputes between the two.

Desecuritisation, which will be used as a category of analysis, is simply the inverse process, indicating 'the shifting of issues out of emergency mode and into the normal bargaining process of the political sphere' (Buzan et al. 1998, 4). In other words, desecuritisation is the process of 'moving [. . .] issues off the "security" agenda and back into the realm of public discourse and "normal" political dispute and accommodation' (Williams, 2003, 523). It is generally acknowledged that desecuritisation figures more prominently in Wæver's initial works (such as Wæver, 1995, 2000) than in the scholarship of the Copenhagen School, which spends less time exploring desecuritisation (Peoples and Vaughan-Williams, 2010, 83). Lene Hansen (2012, 530) has argued that '[d]esecuritisation is derivative of securitisation semantically (modified through "de"), and in terms of the political modality, the concept identifies: desecuritisation happens "away from" or "out of" securitisation'.

Understanding the shift from securitisation to desecuritisation is very difficult considering that the latter is much more abstract than the former. As Behnke (2006, 65) has pointed out, '[i]f securitisation is a speech-act, desecuritisation should be marked by the lack of any such speech acts'. Aras and

Polat (2008, 499) put it differently: 'Desecuritisation occurs not through further speech but through its absence'. Wæver (2000, 252) has also emphasised this sentiment, asserting that 'one cannot desecuritise through speech-acts such as, "I hereby declare this issue to no longer be a threat"'; he proposed the idea of 'desecuritisation through avoidance of security speak' (2000, 253). To that end, Behnke (2006, 64) has argued that 'desecuritisation can never really happen':

> States continuously securitise issues and actors in order to produce a national identity. Desecuritisation is perhaps best understood as the fading away of one particular issue or actor from the repertoire of these processes. At some point, certain 'threats' might no longer exercise our minds and imaginations sufficiently and are replaced with more powerful and stirring imageries.

There also exists a dilemma in the Copenhagen School's concept of securitisation. According to Williams (2003, 523), the Copenhagen School does not regard an act of securitisation as a positive value or as a required development to tackle specific issues. Instead, societies should, as much as possible, operate within the realm of normal politics, where issues can be debated and addressed within the boundaries of politicisation. Desecuritisation, therefore, is the 'optimal long-range option' or 'the ultimate aim' for the scholars of the Copenhagen School, since they consider that 'security should be seen as negative, as a failure to deal with issues as normal politics' (Wæver, 1995; Buzan et al., 1998, 29). Jef Huysmans (1998, 576) has provided an alternative approach based on an ethical-political framework while investigating sources of desecuritisation:

> Desecuritisation unmakes politics which identify the community on the basis of the expectations of hostility. Instead of simply removing policy questions from the security sector and plugging them into another sector, desecuritisation turns into a political strategy which challenges the fundaments of the political realist constitution of the political community head on.

Following the logic of the theory, Bilgin (2007, 557–59) has identified 'universal desecuritisation' as the best choice for the Copenhagen School, referring to the assumption that 'desecuritisation is the preferable ethico-political strategy for scholars and societal actors, regardless of time and space'.

Peoples and Vaughan-Williams (2010, 83) have also stressed that more security is not better, as securitisation of any issue accompanies a particular type of emergency politics and a militarised mode of thinking.

While securitisation theory scholars provide a comprehensive framework to analyse how securitisation occurs, a comparable framework for desecuritisation is lacking. Contrary to the collective efforts to produce a securitisation theory, Wæver (2000, 253) has outlined three options for desecuritisation: to not 'talk about issues in terms of security in the first place', to 'not generate security dilemmas and other vicious spirals' once an issue is securitised and, finally, 'to move security issues back into normal politics'. The lack of a systematic framework for desecuritisation has resulted in a slew of divergent scholarly interpretations. Lene Hansen's 'four forms of desecuritisation', as proposed in her 2012 article, provide a thoroughly constructed scaffold for various empirical studies. Hansen's framework is a broad categorisation that includes most other approaches to desecuritisation. She has responded to debates around the need for a desecuritisation framework with the following words (2012, 539): 'We are unlikely to find – at least at the moment – instances of desecuritisation, which cannot be analysed through these four forms of desecuritisation'. The first form, *change through stabilisation*, was derived from the Cold War détente period and gave Wæver a reason to invent the concept of desecuritisation (Hansen 2012, 536–39). According to Hansen (2012, 539), this form of desecuritisation refers to the 'rather slow move out of an explicit security discourse, which in turn facilitates a less militaristic, less violent and hence more genuinely political form of engagement. It also requires that parties to a conflict recognise each other as legitimate'.

Although *change through stabilisation* is associated with 'macro-desecuritisation' – such as the Cold War détente – Hansen has listed instances that are consistent with this component of the theory, such as cross-border minority conflicts. The second form, *replacement*, refers to a process in which 'one issue is moved out of security, while another is simultaneously securitised' (Hansen 2012, 541). This form of desecuritisation aligned with Behnke's (2006, 65) argument about the replacement of threats with more powerful, stirring imagery. The third form, *rearticulation*, denotes the fundamental transformation of an issue that is no longer securitised, through the resolution of threats and dangers and without any looming conflict. It is therefore a more radical form of political engagement (Hansen 2012, 542–43). The fourth and final form of desecuritisation, *silencing*, depicts the disappearance of or failure to register an issue in the security discourse (Hansen 2012, 544–45).

In the context of Turkish–Greek relations, the book borrows from Hansen the different forms of desecuritisation in order to understand the relation between rapprochement and desecuritisation. By doing so, this study reaches the conclusion that the rapprochement process, as an outcome of several factors, can also be read from the viewpoints of *change through stability* and, to a certain extent, *rearticulation*, while other forms such as *replacement* and *silencing* are not suitable. Before my analysis of the transformation from the viewpoint of desecuritisation, the following section will focus on all root causes behind the rapprochement process, which will also provide a fruitful ground for desecuritisation. As discussed in more depth in the following section, this part of the book argues that there exists significant evidence showing that actors have preferred to desecuritise issues by employing various strategies for taking these very issues out of the military/security sphere.

5

THE ROOT CAUSES OF RAPPROCHEMENT

The rapprochement process between Turkey and Greece, like many other aspects of their relations, has been an attractive topic for scholars. There exists a large number of studies investigating this process from different perspectives. Analysing all of these studies in detail is beyond the scope of this chapter; however, it is possible to classify them within four main categories: the impact of the earthquakes and the empowerment of civil society; the Europeanisation process in both Turkey and Greece; the role of the two solution-oriented ministers of foreign affairs; and, finally, the role of third parties. The following sub-sections will briefly focus on each explanation in order to familiarise readers with the context, as well as to show that it is possible to explain the same period through the different forms of desecuritisation.

Earthquakes and the Empowerment of Civil Society

Turkey and Greece experienced the same destiny in August and September of 1999, respectively, when disaster struck both countries. İzmit, an industrialised town in western Turkey, was hit by a powerful earthquake on 17 August 1999. The earthquake and its aftershocks left approximately 20,000 people dead and more than 50,000 injured. Immediately after the earthquake, as did many other countries, Greece sent to Turkey several teams on a transport plane of the Greek Air Force, including two medical aid teams of eleven nurses and twenty-five fully equipped rescue teams with sniffer dogs and emergency supplies (*Hürriyet*, 18 August 1999). In fact, this was not the first time that Greeks had given support, as Greece had also sent relief aid and non-governmental relief teams to conduct search-and-rescue operations and provide medical care in Turkey immediately after the Erzincan and Dinar earthquakes in 1992 and 1995, respectively (Ganapati et al., 2010, 165). In addition to the efforts of the rescue teams, the Greek public also tried to help the earthquake victims in Turkey by raising money and donating food, medicine and other items (Ker-Lindsay, 2000, 221).

Just twenty-two days after the İzmit earthquake, on 7 September 1999, Athens was hit by an earthquake that killed hundreds of people and injured hundreds more. Despite the fact that Turkey was trying to recover from its own disaster, it quickly sent a Turkish twenty-member search-and-rescue team to Greece to assist in the rescue efforts in cooperation with the Greek teams (*Hurriyet Daily News*, 10 September 1999). During the natural disasters that shook both countries within several weeks, the media, which had been manipulating nationalist sentiments on both sides by using patriotic language, also acted in a prudent manner, resulting in a breakthrough in relations. One of the most striking indicators, as Gündoğdu (2001, 112) has shared in her article, reflected the mutual empathy/solidarity between Turkey and Greece, as the Greek daily *Ta Nea* wrote in its issue following the earthquake in Turkey: 'We are all Turks'. The Turkish daily *Hürriyet* responded in Greek: '*Efharisto Poli, File*' (Thank You, Neighbour). The media widely broadcasting the suffering of both countries' people after the earthquakes triggered mutual empathy.

While there had been no cordial relationship between Turks and Greeks before the natural catastrophes, both communities were more willing to accept the improvement of relations than had previously been thought (Grigoriadis, 2011, 121). However, the spirit of solidarity and the interrelated positive developments played a catalytic role for the growing mutual empathy in both communities, improving the interaction among Turkish and Greek civil societies as well as allowing the leaders to change their rhetoric towards each other. As seen during and after the earthquake, the statements of decision-makers from both countries were very friendly and in harmony with the demands of civil society. Following the Athens earthquake, Turkish President Süleyman Demirel sent a message to his Greek counterpart to share his feelings: 'We are in solidarity with the people of Greece. Please be certain that Turkey will not withold any support or help for your country and people in the face of this calamity' (*Milliyet*, 8 September 1999).

Likewise, Prime Minister Bülent Ecevit emphasised the friendship between the two countries and their citizens as follows:

> Through these two earthquakes, which have shaken these two neighbouring countries, nature has once again reminded us of the shared fate of the two countries. We [Turkey] share Greece's grief resulting from the earthquake just as Greece shared ours [Turks]. We are determined to exert every possible effort to ease this pain. (*Milliyet*, 9 September 1999)

Apart from the positive messages by the decision-makers, there also existed other initiatives that provided fertile ground for the improvement of relations between the two countries. Right after the disasters, Turkish Minister of Foreign Affairs İsmail Cem offered 'the idea of the establishment of a joint Greek and Turkish disaster relief force' (Ker-Lindsay, 2000, 226; Ganapati et al., 2010, 166). This was a result of the positive atmosphere that emerged after the 1999 earthquakes, as the two governments actively pursued bilateral disaster-related collaboration. This joint initiative proposal, referred to as the 'Joint Hellenic-Turkish Standby Disaster Relief Unit' (JHET-SDRU), by the governments of Turkey and Greece was adopted in the 54th session of the UN General Assembly held on 6 December 1999 (UN A/RES/54/30). After several meetings, Turkey and Greece signed a protocol on the formation of JHET-SDRU on 8 November 2001, which came into force in Turkey in 2004 and in Greece in 2006 (*Turkish Official Newspaper*, 24 May 2004). According to the protocol between Turkey and Greece, the JHET-SDRU consisted of forty persons from governmental and non-governmental institutions from both countries, with the 'aim to increase their collective capacity to provide timely and effective humanitarian assistance to populations affected by sudden onset natural disasters' (*Turkish Official Newspaper*, 24 May 2004). In line with the protocol, both countries continued to work with the UN Office for the Coordination of Humanitarian Affairs in order to ensure that the efforts of the JHET-SDRU complemented international and regional activities. Thus, it is possible to argue that decision-makers followed the public preference for solidarity and peace, and the diplomatic process that had started months before the earthquakes automatically gained pace.

One of the positive developments of the natural disasters in both countries, along with their transformative effect on the media and decision-makers, was the empowerment of civil society contacts and initiatives between the two states. Civil society had a serious impact on reversing the process of antagonism that had caused long-lasting prejudices on both sides. One of the instances that showed the positive atmosphere and mutual trust between Turks and Greeks was the fact that Greek cross-border shoppers were allowed to enjoy a traditional Turkish retail business practice: credit lines for regular customers (Güvenç, 2004, 1). The increase of civil society activities entailed institutionalism as well. As Rumelili (2005, 8) has pointed out, the activities of civil societies are 'no longer just meetings of "Greeks" and "Turks" for dialogue and friendship, but joint efforts around common causes and interests, be they promoting the status of women, or exploiting the tourism and trade potential'.

Nevertheless, the impact of civil society had already started to increase within the EU context that had provided legitimacy and funding for joint civil society initiatives related to Turkish–Greek cooperation and dialogue (Öniş and Yılmaz, 2001, 13; Rumelili, 2004, 10). As Özel (2004, 269) has pointed out, 'many concerned Greeks and Turks from different walks of life looked for a workable "second track" diplomatic route', even in the atmosphere of insecurity and mistrust of the 1990s; however, most of these efforts had failed, for several reasons. The EU, as already mentioned, played a significant role in eliminating one of the barriers to cooperative activities specifically at the level of civil society. The generous contribution of the EU can clearly be seen through its funding of two programmes: the Civil Society Development Programme introduced in 2002 with its budget of 8 million Euro to promote civic dialogue and to enhance the capacity of NGOs in Turkey; and the 35-million Euro package approved in 2004 to support cross-border cooperation between the two (Rumelili, 2004, 10). With the empowerment of inofficial organisations, think-tanks and individuals such as private persons, businessmen and journalists, these programmes acted as agents of change, message-carriers and intermediators (Özel, 2004, 270–71). The Greek–Turkish Business Council founded in 1988 in the spirit of the Davos Meetings between Turgut Özal and Andreas Papandreou had remained dormant since then, but now it was re-activated for the continued cooperation between Turkey and Greece (Liargovas, 2003, 133; Oğuzlu, 2004, 95; Heraclides, 2010, 151). Likewise, the Turkish–Greek Forum, one of the most promising initiatives which consists of prominent citizens of different backgrounds in Turkey and Greece, still continues to be an engine for enhancing dialogue and improving relations between the two countries.[1]

It is obvious that the earthquakes in both Turkey and Greece played a fundamental role, even if not a primary one, in increasing dialogue between the two communities, in breaking deep-seated stereotypes, enabling joint civil society initiatives and providing decision-makers with some scope to commit to the rapprochement process. The dialogue between the Turkish and Greek ministers of foreign affairs had already started with İsmail Cem's letter to his Greek counterpart on 24 May 1999, one and a half months before the İzmit earthquake. Thus, in the words of Cem (2009, 138), 'The subsequent earthquakes increased the pace of rapprochement process between Turkey and Greece; however, this process was neither a product of earthquakes, nor started through earthquakes'.

Yet, both sides never under-estimated the importance of the shift in public opinion due to natural disasters. As Turkish Minister of Foreign Affairs İsmail Cem pointed out, 'people of both countries have superseded politicians' in showing a new, progressive direction (Siegl, 2002, 44). Likewise, George Papandreou (2001, 6) has also pointed out:

> The earthquakes that shook Greece and Turkey in summer 1999 create a new climate in our recent diplomatic history. Tragedy generated a genuine feeling of human warmth between two peoples involved in historical strife. Spontaneous and dramatic acts of fraternity and solidarity were expressed between the citizens of Greece and Turkey. These acts short-circuited elaborate diplomatic strategies and exerted powerful pressure on our governments to move ahead boldly. Our mandate became clear. Our people desire to live in peace together.

Minister of Foreign Affairs İsmail Cem, in his speech delivered at the ceremony for the 'Statesman of the Year' award on 2 May 2000, said:

As representatives of Turkey and Greece, George and I are standing before you today for one simple reason: We have faithfully translated the feelings of the Turkish and Greek peoples into policies and acts.

Back in June 1999, we had already initiated, as two ministers, a process of consultation and joint work on our bilateral issues, which was later expedited by the immense solidarity between our two peoples during the tragic earthquakes of last summer. On both sides of the Aegean, Greeks and Turks have rediscovered that they are thinking of each other more than thought in general. (Cem, 2009, 169)

In spite of the new relationship between Turkey and Greece based on mutual trust and cooperation due to civil society initiatives, its reflection on public opinion was quite different because of the prolonged disputes between the two. As Birand (1991, 30) has pointed out, public opinion sometimes acted as an impediment to the improvement of relations. According to one such public opinion survey, 36.1 percent of the respondents answered to the open-ended question of 'which country is Turkey's worst enemy in the international arena' by identifying Greece (Çarkoğlu and Kirişci, 2004, 126–27). Undoubtedly, such a result is to be expected, considering the burden of their shared history, as both Turkey and Greece continued to perceive each other as a source of threat. Accordingly, the media's stance is a significant determinant for the course of relations, as the prevailing sentiments in both communities are open to re-ignite any time.

When senior officials from the Turkish and Greek Ministries of Foreign Affairs gathered in early September, the impact of the new positive atmosphere and the encouraging stance of the media became most obvious. Both sides found themselves under the pressure of the media to achieve results in their meetings (Ker-Lindsay, 2000, 225). At that time, prominent columnists such as Sami Kohen, Mehmet Ali Birand and Cengiz Çandar began to criticise Turkey's traditional nationalist stance and securitised discourse on taboo issues such as Cyprus or the Kurdish question, and the lack of bold steps in Turkey's integration process with the EU (Heraclides, 2010, 150–51). The impact of the prevailing positive atmosphere maintained over the following months paved the way for Greece's support for Turkey's candidacy to the EU, which was confirmed by the European Council's Helsinki Summit on 10–11 December 1999.

The Europeanisation Process in Turkey and Greece

Since the foundation of the EU, both Turkey and Greece have been interested in becoming a member of this union. While the EU accepted Greece as one of its member-states in 1981, Turkey's long-lasting accession process has proceeded at a snail's pace. Therefore, it would not be exaggerated to say that Turkey's lasting desire to become a member-state is still a distant dream. However, the process of 'Europeanisation' – one of the meanings of this term is the adoption of EU rules and regulations not only by member-states, but also by candidate or other associated countries – has seriously impacted both Turkey and Greece's domestic and security policies.

For Greece, this process has led to a shift in its foreign policy behaviour, from a nationalistic stance towards an approach based on diplomacy, negotiation and compromise, which is more compatible with the European model (Öniş and Yılmaz, 2001, 14; Liaropoulos, 2008, 29). In the 1990s, Greece was marginalised within the EU due to its economic problems, along with multi-faceted problems in both domestic and foreign policy. Despite the fact that Greece was struggling, the headlines in the post-election period (such as that featured by the *Frankfurter Algemeine Zeitung* – 'Greece, Welcome to the European Club') reflected the prevailing optimism in Europe towards the new prime minister Kostas Simitis (Verney, 1997, 193). The Simitis government declared in its 'Government Programme' on 29 January 1996:

> Greece's power lies in its ability to compete successfully inside an interdependent world. This requires a national strategy, whereby a set of policies with the aim of generating and maximising the inner components of power, which are: economic stability, self-sustainable development, effective public administration, social cohesion and high standards in education. (Kazamias, 1997, 74)

Although Kostas Simitis was in favour of a Europe-centred foreign policy and wanted to change its course, including restoring relations with Turkey, he faced several difficulties immediately after he took office. The Kardak incident and other subsequent crises in that period, which might be evaluated as the tensest phase in Turkish–Greek relations, revealed how difficult it would have been to reach his goals and to change entrenched Greek perceptions of Turkey. In any case, his term was closely associated with the Europeanisation process in several areas such as economics, as well as domestic and foreign policy.

Moreover, the existence of hard-liners in Greek politics and the resistance to change counted among the barriers to a transformation in foreign policy. As already mentioned above, one of the diplomatic crises in his era – the involvement of several Greek politicians in PKK leader Abdullah Öcalan's escape – aided him in eliminating the hard-liners in the government. The forced resignation of three members of the Greek cabinet paved the way for an adjustment of Greek foreign policy, with a special focus on relations with Turkey and the EU.

Last but not the least, Greece's traditional foreign policy approach was based on a balance-of-power thinking; this thinking was designed to counter potential military threats such as Turkey or the Soviet Union (at least before it collapsed) and used Greece's membership in international organisations as leverage against such threats (Ker-Lindsay, 2007, 120; Liaropoulos, 2008, 27). This traditional security perception required the allocation of substantial resources, which for many years constituted a serious economic burden for the Greek economy. As Kollias, Manolas and Paleologouc (2004, 190) have pointed out, in comparative terms, Greece is the most militarised country in the NATO and the EU in terms of human and material resources invested in defence. For the period between 1990 and 1999, Greece's military expenditure as part of its GDP was on average 3.5 percent, the highest after the US and Turkey's 3.8 percent for the same period (see Table 5.1).

Thus, Kostas Simitis wanted to reduce the arms spending, which constituted a serious burden to the Greek economy and a barrier for Greece to join the European Monetary Union (EMU) in order to reach his goal of increasing Greece's integration and reputation with(in) the EU (Heraclides, 2010, 138). In the mind of Simitis, becoming a member of the EMU was a political rather than an economic issue. At this point, the Turkish bid to become an EU member inevitably provided the Greek government with leverage concerning the differences between Turkey and Greece, by moving their bilateral disputes to the EU level. This would make it much easier to discuss and solve any Turkish–Greek disputes, as well as the Cyprus problem in a broader context of European integration rather than in a bilateral framework (Eralp, 2009,

Table 5.1 Military Expenditure of NATO Countries in Percentage of GDP (1990–99)[2]

Country (NATO accession year)	USA (1949)	France (1949)	Greece (1952)	The Nether. (1949)	Norway (1949)	Poland (1999)	Portugal (1949)	Turkey (1952)	UK (1949)
1990	5.3%	3.4%	3.8%	2.5%	2.9%	2.6%	2.4%	3.5%	3.6%
1991	4.6%	3.4%	3.5%	2.4%	2.7%	2.3%	2.4%	3.8%	3.7%
1992	4.7%	3.3%	3.6%	2.4%	3.0%	2.2%	2.4%	3.9%	3.5%
1993	4.3%	3.3%	3.6%	2.2%	2.7%	2.5%	2.4%	3.9%	3.2%
1994	3.9%	3.3%	3.6%	2.0%	2.7%	2.3%	2.2%	4.1%	3.0%
1995	3.6%	3.0%	3.2%	1.9%	2.4%	2.0%	2.3%	3.9%	2.8%
1996	3.4%	2.9%	3.3%	1.9%	2.2%	2.0%	2.1%	4.1%	2.6%
1997	3.2%	2.9%	3.4%	1.8%	2.1%	2.0%	2.1%	4.1%	2.5%
1998	3.0%	2.7%	3.5%	1.7%	2.2%	2.0%	1.9%	3.3%	2.4%
1999	2.9%	2.6%	3.6%	1.6%	2.1%	1.9%	1.9%	4.0%	2.3%
AVERAGE	3.9%	3.1%	3.5%	2.0%	2.5%	2.2%	2.2%	3.9%	3.0%

Source: Stockholm International Peace Research Institute's (SIPRI) Military Expenditure Database - https://www.sipri.org/databases/milex.

4). In other words, alignment with the EU would bring about an 'external balancing' factor vis-à-vis Turkey, a factor that was also in accordance with Greece's new strategic needs and priorities, mainly its ability to integrate itself into the EU (Tsakonas, 2001b, 154). Moreover, Greece would have a stronger hand in lobbying for its interests if it could prove a solid integration with the EU. Dimitrios Triantaphyllou (2005, 332) has evaluated the Europeanisation process of Greece's foreign policy as the 'panacea for eventually resolving or impacting on all of Greece's key foreign policy concerns'. This approach brought with it Greece's withdrawal of its long-standing veto strategy against Turkey's EU bid, which meant a 'U turn in Greek politics' – that is, a long-term strategy of binding it with, or even integrating it into Europe (Siegl, 2002, 45; Liaropoulos, 2008, 28). Greece seemed to have achieved its strategy at the Helsinki Summit on 10–11 December 1999, through bringing several issues to the EU, which would provide some space for its security concerns by avoiding further crises.

For Turkey, a similar process of Europeanisation became much more evident right after the formal recognition of its candidate status at the EU's Helsinki Summit of 1999, which reversed the negative effects of the 1997 Luxembourg Summit, with the support of Greece (Tsakonas, 2001, 3). As

Akgül Açıkmeşe (2013, 303) has underlined, 'Turkey, as an EU candidate since 1999 and a negotiating country since 2005, has been in a process of substantive, if contradictory, transformation in every aspect of politics, economics and foreign policy'. In return for granting Turkey's candidacy status, the break-through Helsinki Summit set certain political conditions about Turkish–Greek relations and the Cyprus issue for Turkey's ultimate accession to the EU. According to the Helsinki Summit Presidency Conclusion, the paragraph related to Turkey emphasised the political conditions as such:

> Turkey, like other candidate States, will benefit from a pre-accession strategy to stimulate and support its reforms. This will include enhanced political dialogue, with emphasis on progressing towards fulfilling the political criteria for accession with particular reference to the issue of human rights, as well as on the issues referred to in paragraphs 4 and 9(a). (Helsinki Summit Presidency Conclusion, 10–11 December 1999)

While paragraph 4 referred to the resolution of outstanding disputes, particularly with Greece, paragraph 9 related to the political settlement concerning Cyprus. The resolution of these preconditions was combined with Turkey's accession negotiations. These paragraphs once more show that the resolution of its border disputes with Greece and the Cyprus issue – in which the EU decided to evaluate the RoC (as the representative of the entire island) and its full membership independent of a resolution of the conflict – constructed another requirement for Turkey's accession to the EU (Gündoğdu, 2001, 112; Müftüler-Baç and Güney, 2005, 289; Grigoriadis, 2011, 121). As Aydın and Akgül Açıkmeşe (2007, 268–71) have underlined, the EU had already applied such requirements under the Common Foreign and Security Policy chapter in the previous enlargements; however, 'for Turkey and all current candidates, this criterion has been elevated onto an equal footing with the political criteria'. Accordingly, the EU began to review the situation under the political criteria in the Accession Partnership Documents and the progress reports for the candidate countries. For instance, the Accession Partnership Document of Turkey dated 8 March 2001 urged the candidate countries 'to make every effort to resolve any outstanding border disputes and related issues' by referring to the Helsinki Conclusion. Likewise, the EU has continued to put the same emphasis on the border disputes in the following Accession Partnership

Documents, as well as the Negotiation Framework Document of 3 October 2005, with a similar tone highlighting 'Turkey's unequivocal commitment to good neighbourly relations and its undertaking to resolve any outstanding border disputes in conformity with the principle of peaceful settlement of disputes in accordance with the United Nations Charter, including if necessary jurisdiction of the International Court of Justice'. Likewise, since 2001 the annual progress reports have been regularly stressing the same issue under the political criteria.

Apart from these preconditions, Turkey had to continue its reform process in compliance with the Copenhagen Criteria that had been established by the 1993 Copenhagen European Council for countries wishing to become an EU member. These criteria refer to conditions such as a functioning market economy, preserving democracy, rule of law and human rights, and accepting the EU's obligations. Since then, Turkey has entered an intense reform process through harmonisation packages and constitutional amendments in order to fulfill the Copenhagen Criteria. Nevertheless, the most striking impact of Europeanisation showed itself in the decision-making mechanism of Turkish foreign and security policy. Even with these fundamental changes, Europeanisation could not successfully prevent statements from military authorities on important foreign policy issues, which had serious repercussions for Turkish foreign policy.

The process of Europeanisation coincided with the new foreign policy line of Turkey, which necessitates moving beyond long-lasting problems and establishing good economic relations as well. The liberalisation of Turkey's economy and development strategy – from import-substitution to export-led growth in the 1980s – reflected itself in the traditional security-oriented foreign policy considerations. Kemal Kirişci (2009, 39) has defined this modification as a 'trading state' in which 'foreign policy has increasingly been shaped by economic considerations'. The Customs Union between Turkey and the EU provided a fruitful environment for the eventual emergence of a trading state (Kirişci, 2009, 39). The coalition governments' period of the 1990s as well as the crises in foreign policy interrupted the successful implementation of this new trend in foreign policy. The new trend in foreign policy, which began with İsmail Cem, was based on expanding political and economic relations into new regions and countries, and it continued after the Justice and

Development Party (*Adalet ve Kalkınma Partisi*, AKP) came to power in 2002. The AKP also emphasised the importance of economic prosperity and stability in the region but shifted Turkey's perspective in several aspects. Rather than focusing on long-standing problems, such as the Aegean or the Cyprus issue, the AKP used new policy tools to improve its relations with the region's countries. The policy of 'zero problems with neighbours' associated with then Minister of Foreign Affairs Ahmet Davutoğlu was the driving force behind this new vision. New tools such as visa liberalisation, mediation, trade zones and High-Level Cooperation Councils have been used successfully for the institutionalisation of the new process. Nevertheless, the European transformative process through 'conditionality' played an 'effective anchor' in Turkey's new foreign policy trend (Aydın and Açıkmeşe, 2007, 272; Keyman, 2009, 15).

The most striking divergence in foreign policy showed itself in Turkey's established policy line in Cyprus. Traditionally, Turkey's Cyprus policy was based on a nationalistic perspective, which considered the issue through a security lens and evaluated it as 'existential threat' to its security. However, the first AKP government (2002–7) changed the discourse of Turkey's Cyprus policy and acknowledged the link that had been denied by the previous coalition governments, between Turkey's accession process and a Cyprus settlement. As Çelenk (2007, 351–54) has stressed, the most obvious desire for change at that time was the AKP government's effort to restart negotiations between the parties under the auspices of UN Secretary General Kofi Annan and to resolve the dispute before the RoC would join the EU on 1 May 2004. The AKP government's Cyprus policy was based on supporting the resolution of the issue through a peace plan, known as the Annan Plan, which would also reconstruct the Turkey's image in the international realm vis-à-vis the EU, the US and the UN (Çelenk, 2007, 353). As a result, Turkey supported a 'yes' vote in the referendum on the Annan Plan held on 24 April 2004. In the break-through referendum on the island's unification, Turkish Cypriots approved the plan by 64.9 percent, whereas Greek Cypriots rejected it by 75.8 percent. Even though Greek Cypriots shattered any hopes regarding the fate of the island, the EU accepted the RoC as representative of the island and welcomed it among nine other countries. Although the Europeanisation process had paved the way for beginning accession negotiations between Turkey and the EU on 3 October 2005, the settlement of the Cyprus issue still constitutes an important barrier to Turkey's accession to the EU. Turkey's decision to extend the Ankara Agreement to the RoC, in line with the Brussels Summit, has caused the suspension of eight of the thirty-five chapters in Turkey's accession negotiations since 2005.

In terms of Turkish–Greek relations, the above-mentioned EU documents (such as the Accession Partnership, the Regular Progress Reports and the Negotiating Framework) set a new framework for relations. The EU welcomed the progress in bilateral relations, while it continued to emphasise the jurisdiction of the ICJ for the unresolved disputes between the two countries, without mentioning a deadline. The positive impact of the Europeanisation process was reflected in the statements of Turkish decision-makers as well. Then Prime Minister Bülent Ecevit stated that 'our status as a EU member candidate is helping the development of our relationship with Greece as well' (*Milliyet*, 31 January 2001), whereas Prime Minister Erdoğan stressed the role of the EU as follows:

> We [Turks and Greeks] have a common history, cultural values. Our cuisine, culture of music, clothes are nourished from a common pool of the Mediterranean and the Aegean. But beyond that we [Turkey and Greece] are two neighbouring countries, one is an EU member and the other is a candidate to the EU [. . .] (*Anadolu Agency*, 25 January 2008)

Although the dynamics of Europeanisation existed in different ways in both Turkey and Greece, they constitute a common denominator for both sides, which in turn has contributed to the easing of tensions between the two countries and consolidated the gains of earthquake diplomacy (Kutlay, 2009, 116; Çarkoğlu and Kirişci, 2004, 117). Both Turkey and Greece have tried to improve relations within the framework of the EU. As Aydın and Akgül Açıkmeşe (2007, 272) have pointed out, Turkey would not be able to change the course of relations on such a sensitive foreign policy issue without the encouragement of or pressure from the EU through 'conditionality'. A similar process took place in Greece, albeit in a different way, as Greece promoted the EU perspective in order to reduce tension and lead to the resolution of outstanding disputes (Triantaphyllou, 2005, 332). This positive atmosphere in bilateral relations can also be traced in the developments in both countries' foreign policies, as both searched for ways to change and modernise their traditional foreign policies as well as to improve their positions in the international arena. Last but not least, the fertile domestic environment, where civil society and private sector were demanding cooperation rather than conflict, also helped in deepening relations between Turkey and Greece. In a globalised world, decision-makers in foreign policy operate within the context of an aspiring civil society, vibrant media and private economic interests (Keridis, 1999, 7). Therefore, instead of maintaining old foreign policy habits, decision-makers in both countries were forced to pay attention to the demands of the public. At this point, it is important to analyse the role of the two ministers of foreign affairs in Turkey and Greece, İsmail Cem and George Papandreou, respectively, who might be evaluated as the architects of the rapprochement process.

The Role of İsmail Cem and George Papandreou

The winds of change in Turkish–Greek relations began to appear in the mid-1990s with the transformation of both countries' foreign policy; however, the conflicts popping up at that time prevented tangible changes in relations. The simultaneous presence of two solution-oriented ministers of foreign affairs, İsmail Cem in Turkey and George Papandreou in Greece, eased the process of change. As already noted in the section on the earthquakes, İsmail Cem's letter to his Greek counterpart on 24 May 1999 – two months before the earthquakes – constituted a milestone in the relationship between Turkey and Greece. The exchange of letters between the ministers of foreign affairs initiated a dialogue channel in bilateral relations, despite the turbulent times and hostility between the two countries. This was reflected in Papandreou's letter as follows: 'In this context, we could meet when the opportunity arises in order to have a sincere and constructive exchange of views. I have always been of the view that personal contacts between us can in many ways be productive' (Cem, 2009, 133).

Apart from their influential role in bilateral relations, the two ministers had played a significant role in shaping their respective countries' foreign policy. George Papandreou, who had replaced Theodoros Pangalos, the former minister of foreign sffairs, was initially considered a risky choice for Greece, as Ker-Lindsay (2007, 37) has stressed, since he was seen as too soft and too 'ineffectual' a character for such an important post. However, his moderate stance in terms of Turkey had a positive impact on then Prime Minister of Greece Kostas Simitis' Europe-centred foreign policy. In contrast to his negative image in Greece, he was an asset on the wider international stage when it came to relations with Europe and the US (Ker-Lindsay, 2007, 37).

George Papandreou's positive stance had already appeared while serving as a deputy minister of foreign affairs. On 12 February 1998, İsmail Cem issued a verbal note to his Greek counterpart, Theodoros Pangalos, and called for the settlement of all Aegean disputes between the two countries. The five-point proposal contained the following:

1) Jointly identifying the Aegean problems between the two countries;
2) Formalizing the 'Madrid Declaration' of 8 July 1997, which was agreed upon by Turkey and Greece with the initiative of the US Secretary of State, Mrs Albright;
3) Developing and mutually implementing the 'Confidence Building Measures (CBMs) in the Aegean' with the collaboration of the NATO Secretary General;
4) Jointly initiating the Personalities Group process, composed of respected Turkish and Greek personalities assigned to come up with proposals concerning the resolution of bilateral problems between the two countries;
5) Upon the positive reply from the Greek Government to the Turkish initiative, convening a high-level meeting between the two Foreign Ministries to discuss these proposals, before the end of March 1998, either in Ankara or in Athens. (*Turkish Ministry of Foreign Affairs*, 12 February 1998)

In response to İsmail Cem's verbal note, George Papandreou said: 'The proposals are considered by the government and a diplomatic response will be given only after the evaluations of Prime Minister of Greece Kostas Simitis and Minister of Foreign Affairs Theodoros Pangalos' (*Hurriyet Daily News*, 14 February 1998). However, Turkey's proposal was rejected by Pangalos, with a letter dated 20 February 1998. Still, both parties continued to work on the proposal to develop and mutually implement the 'Confidence Building Measures (CBMs) in the Aegean' in collaboration with the NATO Secretary-General. The CBMs were agreed upon by the parties during the NATO meeting in Luxemburg on 28–29 May 1998, and NATO Secretary-General Solana declared them on 4 June 1998. In fact, Papandreou's statement was a reaction, as it came right after the statement of government spokesman Dimitris Reppas, who tried to turn down the Turkish initiative (Fırat, 2006, 274). Thus, he played an instrumental role in institutionalising cooperation with Turkey, in that he initiated a dialogue with his Turkish counterpart, İsmail Cem.

Similarly, the appointment of İsmail Cem as the minister of foreign affairs in 1997 brought about a certain change in Turkish foreign policy. As mentioned above, the liberalisation process in the foreign policy of Turkey, which has been identified as 'trading state' by Kemal Kirişci (2009, 39), was interrupted during the era of coalition governments in the 1990s. In this period, Turkey was governed by coalitions consisting of two or three political parties; there was no single-party government until the AKP came to power in 2002. As Tuğtan (2016, 5) has underlined, İsmail Cem, who acted as minister of foreign affairs for five years (1997–2002), was the only exception of a constant appointment between 1991 and 2002. There were frequent changes of ministers of foreign affairs, and the average duration of each minister was eight months. İsmail Cem's 1997 appointment brought significant changes in several areas, ranging from Turkish–Greek relations, over Turkey's bid to join the EU and the negotiations of the Baku-Tbilisi-Ceyhan Pipeline, to the Adana Protocol with Syria in 1998 (Örmeci, 2011, 102; Tuğtan, 2016, 7).

Cem and Papandreou's constructive role at the beginning of the dialogue between the two countries and the personal relationship between the two ministers are worth noting. The attendance of both ministers of foreign affairs, with their families, at the Turkish–Greek Economic Forum held in Samos (*Sisam*) in June 2001 was important to demonstrate their close ties. During the dinner in honour of Cem, Papandreou performed a *Sirtaki*, a traditional Greek folk dance, in honour of the fifth anniversary of his father Andreas Papandreou's death (*NTV*, 21 June 2001). The friendship between the two foreign ministers was even referred to as 'sirtaki diplomacy' by columnist as well as representatives from the Turkish Ministry of Foreign Affairs. Senior columnist Yusuf Kanlı (2009), in his piece about the return of Papandreou as prime minister, evaluated the empathy among Turkish social democrats and conservatives towards the Greek politician with a particular emphasis on this so-called 'sirtaki diplomacy'. Likewise, in an interview with the Greek daily *Kathimerini* on 17 March 2014, Kerim Uras, Turkish Ambassador to Athens, said:

> [D]iplomats from both Turkey and Greece evaluated the atmosphere between Greek Minister of Foreign Affairs George Papandreou and his Turkish counterpart İsmail Cem as an affirmative process. We called it as 'sirtaki diplomacy', which reflects the public view after the performance of two foreign ministers. (*Embassy of the Republic of Turkey to Greece*, 23 April 2014)

When İsmail Cem passed away on 24 January 2007, George Papandreou as then prime minister of Greece, attended his funeral and left an olive branch on his grave. During the funeral George Papandreou shared his feelings with the following words:

> Today, when I came here to the cemetery to leave an olive branch from my garden, I wanted to pay my last respects to my friend and remind all, that years ago [in 2001] we were on the island of Samos [*Sisam*], where together we planted an olive tree to symbolize peace. [. . .] I wanted to say to İsmail that this olive tree is strong, and I will work very hard to make it stronger for peace between our countries and our peoples. [. . .] We had many moments together, many difficult, but also many happy moments in making our vision come true. (cited from the webpage of the 'Cem Papandreou Peace Award')

In 2015, George Papandreou and İpek Cem Taha, daughter of İsmail Cem, decided to establish the 'Cem-Papandreou Peace Award' to honour individuals or institutions that contribute to peace.[3] This award reflects the spirit of the olive tree, which was planted on the island of Samos in 2001. Despite all problems in bilateral relations, the two countries have been finding ways to solve their problems either through bilateral dialogue, as exemplified by these two politicians, or with the involvement of third parties. The next section will focus on the role of such third parties in bilateral relations, with a particular focus on the US.

The Role of Third Parties: The USA

The relationship and the long-standing disputes between Turkey and Greece have always been important for the US, due to their implications for NATO's southern flank. As strategic partners for the US as well as the NATO allies, both countries have played important roles in regional security and other issues, such as energy. Thus, a confrontation between Turkey and Greece has never been in the interests of the US and the NATO. Especially during the Cold War, stability and cohesion in the southern flank were essential for the effective balance of power against the Soviet Union. As Lesser (2001, 6) has stressed, 'the US has a stake in the evolution of Greece and Turkey as "pivotal" states – pivotal because what happens there involves not only the fate of two longstanding allies (with NATO security guarantees) but also influences the future of the regions that matter to Washington'. The US would continue to have good relations with both Turkey and Greece, as long as its security interests and the NATO's effectiveness necessitated this (Athanassopoulou, 1997, 77). Therefore, it is useful to examine the role of the US (along with that of the EU, as already discussed above) in Turkish–Greek relations in order to comprehend more fully its influence on the latest rapprochement process.

In the aftermath of the World War II, both Turkey and Greece sided with the US-led Western bloc due to fear of Soviet expansionism. The US support to both Turkey and Greece under the Truman Doctrine, which US President Harry S. Truman had launched with a speech to US Congress on 12 March 1947, marked a turning point in the Cold War strategy of the US (Hale, 2002, 115). In this speech, President Truman asked for 400 million US dollars to fund an aid programme for Greece (300 million) and Turkey (100 million), in order to 'support free people who are resisting attempted subjugation by armed minorities or by outside pressures'. This was a breakthrough, as the US provided economic and military aid for both countries and 'took the advantage of a favourable opportunity to enhance the strategic interests of the US in the Middle East and the eastern Mediterranean' (Leffler, 1985, 808). The relationship between the US, Greece and Turkey was consolidated with the accession of the latter two countries to the NATO in 1952.

Previously, there had existed harmony in the US-Greece-Turkey triangle, as both Turkey and Greece were willing to subordinate their national interests to focus on the external threat of the Soviet Union (Kalaitzaki, 2005, 106; Larrabee, 2012, 472). However, this cordial relationship began to experience great strain with the outbreak of the Cyprus problem in the mid-1950s as one of the contentious issues between Turkey and Greece. Both sides expected the involvement of the US, but Washington had no reason to become involved in a bilateral dispute over Cyprus, where it had no interest per se (Athanassopoulou, 1997, 77; Kalaitzaki, 2005, 106; Larrabee, 2012, 472). As Secretary of State John Foster Dulles' letter to the prime ministers of both countries in September 1955 showed, the US kept itself at an equal distance to each country, while he was calling the other parties for restraint (Stearns, 1992, 25–30). However, in the early 1960s, the intercommunal disputes on the island forced the US to intervene, through a letter by US President Lyndon Johnson to Prime Minister İsmet İnönü, in order to prevent Turkey's intervention on the island. As a result, there began a tense period between Turkey and the US, which lasted until the 1980s, since Turkey realised that it could not trust US commitments to its security.

In the subsequent crisis of 1967, US mediation between Turkey, Greece and Cyprus paved the way for a quick solution. Cyrus Vance, President Johnson's special envoy, convinced the Greek side to withdraw its fighters from the island, which satisfied Turkey's demands and prevented escalation. In contrast, during the Turkish intervention on the island in the wake of the coup d'état by the Greek junta administration in 1974, the US did not play a decisive role to prevent Turkey's intervention. Moustakis (2003, 33) has explained the general attitude of the US towards Cyprus as follows: '[T]he US concern was not the rights or wrongs of either side or the fate of the two communities on the island, but rather a way to limit the potential damage to NATO and to the US strategic position in the Mediterranean'. The ineffectiveness or passive stance of the US caused Greece's withdrawal from the NATO's military wing until 1980. In response to the Turkish operation, the US Congress secured a resolution on an arms embargo on Turkey, which also included banning military sales and aid to Turkey, under the pressure of the pro-Greek lobby in Congress (Hale, 2002, 160). The arms embargo came into effect on 5 February 1975 (it was completely lifted in August 1978) and had a serious impact on Turkish foreign policy, as the Turkish government decided to suspend all US operations at all military installations within Turkey (Uslu, 1997, 14; Hale, 2002, 161; Kalaitzaki, 2005, 116).

The US role in the Cyprus problem, one of the core disputes between Turkey and Greece, proved that US policies were shaped around its own strategic interests rather than considering the interests of Turkey and Greece. According to Güvenç (1998–99, 105), 'as long as [Greece and Turkey] did not tend to destabilise the region or pose a threat to the superpower balance in the Mediterranean basin, leaving these problems unresolved was a manageable solution for Washington'. As a result of the hesitant stance of the US, both Turkey and Greece realised that they needed alternative policies to improve their national security. Within this context, Turkey started to develop new relations with Muslim countries from the Middle East and to improve its relations with the Soviet Union beginning in the 1970s (Ifantis, 2004, 24). Greece also tried to decrease its dependency on the US and shifted its focus towards the EU, which altered the nature of its relations with the US (Ifantis, 2004, 24; Kalaitzaki, 2005, 116). It is also important to highlight that US policy was to encourage the UN to become the lead in the conflict's settlement, rather than to offer the active and direct involvement of the US (Larrabee, 2012, 475).

The US continued to remain hesitant and stayed out of the bilateral disputes in the Aegean Sea that had existed since the mid-1960s; it encouraged both parties to settle their problems via dialogue. As Kalaitzaki (2005, 119) has stressed, 'the US attempted neither to take a more active role as a mediator nor to take public positions on the bilateral dispute'. However, Greece continued its efforts to receive a guarantee from the US in terms of maintaining the status quo in the Aegean Sea, whereas Turkey sought to gain the upper hand in the bilateral relations via blocking Greece's return to the NATO (Kalaitzaki, 2005, 118). In contrast to what had happened in the context of the Cyprus problem, neither Turkey nor Greece attempted to involve the US in its disputes over the Aegean Sea.

The Cold War caused profound changes in US priorities in international politics; however, its quest of preserving stability within NATO boundaries continued. The successive US administrations pursued a strategy of enhancing the country's superpower capabilities and primacy as well. Considering the developments in US foreign and security policies, the disputes between Turkey and Greece did not constitute a priority on the US agenda. However, stability in the southern flank continued to be paramount for US strategic interests, as instability there could imperil the Balkan stability that the US administration sought (Athanassopoulou, 1997, 85). In any case, US policy towards Turkish–Greek disputes might be evaluated as more active considering its role during the Kardak incident and the S-300 missile crisis. As Kalaitzaki (2005, 120) has emphasised, when compared to the period between 1974 and 1989, the US has been more active since the end of the Cold War.

During the Kardak crisis in late 1995, the worsening situation between Turkey and Greece stimulated third-party intervention to defuse the crisis. Alongside with US President Bill Clinton, senior members of the US administration initiated an intense telephone diplomacy with Ankara and Athens to ease tensions and secure an agreement (Ker-Lindsay, 2007, 30). Intense mediation by US officials, particularly the US special envoy Richard Holbrooke, paved the way for the return to the *status quo ante* in the Aegean Sea without any incident. Likewise, when relations between Turkey and Greece were once more strained over the Greek Cypriot administration's decision to acquire a Russian medium-range S-300 surface-to-air missile defence system in January 1999, the US put pressure on both sides to stop the deployment of missiles as well as the Turkish threat of military action. Another crisis was prevented when Simitis' administration, under the pressure of the US and the EU, suggested putting missiles on the Greek island of Crete instead of Cyprus.

In both cases, the role of the US as mediator served to decrease tensions between the two allies and to preserve the status quo in southeast Europe. However, the US involvement in the crises did not help to find a comprehensive solution to the long-standing disputes between the two countries. Moreover, the increasing role of the EU in the 1990s, with the quests of both Turkey and the RoC to gain EU membership status, became a dominant factor in the future of bilateral disputes. The EU's involvement in the Greek–Turkish disputes was strongly welcomed by the US, as it provided an opportunity for the US to disengage itself (Kalaitzaki, 2005, 124). The US administrations believed that there was a strong correlation between Turkey's integration to the EU and its cooperation with the West. The EU integration process would 'anchor' Turkey ever more closely in the West and provide stability in Turkish–Greek relations (Siegl, 2002, 47; Ifantis, 2004, 34). Friction between Turkey and the EU would impinge on Turkey's cooperation with the West and might encourage a more nationalist stance in foreign policy (Lesser, 2001, 6). This is the reason why, from the late 1990s onwards, the US started to play an active role in promoting Turkey's accession to the EU.

In terms of the rapprochement between Turkey and Greece, the US government has been in favour of reinforcing that process. It is reasonable to believe that the rapprochement process and Turkey's integration with the EU will transform Turkey into a more predictable partner for both the US and the EU. As long as the rapprochement process continues, the US will make sure that Greek–Turkish brinkmanship no longer threatens the broader interests of the regional détente and integration (Ifantis, 2004, 35). As the historical context shows, the 'equidistance' policy of the US towards Turkish–Greek relations is based on its pragmatic calculations, which is to keep Turkish–Greek relations constant so as to allow the NATO's effective functioning.

Notes

1. On the history of the Turkish–Greek Relations Forum and the importance of second-track diplomacy, see Özel, 2004.
2. The table only covers the NATO member-states that committed to a minimum of 2 percent of their Gross Domestic Product (GDP) for their defence expenditures. On the defence expenditure trends of the member-states, see NATO's official webpage, http://www.nato.int/cps/en/natohq/news_127537.htm.
3. For details of the Cem-Papandreou Peace Award, see http://www.cempapandreouaward.org.

6

INSTANCES OF RAPPROCHEMENT AND FORMS OF DESECURITISATION

The rapprochement process between Greece and Turkey began with a letter that broke the orthodoxy of the securitised discourse about Greece in Turkish foreign policy. Hence, the letter by Turkish Minister of Foreign Affairs İsmail Cem to his Greek counterpart, George Papandreou, on 24 May 1999 in order to discuss terrorism constitutes a milestone in the relationship between Turkey and Greece. Cem's letter triggered a change in discourse which was followed by political engagement between the two countries. Accordingly, this chapter will focus on the instance of a slow but sure rapprochement process, which lasted until 2016; it will analyse the period based on different forms of desecuritsation. The rapid changes from securitisation to desecuritisation, or vice versa, in Turkish foreign policy towards Greece reveal the constructed nature of security and shed light on the overarching politics of securitisation and desecuritisation, in line with the various objectives of the ruling governments (Baysal and Dizdaroğlu, 2022).

Several days after the exchange of letters between the two foreign ministers, İsmail Cem and George Papandreou met at Kosovo's Friends meeting in New York, under the auspices of the UN Secretary-General, on 3 July 1999. They agreed on an action plan, which paved the way for establishing five working groups in the areas of 'organised crime, drug trafficking, illegal migration and terrorism', 'tourism', 'environment' and 'culture' and 'trade'. Upon his return from the meetings in New York, Cem evaluated the negotiations with his Greek counterpart as follows: 'Turkey has agreements with various countries on the fight against terrorism. Therefore, dealing with an agreement with Turkey on the very same issue would be the first step for Greece to get over the shadow of terrorism' (*The Directorate General of Press and Information*, 1 July 1999). Moreover, he pointed out the importance of the action plan by saying that an effort was being made 'without raising high expectations, without being too assertive' (*Turkish Daily News*, 4 July 1999).

Following the two foreign ministers' consensus on the establishment of working groups during their meeting in New York, the first working group met in Athens on 5–6 July 1999, to initiate cooperation in the proposed fields (Evin, 2005, 397). As a result of these efforts, both countries through the initiative of their foreign ministers established an intense diplomatic traffic, including paying high-level reciprocal diplomatic visits, signing agreements and protocols, and staging joint military exercises. Accordingly, Greek Minister of Foreign Affairs George Papandreou came to Turkey for an official visit, the first official visit in twenty-five years, in January 2000, and Turkish Minister of Foreign Affairs İsmail Cem returned the visit, for the first time in thirty years, in February 2000. Likewise, between 20 May and 10 June 2000, the two countries staged joint military exercises in Greece, under the NATO's aegis. One of the indicators of the transformation in bilateral relations was the sheer number of documents signed between the two countries. After three decades of dormancy – the last major agreement had been the 'Agreement on International Land Transportation' in 1970 – the signing of twenty-five new agreements and protocols between 2000 and 2004, pertaining to economic, social and cultural relations and providing the legal framework for enhanced interaction, constituted a very significant development (Öniş and Yılmaz, 2008, 130).

In parallel with these efforts, there have been considerable changes in the decision-makers' discourses that led to the securitisation of Greece. First and foremost, the decision-makers began to stress the importance of a 'friendship between the peoples of the two countries', while ignoring the existence of issues of contention. With the desired result being the potential disappearance of issues from the security realm, the form of *change through stabilisation* (where the larger conflict still looms in the background) is best suited for the case of Turkish–Greek relations. The two countries are still dealing with major contentious issues over the Aegean and Cyprus, along with new ones emerging in the Eastern Mediterranean. The regular dogfights occuring over the Aegean airspace might serve as a good example in this respect. There are various instances regarding the changing security discourse in the statements of decision-makers, even though problems between the two still exist. For instance, during George Papandreou's visit to Turkey on 20 January 2000, Minister of Foreign Affairs İsmail Cem said that 'recent developments have shown that the peoples in these two countries are much closer to each other than we thought they were' (*Milliyet*, 20 January 2000). Likewise, Prime Minister Bülent Ecevit stressed in an interview: 'I wish the Aegean Sea to be a perpetual link of friendship between Greece and Turkey, which will be based on a just foundation'. President Ahmet Necdet Sezer, in a dinner with nineteen chiefs of general staff (including the Greek one), stated: 'Turkey wants to be in good relationship and cooperation with Greece, just like with all of its neighbours' (*Milliyet*, 9 June 2000; *Sabah*, 16 September 2000). The two foreign ministers even began to address each other as 'my friend' (*Hürriyet*, 9 November 2001).

The transformation in discourse naturally reflected itself in several aspects of foreign policy practices. The high-level reciprocal visits for the first time after many long years, the creation of dialogue channels such as the Turkey-Greece EU Committee and the 'exploratory talks' between foreign ministry officials, the joint military exercises, the expansion of economic ties and increases in tourism are all results of such a transformation.

The Rapprochement in Practice

Apart from the working groups between the two countries, Turkey and Greece also initiated a cooperation in order to accelerate Turkey's accession process to the EU after Turkey's official candidacy status had been recognised at the Helsinki Summit in 1999. Within this framework, the two parties established a Turkey-Greece EU Committee that held its first meeting in Ankara on 28 February 2000, with the participation of officials from both ministries of foreign affairs. In the committee meetings, Greek officials shared with their Turkish counterparts Greece's experience with customs and financial issues, judicial and agricultural matters (Oğuzlu, 2004, 97). These meetings facilitated a deeper cooperation and more extensive dialogue between the two countries.

During the same period, attempts to resolve the many disputes between Turkey and Greece in the Aegean took place behind closed doors. Teams led by the respective under-secretaries of the Turkish and Greek foreign ministries began exploratory talks on 12 March 2002 in Ankara (Turan, 2010, 2). The outcome of these talks was a willingness to discuss at least the disputes between Turkey and Greece over the Aegean Sea. Before the beginning of these exploratory talks, İsmail Cem said in a TV interview on CNN Türk that 'there can be a development concerning the Aegean. Be it dialogue, mediation, arbitration or even the international tribune, we're open to all' (*Hurriyet Daily News*, 30 January 2002). The nature of this communication, as evaluated by the Under-Secretary of Turkish Ministry of Foreign Affairs Uğur Ziyal after the first exploratory talks, in Ankara was as follows:

> We had a broad and constructive discussion with my Greek colleagues. We looked into a number of issues and we decided to continue [. . .] The exploratory dialogue had no deadline and its aim was to promote Greek–Turkish relations. The talks dealt with the procedures, framework and substance of the problem. (*Ekathimerini*, 13 March 2002)

Due to the conditions of the Helsinki Summit, the talks began in and maintained high gear; so far, sixty-four rounds of exploratory talks have been held between the representatives of the two countries.[1] Yet, so far no substantive changes have occurred in eithers side's position, based on the principle that 'nothing is agreed until everything is agreed'. In any case, various crises between the two have already confirmed the significance of direct channels for dialogue between Turkey and Greece. Through the idea of the exploratory talks, an essential high-level dialogue mechanism has been established between Turkey and Greece.

In the military field, Greece and Turkey along with Italy hosted a major training exercise in mid-2000, under the NATO's aegis, involving forces from fourteen NATO countries. During the three-week-long military exercise, code-named Dynamic Mix 2000, over 15,000 troops, sixty-five ships and 290 aircraft from fourteen countries demonstrated the full range of the NATO's capabilities and power in the southern region. The operation was important in terms of Turkish–Greek relations since during the exercise Turkish military aircraft arrived at a Greek airbase and 150 Turkish marines landed on a Greek beach located 200 km southwest of Athens (Ker-Lindsay, 2000, 226; *BBC*, 2 June 2000). Another NATO exercise, code-named Destined Glory 2000, was held in the Aegean Sea, Western Anatolia and the Eastern Mediterranean between 9 and 25 October 2000. Some problems arose between Turkey and Greece during the exercise when Greek aircraft flew over the demilitarised islands off the Turkish coast. Following Turkey's objections, Greece withdrew its military participation from the last series of the exercise on 22 October 2000 (*Turkish Ministry of Foreign Affairs*, 23 October 2000). Despite this tension between the two countries, both showed their willingness to continue to cooperate with each other. Prime Minister Bülent Ecevit stressed the importance of dialogue, which paved the way for joint exercises:

> The separations and disagreements between Turkish and Greek peoples are artificial while friendship is natural [. . .] warming friendship and public support to our relationship have made the handling of problems via dialogue easier. [. . .] Friendly relations between the militaries of the two countries were developed [. . .] soldiers are able to participate jointly on each other's soil in exercises that are organised for the common security of the two countries. (*Milliyet*, 9 October 2000)

Likewise, after a meeting with his Greek counterpart in Skopje, Turkish Minister of Foreign Affairs İsmail Cem pointed out the continuation of the dialogue process and military exercises: 'Sudden ups and downs may occur between two countries. We may face even bigger problems in the future. However, we have to continue the dialogue [including joint military exercises] because it is to the interest of both peoples' (*Hürriyet*, 1 November 2000).

If we consider the statements of those same actors in the not-too-distant past, there was substantial change in the decision-makers' securitised discourse. While Turkey and Greece had come to the brink of war due to the Kardak incident five years earlier, the two countries now even began to conduct joint military exercises by deploying troops on each other's soil. The emphasis on 'friendship' or 'the interests of both peoples' rather than focusing on an 'existential threat to the referent object' is the reflection of the political dialogue between the two countries.

Furthermore, in 2002 Turkey cancelled one of its scheduled military exercises, called Efes-2002, in the Aegean, in accordance with the CBMs

(*Sabah*, 4 June 2002). As Aksu (2004) has stated, the CBMs 'were meant to avoid risk of confrontation of the military forces of both countries during routine military practices in the open-seas region and international aviation zone in the Aegean and to sustain mutual respect for sovereignty and territorial rights'. By agreeing to these measures in 1998, in collaboration with NATO Secretary-General Javier Solana, both Turkey and Greece defused the risk of a military confrontation in the Aegean Sea. The positive atmosphere was also reflected in the national security perception. As Oğuzlu (2004, 98) has pointed out, Turkey's new National Security Policy Document dated August 2002 did not mention Greece as the top external threat to Turkey's national security.

Given the positive relationship, in April 2001, Turkey and Greece also agreed on an essential decision about the elimination of the anti-personnel landmines along their shared borders over the following ten years. This was a significant example of the CBMs between the two countries. During the one-day work meeting between the two foreign ministries, officials decided to start the process necessary to become signatories to the 1997 Ottawa Convention,[2] which required the destruction of their existing landmines and prohibited future landmine use and production (Oğuzlu, 2004, 97). Both Turkey and Greece formally agreed to be bound by the Ottawa Convention on 23 November 2003, and it entered into force on 1 March 2004 following official ratification in their respective parliaments. İsmail Cem evaluated the common decision with Greece as follows: '[W]e agreed upon every issue and took concrete decisions. We are progressing slowly but surely in our relations' (*Sabah*, 7 April 2001).

Apart from the diplomatic and militarily initiatives between Turkey and Greece, the thaw in bilateral relations had a positive impact on bilateral trade and economic relations. The growth in bilateral trade was supported by administrative adjustments and political agreements in light of the agenda that had been agreed upon between Cem and Papandreou in 1999 (Tsarouhas, 2009, 46). During the reciprocal high-level visits by the two foreign ministers to Ankara and Athens, respectively, in January and February 2000, the parties signed several agreements. One of these agreements on Economic Cooperation signed on 4 February 2000, during Cem's visit to Athens, aimed to promote and develop bilateral economic cooperation. Based on the Agreement on Economic Cooperation, the parties agreed on encouraging their respective nation's enterprises, organisations and businesses to develop economic cooperation, creating a favourable climate for investment, as well as establishing a Turkish–Greek Joint Economic Commission (*Official Gazette of the Republic of Turkey*, 25 June 2001). Likewise, the ministers of foreign affairs of both countries met at the 'Turkish–Greek Economic Forum' held on the island of Samos in June 2001, with the participation of a large number of businessmen, journalists, academics and representatives of the Chambers of Commerce. While there were conducted negotiations to boost trade and economic relations between the two countries at the forum, the foreign ministers also discussed possibilities to lift or ease the visa requirement for day excursions to the islands (*NTV*, 23 June 2001). Turkish Minister of Foreign Affairs İsmail Cem in his interview emphasised the positive atmosphere:

> We are not running away from problems or ignoring them. Both countries perceive the problems in the Aegean differently. Rather than trying to gain an upper hand, the best way is to pay attention to the sensitiveness of each other or to find ways by understanding each other. There is a possibility to reach that point. Maybe it will not happen today or tomorrow, but considering the situation two years ago, now we are much closer to that point. (*NTV*, 23 June 2001)

The transformation in the security discourses of the decision-makers as well as the practices surrounding the relationship between Turkey and Greece, which had started under İsmail Cem's tenure as minister of foreign affairs (1997–2002), continued after the AKP's rise to power. The AKP's decision-makers followed the new policy line and expanded political and economic relations into new regions and countries, focusing on economic prosperity. Rather than concentrating on long-standing problems, such as the Aegean or Cyprus issue, the AKP used new policy tools to improve its relations with regional countries.

As a continuation of the positive atmosphere, Turkey and Greece reciprocally cancelled their routine military exercises in the Eastern Mediterranean in 2003. Turkish Prime Minister Recep Tayyip Erdoğan evaluated this reciprocal cancellation in an interview with Greek television as follows:

> Military exercises were mutually cancelled. These are positive developments. Our principle on this area is that a lack of a solution is no solution. I do not mean to say that we will give everything for the interest of one party. Both sides should approach each other honestly and reciprocally, meeting on common

ground. I am saying this to Mr Kostas Simitis and George Papandreou as well. If we can find a common ground, I think that there will be no reason for a lack of resolution of the problems. (*Milliyet*, 28 November 2003)

Despite several small-scale problems between the two countries during the rapprochement period, the political actors insisted on a positive language in their statements so as to ensure stability and friendship between Turkey and Greece. While no break-through was achieved with regard to the main disputes in the Aegean and the Eastern Mediterranean, the détente bore undeniable fruit at the economic level (Grigoriadis, 2011, 123). The improvement in economic relations was absolutely in favour of the business elites and gained momentum in the post-1999 period. Although a Customs Union was established between Turkey and the EU in March 1996, which could have led to a significant increase in economic relations, the two business communities only managed to keep the dialogue channels open instead of utilising the prospects of the Customs Union (Tsarouhas, 2009, 44). As can be seen in Table 6.1, the bilateral trade – as one of the economic sectors – amounted to less than 700,000 US dollars throughout the 1990s due to political tensions, and it took time to exceed the one-million-dollar mark, which occurred in 2003. The gradual increase in trade volume continued until the Euro-crisis hit Greece in 2008, causing a decrease in trade volume over the following two years. However, the establishment of the Turkish–Greek High-Level Cooperation Council (HLCC) in May 2010 doubled trade volume, which then reached 5 million US dollars between 2011 and 2014. In 2014, the trade volume between the two countries reached the highest amount ever recorded. However, economic interaction has declined since 2015; this can be explained as the outcome of several factors, such as political unrest in Greece, the influx of migrants into both countries in 2015, the 2016 coup attempt in Turkey and so on. As Tsarouhas (2019, 204) has argued, 'the EU-Turkey migration deal had offered potential cooperation areas for Greek and Turkish authorities, [but] the confrontation over the sea border demarcation has not helped its realization'. In any case, the trade volume between the two countries has reached a significant level when compared with the unstable environment of the 1990s. Even though there have been signs of re-securitisation in Turkish foreign policy towards Greece after 2016, the economic interaction between the two has been increasing, despite some fluctuation.

Table 6.1 Trade Volume of Turkey and Greece (1990–2021, in USD 1,000)

	EXPORT	IMPORT	TRADE VOLUME
1990	139,386	128,591	**267,977**
1991	143,681	77,059	**220,740**
1992	145,704	88,150	**233,854**
1993	118,124	120,460	**238,584**
1994	168,854	105,064	**273,918**
1995	209,952	200,673	**410,625**
1996	236,473	284,959	**521,432**
1997	298,237	430,780	**729,017**
1998	370,039	319,751	**689,790**
1999	406,794	287,556	**694,350**
2000	437,725	430,813	**868,538**
2001	476,095	266,254	**742,349**
2002	590,382	312,462	**902,844**
2003	920,401	427,743	**1,348,144**
2004	1,171,203	594,351	**1,765,554**
2005	1,126,678	727,830	**1,854,508**
2006	1,602,590	1,045,328	**2,647,917**
2007	2,262,655	950,157	**3,212,812**
2008	2,429,968	1,150,715	**3,580,683**
2009	1,629,637	1,131,065	**2,760,702**
2010	1,455,678	1,541,600	**2,997,277**
2011	1,553,312	3,539,869	**5,093,181**
2012	1,401,401	3,539,869	**4,941,270**
2013	1,544,239	4,072,881	**5,617,120**
2014	1,668,860	4,371,046	**6,039,906**
2015	1,488,662	1,851,355	**3,340,017**
2016	1,472,536	1,289,474	**2,762,010**
2017	1,724,184	1,864,022	**3,588,206**
2018	2,323,001	2,059,363	**4,382,364**
2019	2,245,318	1,474,999	**3,720,317**
2020	1,799,836	1,320,976	**3,120,812**
2021	3,118,808	2,162,133	**5,280,941**

Source: Turkish Statistical Institute, Data Portal for Statistics, www.data.tuik.gov.tr.

Another striking development worth mentioning is the 'Agreement for the Avoidance of Double Taxation with Respect to Taxes on Income' – signed on 2 December 2003, it entered into force as of January 2005 – in order to eliminate double taxation on the profits of businesses operating in either country. This development was supported by Turkish officials, and Prime Minister Recep Tayyip Erdoğan stated: '[R]ecently, dual taxation between Greece and Turkey was rescinded. [. . .] If we can find a common ground, I think that there will be no reason for a lack of resolution of problems' (*Milliyet*, 28 November 2003). The business elites also supported the improvement of economic relations. Tuncay Özilhan, Chairman of TÜSİAD, said that 'he hoped that new ways would be found to develop the Turkish–Greek relations contacts. Obstacles preventing both Turkey and Greece's mutual benefits abroad could only be overcome through efficient, collective and consistent policies, and the appropriate practice of these policies' (*Hurriyet Daily News*, 2 December 2003).

The field of foreign direct investments (FDI) and joint ventures presents another indicator of the positive relations between Turkey and Greece. Although members of a nation that still remembers negative past events such as the September 1955 anti-Greek riots in Istanbul, Greeks started to invest in Turkey thanks to the dialogue and cooperation between the two countries. As Tsarouhas (2019, 198) has reported, the number of companies with capital originating from Greece amounted to 439 by the end of 2010; however, this number significantly increased over seven years and reached 752 by the end of 2017. The newly established business routine between the communities expanded to new fields such as information technology, construction, banking and so on. The most striking example of a joint initiative in this vein was the Turkish–Greek construction consortium's bid for a project in Oman (Tsarouhas, 2009, 46–47). In the banking sector, the National Bank of Greece's acquisition of Finansbank, the fifth-largest bank in Turkey, serves as another indicator of the deepening economic relations (Tsarouhas, 2009, 46). Even though Turkish companies experienced several bureaucratic barriers to operating in Greece, the state-owned Ziraat Bank's branches in Athens, Xanthi, Komotini and Rhodes might be evaluated as the most remarkable Turkish investments in Greece. Furthermore, there exist a few companies operating in Greece in the textile and information technology sectors. Finally, the increase in mutual tourist visits likewise broadened the dialogue channels, eliminating negative historical perceptions between the two communities. Visa-free travel for Turkish citizens to the Greek islands close to Turkish shores, which came into effect in 2012, was another instrumental arrangement between the two countries.

Despite all these positive developments in bilateral relations, the course of foreign policy has started to change in both countries. The political transformation and emergence of new actors in Turkey, problems in Turkey's accession negotiations with the EU and the economic crisis in the US and the EU resulted in a change in Turkish foreign policy. Greece has experienced the same due to the intensification of the economic crisis. Particularly in the AKP's second term (2007–11), Turkey began to develop stronger relations with Middle Eastern countries, under the influence of new actors such as the Independent Industrialist and Businessmen's Association (MÜSİAD) of small to medium-sized businesses from Anatolia. These businesspersons, through their connection with the government, pushed for closer economic relations with countries in the wider Middle East (Tür, 2011). Despite the change in foreign policy priorities in both countries, the cordial atmosphere was maintained. In the end, the efforts to institutionalise bilateral relations came to fruition with the establishment of the Turkish–Greek High-Level Cooperation Council (HLCC) on 14 May 2010, during Turkish Prime Minister Recep Tayyip Erdoğan's visit to Athens with an entourage of more than 300 persons, including bureaucrats and businesspersons. The HLCC aims to bring together from time to time the two countries' representatives at different levels. In line with this institutionalisation, the two countries signed twenty-two bilateral agreements, and the two prime ministers agreed to meet at least annually in Turkey or Greece, while the foreign ministers would come together at least twice a year, and other ministers three or four times a year. The positive atmosphere reflected itself on Turkey's security considerations as well. As seen in the press release of the NSC meeting on 19 February 2010, Turkey's official discourse also changed with the stabilisation in relations:

> The interrelated issues between Turkey and Greece such as disputes in the Aegean, and Turkey's vital and legitimate rights and interests in the Aegean and the Eastern Mediterranean were evaluated in detail in the light of

current developments. The NSC reiterated its determination to solve all disputes between Turkey and Greece that stemmed from the Aegean Sea based on the principles of good neighbourhood, close cooperation and constructive dialogue.

The Arab Spring throughout the Middle East and North Africa at the end of 2010 – triggered by the local population's quest for freedom, equality and better living conditions – has created unexpected and serious challenges for the entire region and beyond. This upheaval's influence on the immediate neighbourhood of Turkey as well as the adverse effects of the economic crisis in Greece have naturally affected the domestic and foreign policy agendas of both countries. While there did occur a decrease in interaction, high-level Turkish and Greek politicians and diplomats continued to come together on several occasions. The prevailing positive discourse was maintained in statements by the Turkish decision-makers. For instance, Turkish Minister of Foreign Affairs Ahmet Davutoğlu's visit to Athens on 10 October 2012 and the reciprocal visit by his Greek counterpart, Dimitris Avromopoulos, to Ankara on 15 February 2013 in order to discuss the preparations for the HLCC, held on 4 March 2013, illustrates the continuation of a positive discourse. The HLCC met for two more rounds, in December 2014 and March 2016, held in Athens and İzmir, respectively. According to the Turkish Ministry of Foreign Affairs, in line with the HLCC's mission, both countries have signed fifty-four agreements in total.

In the aftermath of the reciprocal visits by the foreign ministers, Ahmet Davutoğlu evaluated the prevailing atmosphere between the two countries in separate press conferences:

> The problems in the Aegean Sea will be solved with Greece in a positive manner and I believe that this would transform the Aegean into a sea of peace and prosperity. (*Turkish Ministry of Foreign Affairs*, 10 October 2012)

> The ongoing efforts would strengthen the awareness of a common destiny among the people of the two countries. The two countries would share a common vision concerning the future of Turkish–Greek relations. (*Turkish Ministry of Foreign Affairs*, 15 February 2013)

The rapprochement process that had started in 1999 thus lasted until late 2016. Although there are no tangible changes in any core disputes between the two countries, there have been regular ties between the officials from both sides of the Aegean Sea. The dialogue and cooperation were much more progressive in the first five years of the process, due to both countries' desire for integration with the EU. Although Turkey's accession negotiation has slowed down due to Turkey's domestic problems as well as the EU's internal debates, the transformative potential of the EU for both countries has played a significant incentive role for the constructive atmosphere between the two (Kirişci, 2002, 48). The EU's role in the relationship between the two became more apparent with the flow of migrants into Europe. According to the United Nations High Commissioner for Refugees (UNHCR), in 2015 alone over 800,000 migrants fleeing from their homes in war-torn countries crossed the Aegean Sea from Turkey into Greece (Clayton and Holland, 2015). Therefore, the migration issue added a new layer to the bilateral relations between Turkey and Greece.

At a time when the relationship between Turkey and the EU was moving forward at a snail's pace, the agreement on a Joint Action Plan between Turkey and the EU on 29 November 2015, aiming to tackle the migration crisis, reactivated the stalled relations. The main goal of the Joint Action Plan was to step up cooperation on both sides to prevent the flow of irregular migration from Turkey to Europe.[3] In line with this development, Turkey and Greece signed a bilateral re-admission agreement for illegal migrants on 8 March 2016, during the fourth HLCC meeting in İzmir, alongside other agreements focusing on trade, transportation and tourism (*Ekathimerini*, 8 March 2016). According to the agreement signed by Turkish Prime Minister Ahmet Davutoğlu and his Greek counterpart, Alexis Tsipras, the two countries agreed on the re-admission of those migrants who are ineligible for international protection to Turkey after having crossed into Greece. During a joint press conference, Ahmet Davutoğlu said: '[I]n the decision we have taken yesterday in the execution, the cooperation of Turkey and Greece will be critical. In the forthcoming process, the Aegean will turn from a sea of despair where people lose their lives into a sea of happiness and joy' (*Millet*, 8 Mart 2016). The following negotiations between Turkey and the EU also reconfirmed the commitment of both sides to implementing the Joint Action Plan on 18 March 2016. Accordingly, the two countries simply agreed on the re-admission of irregular migrants to Turkey from 20 March 2016 onwards; on resettling legal refugees from Turkey to the EU, up to a total of 72,000, for every Syrian who is being returned to Turkey from Greece; on lifting the visa requirements for Turkish citizens by the end of June 2016 at the latest, if Turkey fulfilled all benchmarks; on providing an additional 3 billion Euro for the health, education, infrastructure and other living costs of migrants in Turkey; and finally on re-energisiung the accession process of Turkey (*European Council Press Release*, 144/16, 18 March 2016).

While these adjustments and agreements between Turkey and the EU have had considerable impact on the migrant-related responsibilities of Greece as the southeastern gate of the EU, the agreements also paved the way for new cooperation areas between Turkey and Greece. According to the UNHCR, the number of refugees crossing the Aegean to reach Greece by sea decreased from over 800,000 in 2015 to 170,000 in 2016, thanks to the Joint Action Plan between Turkey and Greece (UNHCR, 31 December 2016). In the short and mid-term, the agreement facilitated a dramatic drop in the numbers of migrants despite all criticism. As of December 2020, Turkey had received 3.9 of the committed and contracted 6 billion Euro (Kirişci, 2021b); however, other promises – mainly visa liberalisation for Turkish nationals – did not become reality, as Turkey has met only sixty-five out of seventy-two benchmarks. All these problems have caused regular criticism by President Erdoğan, who has complained about the disbursement of funds and the failed visa liberalisation while threatening the EU with opening Turkey's borders (Kirişci, 2021b). This threat materialised in February 2020, as an immediate reaction to the killing of Turkish soldiers in Idlib, Syria. This humanitarian crisis triggered some blame-shifting between Turkey and Greece over 'pushbacks' and 'mistreatment'.

In terms of cooperation, Greece and Turkey conducted several high-level meetings to discuss migration, along with other bilateral issues. Greek and Turkish Ministers of Foreign Affairs Nikos Kotzias and Mevlüt Çavuşoğlu met in Athens on 4 March 2016. In the press conference following the meeting, Turkish Minister of Foreign Affairs Çavuşoğlu evaluated the negotiations with his Greek counterpart by emphasising 'dialogue':

> Naturally we know, and we said this again in our one-on-one meeting, that there are differences and problems that need to be resolved in Greek–Turkish

relations. [. . .] Both sides believe that we need to avoid any intervention, any statement that will cause the climate that exists between Greece and Turkey to deteriorate. [. . .] There is a joint action plan that was decided on at the end of November. As Nikos said earlier, the refugee issue is not Turkish or Greek. Our issue is how we will resolve it, how this huge influx, this refugee and humanitarian crisis, will be resolved. Of course, we support and will always support the NATO forces operating in the Aegean to assist with this refugee crisis. We are aware, and we reiterate once again, that Greece is the neighbour of Turkey with which Turkey wants to cooperate, and we must capitalise on every opportunity to deepen the existing cooperation framework. (*Greek Ministry of Foreign Affairs*, 4 March 2016)

Similar to previous statements of decision-makers in Turkey, Mevlüt Çavuşoğlu's statement also indicated the existence of disputes; however, the minister pointed out the need for a prudent attitude on both sides of the Aegean, in accordance with the détente. During this period, Turkish decision-makers continued to stress the importance of cooperation and stability in relations rather than the continuation of disputes; it is also possible to interpret this emphasis as the desecuritisation of the issues between Greece in Turkey.

The Rapprochement Period: An Analysis Based on Forms of Desecuritisation

The rapprochement between Turkey and Greece since the 1990s has included direct attempts at resolving any outstanding disputes (for instance, exploratory talks to discuss disputes over the Aegean Sea), as well as indirect attempts that did not address the resolution of disputes but aimed at deepening cooperation at various levels (such as the military, tourism, environment, culture, trade, organised crime, drug trafficking, illegal migration and terrorism). All these direct and indirect attempts also found reflection in the elites' discourses, which included a positive and cautious pattern instead of a highly securitised discourse containing a 'threatening' or 'hostile' tone. In any case, the period of rapprochement in the 1990s differed greatly from earlier periods, as the emphasis on friendship and the elimination of hostilities can be clearly discerned in the decision-makers' statements. The most important indicator consists of the fact that, instead of securitising problems, decision-makers preferred to discuss the relations within normal bureaucratic spheres and created a dialogue mechanism (Baysal and Dizdaroğlu, 2022).

In this context, Turkey's securitisation of Greece, which had existed before the rapprochement, seems to have ended. But how did this happen? This question may be answered by employing the concept of desecuritisation, as developed by the Copenhagen School. Analysing the process of desecuritisation is a highly difficult task considering its abstract characteristics; however, Hansen's forms of desecuritisation provide a viable framework for this purpose. Thus, an analysis based on Hansen's forms will unveil the correlation between rapprochement and desecuritisation and enable us to see which forms of desecuritisation fit in the context of Turkish–Greek relations.

This book argues that the amelioration of relations between Turkey and Greece very much fits into the form of *change through stabilisation*, as defined by Lene Hansen. This form of desecuritisation refers to the 'slow move out of an explicit security discourse' that paves the way for the 'political form of engagement' (Hansen, 2012, 539). Immediately following the highly securitised discourse of Turkish decision-makers vis-à-vis several crises – such as Greece's extension of its territorial waters in the Kardak incident, Greek politicians' involvement in sheltering terrorist leader Abdullah Öcalan and so on – the security grammar began to be substituted with a positive and cautious tone. The decision-makers' efforts to move bilateral issues between Turkey and Greece out of an emergence mode and discuss relations within the normal bureaucratic spheres helped to maintain the prevailing atmosphere. Thus, the relationship's stabilisation paved the way for political engagement between the two countries and enabled the change in security discourse in Turkey.

The most significant sign of change consisted of the two ministers of foreign affairs addressing each other as 'my friend'. The same feelings were also shared by the two prime ministers during Kostas Karamanlis' official visit to Turkey in 2008. While evaluating the situation of Cyprus, Turkish Prime Minister Erdoğan stated: '[W]e expect the support of my dear friend, my counterpart, Kostas' (*New York Times*, 23 January 2008). Likewise, during crises such as the burning of the Turkish flag at the Greek Military Academy in April 2005, then Turkish Minister of Foreign Affairs Abdullah Gül said: 'Such behaviours occur sometimes. I guess these will be overcome'. Thus, he signalled that he was sure of positive future relations. In a similar vein, Prime

Minister Erdoğan said in an interview: 'We should not aggrandize trivial matters. All is in friendship, not in enmity (*Sabah*, 25 April 2004).

In 2005, Bülent Arınç, the speaker of the Turkish Parliament, even raised the idea of nullifying the *casus belli* decision, and then Minister of Foreign Affairs Abdullah Gül supported his idea by stating that the *casus belli* decision reflected 'old feelings'. Although there has been no change regarding this decision, the positive atmosphere has been maintained between the two countries. In another crisis, when Turkish and Greek fighter jets collided in mid-air during a clash over the disputed region of the Aegean Sea in May 2006, both sides used a careful tone in order to sustain the prevailing positive atmosphere. Following the incident, Turkish Foreign Minister Abdullah Gül spoke to his Greek counterpart, Dora Bakoyannis, and 'both sides stressed the need not to let the incident harm relations' (*Guardian*, 24 May 2006).

The attitude and statements by Turkish decision-makers following these crises provide useful examples for the choices of the political elites – in other words, of the securitising actors – in terms of securitisation and desecuritisation. When the political elites utilised securitisation policies in the 1990s, they preferred to solve problems such as the Kardak crisis through the lens of securitisation. Of course, particularly during the Kardak crisis, historical threats as well as objective conditions – such as tanks on the border, the distinction between friend and enemy, and sentiments of competition – played a role in facilitating securitisation (Akgül-Açıkmeşe, 2008). In the atmosphere of rapprochement, however, decision-makers chose to resolve the issues in the political sphere rather than in the security realm.

Apart from the change in the decision-makers' discourses, working groups that had been established in 1999, joint initiatives such as the 'Joint Hellenic-Turkish Standby Disaster Relief Unit', joint military exercises, the friendship between Turkish and Greek communities as well as the sheer number of documents signed between the two countries were obvious signs of political and social engagement. It is important to highlight that, without 'recognizing each other as legitimate', as Hansen describes another requirement of this form, such cooperation between Turkey and Greece would not have been possible. Beginning with 'soft issues', the two countries aimed to create a spill-over effect from one sector to another as they consolidated their relations.

As the form of *change through stabilisation* is derived from the détente period of the Cold War – which featured the reduction of both the US and the Soviet Union's armaments in order to enable the strained relations to relax – the relations between Turkey and Greece experienced something similar in terms of landmines. As mentioned above, both countries became a signatory to the Ottawa Convention in 2003 and subsequently started the elimination of anti-personnel landmines on their shared borders as a confidence building measure. Turkey and Greece even initiated dialogue mechanisms with working groups and exploratory talks in order to resolve long-lasting problems between the two countries. Immediately after the jet fighters had collided during a dog fight over the Aegean Sea in May 2006, then Ministers of Foreign Affairs, Abdullah Gül in Turkey and Dora Bakoyannis in Greece, agreed on a hotline between the operational headquarters of the two countries' air forces located in Eskişehir and Larissa (*Hurriyet Daily News*, 12 June 2006). As Hansen (2012, 529) has underlined, the larger conflicts still loom in the background during *change through stabilisation*; thus, in the case of Turkish–Greek relations, the existence of long-lasting disputes over the Aegean Sea fits into this form. While the two countries have focused on cooperation areas in their bilateral relations, both prefer to sweep all their problems under the rug.

In the form of *rearticulation*, which refers to a political solution to the threats, dangers and grievances, there is no political solution to any of the contentious issues. Even though Hansen has pointed out (2012, 542–43) that *rearticulation* is a more radical form of political engagement without any conflict looming in the background and that 'fundamental transformations of the public sphere includ[e] a move out of the friend-enemy distinction', Turkish–Greek relations still are not at that point due to the burden of their divergence on several issues. For instance, in an interview İsmail Cem stated that 'five years ago, the nation that fit the concept of "the other" best was the Turks for Greeks, and the Greeks for Turks. Thank God that today this perception of "the other" is now losing its features and qualities. And we hope that it will disappear very soon' (*Milliyet*, 14 February 2002). Accordingly, it is to be expected that the weight of the disputes between the two and the image of 'threat' or 'enemy' will continue to exist in public opinion. Therefore, public opinion surveys will enable us to gauge the prevailing view on specific issues. A survey conducted in 2016 showed that 42.8 percent – presenting an increase from 26.3 percent in 2015 – of people in Turkey still considered Greece to be the most serious threat to Turkey. Greece ranked in eighth place following Israel, the US, Syria, Iraq, Armenia, Iran and Russia (Aydın et al., 2015 and 2016).

Lene Hansen (2012, 543) has used the example of Mikhail Gorbochev's Murmansk Initiative as a *fundamental rearticulation*, by borrowing from Kristian Åtland's (2008) article titled 'Mikhail Gorbachev, the Murmansk Initiative, and the Desecuritisation of Interstate Relations in the Arctic'. In his article, Åtland (2008, 290) has focused on Gorboachev's launching of policy initiatives ranging from security over economic to environmental issues during his visit to the Soviet polar capital of Murmansk in 1987, in order to demonstrate the fundamental change in Soviet policy towards the region. He has argued (2008, 305) that Gorbachev's successful attempt at moving non-military (or 'soft') issues to the sphere of normal politics, rather than evaluating them in the context of the country's national security agenda, presented an example of desecuritisation. Even though the Turkish–Greek rapprochement process – particularly considering the exploratory talks between the two, as well as the decision-makers' desire to find solutions – resembles *rearticulation*, without a complete solution it might rather be evaluated as a *rearticulation attempt*. As seen in the most recent example of Turkish Foreign Minister Mevlüt Çavuşoğlu, Turkish decision-makers are still eager to come up with a complete resolution for the problems in Turkish–Greek relations. In his statement after his meeting with his Greek counterpart in October 2016, he said: 'We agreed to intensify talks on the thorny issue of the continental shelf, promote confidence-building measures and back a new round of peace talks on Cyprus. It is our shared desire to resolve the problems in the Aegean [. . .] and to reduce tensions and disputes' (*Hurriyet Daily News*, 3 October 2016).

The form of *replacement*, as the third form of desecuritisation, is a process whereby one issue is moved out of the security realm while another is simultaneously securitised. This form is evaluated as an inevitable exit process, in reference to Behnke's (2006, 64–65) argument that 'certain "threats" might no longer exercise our mind and imaginations sufficiently and are replaced with more powerful and stirring imaginaries' (Hansen, 2012, 541). Even though the desecuritisation period of the Greek threat in Turkish foreign policy resembles the form of *replacement*, when considering other critical foreign policy issues, none of them have completely replaced the significance of Greece in Turkish security policy, due to the continued existence of contentious issues between the two countries.

Finally, the fourth form of *silencing* refers to the disappearance from or failure to register an issue in security discourse. The demise of the military authorities in the decision-making mechanism, in accordance with the Europeanisation process in Turkey, paved the way for the disappearance of military officials' discourses from the political sphere, even though the decision-makers are still discussing the issue of Greece and the disputes between the two countries on every occasion, even if in a more prudent and positive tone. Thus, it is not possible to apply the form of *silencing* to the rapprochement process.

To summarise, this study argues that the rapprochement in Turkish–Greek relations has paved the way for the desecuritisation of Turkish–Greek relations, and the best way to explain the correlation between rapprochement and desecuritisation is through the category of *change through stability*. Starting with the changing discourse of decision-makers, the establishment of dialogue channels and the beginning of political engagement in a wide range of cooperation areas such as tourism, economy, military, tourism and trade have constituted signs of this *change through stabilisation*. While the forms of *replacement* and *silencing* cannot explain the rapprochement process, the initiatives between the two countries can however be evaluated as *rearticulation attempts*.

Notes

1. The last (sixty-fourth) round of exploratory talks was held in Athens on 22 February 2022. Following a five-year hiatus, the two countries resumed exploratory talks in 2021; since then, Turkey has renamed them 'consultative talks', which refers to the advisory characteristics of the talks.
2. The Ottowa Convention, the informal name of the 'Convention on the Prohibition of the Use, Stockpiling, Production and Transfer of Anti-Personnel Mines and on Their Destruction', was adopted in September 1997 and entered into force on 1 March 1999. The convention is an international effort to stop the suffering and casualties caused by anti-personnel mines. For further information, see http://www.apminebanconvention.org.

3. In return for Turkey's cooperation in the migration crisis, the EU promised to provide $3 billion Euro to improve the living conditions of the refugees, to revitalise Turkey's EU accession negotiations by opening new chapters – such as Chapter 17 of the Economic and Monetary Policy on 14 December 2015 – as well as to advance visa liberalisation for Turkish citizens.

Part 3

REVERTING TO THE DEFAULT SETTING IN TURKISH FOREIGN POLICY (2016 ONWARDS)

PART 3 INTRODUCTION

The desecuritisation approach towards Greece in Turkey's foreign policy has positively affected political, economic and social issues. The absence of any tangible changes in the core disputes between the two countries is incontrovertible, yet both Greece and Turkey managed to establish a dialogue during the post-1999 period. Despite the promising landscape, new disputes – including the extradition of eight military officers who fled to Greece following the failed 15 July 2016 coup attempt, the migration-related crisis, the Hagia Sophia's conversion into a functioning mosque and the mounting tension in the Aegean and Eastern Mediterranean – have gradually begun to dampen this atmosphere. In an elite survey conducted by Triantaphyllou and Dizdaroğlu in 2016, more than 40 percent of Turkish elites (representatives from academia, the military, journalism, diplomacy and business) evaluated the current state of the relationship as either 'good' or 'rather good', and more than half of elites (53.5 percent) considered a crisis between the two countries within the next five years 'improbable' or 'rather improbable'. However, Turkish decision-makers, or securitising actors, have once again adopted the securitisation approach due to the political tension within Turkey as well as its isolationism in foreign policy. For some, this shift occurred when eight soldiers accused of involvement in the 2016 coup attempt fled to Greece, although other incidents and political dynamics also contributed. This part of the book evaluates these emergent crises, large and small, which accompanied the changes in Turkish domestic politics and precipitated adjustments in the rhetoric of Turkish decision-makers. These adjustments can be evaluated as a reverting to the default securitisation settings in Turkish foreign policy. Particularly, Turkey's official statements, along with naval deployments in the Eastern Mediterranean, present a good example of securitising practices, as argued by the authors of the Paris School. Accordingly, security professionals' practices are crucial for the securitisation of issues (Bigo, 2014). Therefore, this part is devoted to the analysis of the post-2016 period in bilateral relations, so as to understand the shift from the previous period's desecuritisation back to securitisation.

The Coup Attempt and its Repercussions

While Turkish–Greek relations are shaped around traditional disputes such as disagreements over the Aegean Sea, new issues have emerged since 2016. One of these was caused by a domestic event in Turkish politics – namely, the 15 July coup attempt – and has had repercussions for Turkish foreign policy in general, as well as for Turkish–Greek relations.

Turkish political history witnessed the 'bloodiest' coup attempt on 15 July 2016, when a faction of the Turkish army launched operations in major cities to seize power and unseat President Recep Tayyip Erdoğan along with the government. President Erdoğan appeared via Facetime on TV at midnight and called on his supporters to take to the streets and resist the coup. As Esen and Gumuscu (2017, 61) have reported, more than 80,000 mosques all over the country joined President Erdoğan's call and urged resistance to the coup. In a matter of hours, the putschist soldiers were defeated with the help of the crowds, the support from the media and from the political opposition; hence, the coup attempt failed.[1] The coup attempt greatly affected Turkish foreign policy, which had been in crisis mode already before 15 July: 'immediate reactions against a perceived Western abandonment of Turkey emboldened pro-government circles to perpetuate a conspiratorial campaign against Western powers' and demonstrated a 'widening trust deficit between Turkey and its Western allies' in the short and long term (Aras, 2017, 6; Sofuoğlu, 2021). Immediately after the failed coup attempt, eight soldiers affiliated with the Fethullah Gülen movement (FETO), which the Turkish government considers a terrorist organisation, fled to Greece and applied for political asylum; they were arrested in the northern Greek city of Alexandroupolis. As Christofis, Baser and Öztürk (2019, 3) have pointed out, during times of crisis, old enmities and disputes have a way of resurfacing and familiar tensions have a way of simply being reframed; such were the immediate repercussions of the coup attempt on Turkey's relationship with Greece.

The following day, President Recep Tayyip Erdoğan requested the extradition of the putschist soldiers from Greece in his phone conversation with Greek Prime Minister Alexis Tsipras (*Reuters*, 16 July 2016). While the Turkish Black Hawk helicopter used by these soldiers was received by members of the Turkish military and returned to Turkey within a few days, Greece rejected Turkey's demands for extradition several times. However, Turkish officials have constantly reiterated this request on every occasion. For instance, on 7 December 2017 President Recep Tayyip Erdoğan paid a landmark visit to Athens, the first time since 1952 that a Turkish president visited Greece, to discuss economic relations, security and migration issues. President Erdoğan renewed his call for the extradition of the putschists involved in the 15 July coup attempt. During a joint press conference with Prime Minister Alexis Tsipras, he said: 'Justice delayed is justice denied' (*Presidency of the Turkish Republic*, 7 December 2017). In response to Turkey's requests, the Greek government has continuously repeated that the case would be fast-tracked without violating Greek and international law. Other Turkish officials have also reiterated the extradition request. For instance, Turkish Foreign Minister Mevlüt Çavuşoğlu, speaking at a joint press conference with his Greek counterpart, Nikos Kotzias, in October 2017, also raised the issue: 'Turkey does not want Greece to become a refuge for members of FETO' (*Anadolu Agency*, 24 October 2017). In one of his interviews with the Greek newspaper *Ta Nea* on 1 September 2018, he said:

> We are deeply disappointed by the rulings of the Greek judiciary that denied extradition of the putschists several times. [. . .] The Greek judiciary, in contradiction with the norms and principles of international law, leaves the perpetrators without punishment and violates the rights of the victims. Indeed, these eight putschists were granted asylum and released by the Greek courts over the past few months. Greece has clearly exposed itself as a country that provides safe haven to putschists. [. . .] We remain determined to ensure that the fugitive putschists are extradited to and stand trial in Turkey. (*Turkish Ministry of Foreign Affairs*, 1 September 2018)

In the post-2016 period, the growing number of persons affiliated with the Fethullah Gülen Movement who apply for political asylum in Greece has added a new layer to the existing problems between Turkey and Greece. According to the Turkish media, 'Greece became a top destination for members of the FETO fleeing justice', and since 15 July 2016 nearly 20,000 Turkish citizens escaped to Greece via the Aegean islands or the Evros (*Meriç*) River to seek asylum (*Anadolu Agency*, 15 July 2022). However, most of those individuals have ended up in other European countries, including Germany, France, the Netherlands and Belgium. As Taş (2019) has argued, Germany is the EU country where Turkish citizens seek asylum most often, while Greece comes in second.

Turkish decision-makers have consistently reiterated the problem, either warning Greece not to become a 'harbour for FETO' and 'safe haven for terrorists' or blaming Greece for doing so. As reflected in various statements by the Turkish Ministry of Foreign Affairs on different occasions, persons affiliated with terrorist organisations have become one of the most contentious issues between Turkey and Greece:

> With this decision, the putschists will be able to move freely in Greece. Hence, Greece has clearly exposed itself as a country that provides safe haven to putschists. (*Turkish Ministry of Foreign Affairs*, 5 June 2018)

> This reveals once again that the traditional sentiments of the Greek political power against Turkey have not changed. Greece, which provided shelter to PKK Leader Öcalan in the past, today grants asylum to criminals wanted by Turkey and easily ignores the court judgements regarding their extradition [. . .] (*Turkish Ministry of Foreign Affairs*, 5 August 2018)

> We observe with concern that Greece has turned into a safe haven for terrorist organizations, such as DHKP/C, the PKK and FETÖ. It is unacceptable that, in contradiction with the international obligations concerning countering terrorism, Greece shows sympathy and tolerance and provides assistance towards these organizations. The Greek Police arrested nine DHKP/C members back in 2017 in view of serious indications of an assassination attempt against the Turkish President. Despite the fact that Turkey issued arrest warrants and requested extraditions of these individuals, today's decision on dropping charges against them also demonstrates as to why these terrorist elements are nested in Greece [. . .] (*Turkish Ministry of Foreign Affairs*, 15 May 2019)

Apart from the impact on bilateral relations, the failed coup attempt and the subsequent state of emergency, which the Turkish government declared on 21 July 2016 and which lasted for two years (until midnight of 18 July 2018), caused crucial changes in policy-making, by completely eliminating the influence of the military elite. As Christofis, Baser and Öztürk (2019, 3) have argued, under the cover of this state of emergency, 'Erdoğan and the AKP pursued a program of purges and a media clamp down intended to stifle opposition and reinforce the ruling party's hegemony'. Due to the characteristics of the policy-making process in Turkey, some actors have amassed enormous influence on decision-making processes, depending on the particular issue and policy agenda. Specifically, military authorities are recognised as a determinant actor, in foreign and security policy decision-making, although not to the same extent as they were in the 2000s. Considering itself the guardian of the republic, the military has since its foundation assumed an important role in shaping Turkish foreign and security policy. Bilgin (2007, 563) has associated the crucial role of the military with its unquestioned authority over 'security knowledge' and a lack of civilian interest in security issues. Bilgin (2007, 563) has suggested that the military's active involvement in the formulation of the national security policy document, particularly after 1980, has influenced the Turkish security agenda, in which the views of the military have prevailed. The military's autonomy in Turkish politics was not questioned until the late 1990s. Challenges emanating both domestically (the Kurdish issue) and internationally (Greece and Syria) then prompted the military to adopt a more prominent role in conducting foreign and security policies. Following the 1999 Helsinki Summit, attempts were made to diminish the privileged and primary role of the military and the NSC, transforming the Turkish political system in accordance with the EU harmonisation process.[2]

In line with the process of Turkish accession to the EU, constitutional amendments and legal changes to Turkish law between 2001 and 2003, particularly concerning the structure of the NSC, allowed for the demilitarisation of the council (Aydın and Akgül Açıkmeşe, 2007, 269–70; Özcan, 2010, 30). Turkey changed the composition of the NSC to incorporate more civilian members, including a civilian secretary-general, and aligned its role as an advisory body to the government in order to meet the EU's demands for ensuring civilian control over the military (Aydın and Açıkmeşe, 2007, 269).

Furthermore, the military's role in preparing the National Security Policy Document was also constrained when the government took a more active role in its preparation (Özcan, 2010, 30). Özcan (2010, 30) has stressed: 'The document was shorter in comparison to its predecessors and did not include the preparation of "action plans" against certain countries'. All these fundamental changes, which did not successfully prevent the military authorities from issuing statements about important foreign policy issues, have had serious repercussions for Turkish foreign policy. Despite all the changes in its composition and role, the NSC remains a securitising actor in Turkey. As Bilgin (2007, 564) has pointed out, the military is still a major actor that shapes the contours of the National Security Policy Document in Turkey.

Through its declarations, the military retained its influence over political life until the mid-2000s (Karaosmanoğlu, 2011, 253). Thereafter, the public declarations and speeches of the chief of general staff were rendered unwelcome in political circles, compelling military authorities to maintain a low profile and to become less outspoken on foreign policy issues (Özcan, 2009, 87). Military bureaucrats were brought under the control of the civilian government especially after 2016, and their autonomous structure was dissolved by the government (Baysal and Dizdaroğlu, 2022). Accordingly, the government has become the sole securitising actor in Turkey and has used its authority to shape securitisation policies in both domestic and foreign politics. As Baysal and Dizdaroğlu (2022) have argued, 'securitisation has more recently become the dominant understanding of decision-makers, who are regulated by civilian authorities' rather than by military bureaucrats. Although the (already in terms of its power consolidated) government's utilisation of securitisation and security-oriented policies has had an impact on domestic politics since the 2013 Gezi protests, its impact on foreign policy began to appear mostly later on. As mentioned above, the coup attempt provided the government with a fertile ground to plant security-oriented policies and to strengthen its alliance with the Nationalist Movement Party (MHP).

Regarding the relations between Turkey and Greece, the government's securitisation policies showed themselves in the Eastern Mediterranean rather than in the other routine disputes between the two countries. The tension in the Eastern Mediterranean dates to the early 2000s; however, it was limited to Cyprus, and it only became problematic in the post-2016 period. It can be argued that the government utilised securitisation policies in the region because of a variety of factors – such as Turkey's isolation in the region, its exclusion from the regional East Mediterranean Gas Forum (EAST-MED) and the newly emerging cooperation between the government and the retired military officers who developed the Blue Homeland discourse. Even though the cooperation between the government and the retired military officers did not last long, it paved the way for the securitisation of the Eastern Mediterranean issue through either policy practices or speech-acts (Baysal and Dizdaroğlu, 2022). Thus, the following section delves into the details of Turkey's policies towards the region and its implications on bilateral relations.

The Tension over the Eastern Mediterranean

In this process of reverting to the default settings in Turkish foreign policy, as mentioned above, Greek–Turkish bilateral relations are shaped around routine disagreements over the Aegean Sea, albeit without any escalation. The spirit of the rapprochement process, which encouraged the parties to refrain from unilateral acts and to prioritise dialogue, prevailed until the Eastern Mediterranean issue impacted bilateral relations. Turkish elites have already pointed out the significance of the energy resources in the Eastern Mediterranean as one of the problems (along with the disputes over the Aegean Sea and Cyprus) that might create a 'new' crisis between Turkey and Greece (Triantaphyllou and Dizdaroğlu, 2017, 19–21). Previously, the issue did not constitute a dominant subject in bilateral relations, because it had remained limited around the island of Cyprus, and because other issues, such as Syria and Iraq, had dominated the Turkish foreign policy agenda. It can be also argued that Turkish decision-makers wanted to keep the issue out of bilateral relations. However, it is noteworthy that Turkish decision-makers have closely followed developments in the region since the beginning.

Since 2003, the RoC has intensified its efforts to sign bilateral agreements on maritime jurisdiction areas; accordingly, it signed the exclusive economic zone (EEZ) agreements with Egypt on 17 February 2003, with Lebanon on 17 January 2007 and with Israel on 17 December 2010 (Aydın and Dizdaroğlu, 2018, 95). Since Turkey has found these attempts by the Greek Cypriot administration unacceptable, it made several demarches with these countries and the UN to register its concerns. Despite Turkey's criticism, the

RoC also in February 2007 adopted a law to identify thirteen oil exploration fields around the island before issuing licenses to international energy companies for off-shore exploration. In response, Turkey warned all interested parties to act responsibly and not to harm the prospects for a comprehensive Cyprus solution (*Turkish Ministry of Foreign Affairs*, 14 August 2007). Turkey's concerns in the region mainly relate to its own and the Turkish Cypriots' sovereign rights to and benefits of the sea. Turkey also argues that the RoC is not competent to represent both Turkish and Greek Cypriots jointly, or Cyprus as a whole. Turkey has insisted that any resources should belong to all Cypriots, and all Turkish and Greek Cypriots should jointly benefit from potential resources. Otherwise, the parties would have to wait until a comprehensive solution is found to the Cyprus problem.

The intensification of the exploration activities and the consecutive discoveries of energy resources off the coasts of Israel, Cyprus and Egypt (the Tamar field in 2009, Leviathan in 2010, Aphrodite in 2011, Zohr in 2015, Calypso in 2018 and Glaucus in 2019) have caused a rather tense political environment due to the conflicting sovereignty claims over the waters of the Eastern Mediterranean. Turkey's policy formulations changed when a US-registered company, Noble Energy, began drilling in the RoC's Aphrodite field on 19 September 2011. Accordingly, Turkey concluded a continental shelf delimitation agreement with the Turkish Republic of Northern Cyprus (TRNC) on 21 September 2011; in April 2012, it authorised the Turkish Petroleum Company to begin exploration off the coast of the island in areas that overlap with six exploration fields also claimed by the RoC (*Turkish Ministry of Foreign Affairs*, 21 September 2011; Aydın and Dizdaroğlu 2018, 95). In the words of İpek and Gür (2021, 13), Turkey has increasingly contested the RoC's acts and has started redefining its attitude as soon as Turkey's sovereign rights and material interests were directly threatened by foreign energy firms.

From the perspective of securitisation, the Turkish government's responses, either by verbal declarations or by policy practices, to protect both its own and the TRNC's rights and benefits have represented a successful securitisation of the issue in Turkish foreign policy. By dispatching its research ships, accompanied by navy vessels, into the disputed fields around Cyprus, Turkey utilised securitisation practices. In fact, this subject had already been categorised as a security issue in Turkish foreign policy earlier; however, in the post-2016 period – due to the changing Turkish political dynamics – Turkish government strategy was once again dominated by securitisation policy and practices (Baysal and Dizdaroğlu, 2022). Even the rapid increase in the number of seismic and drilling ships under Turkish flag confirmed such a cautious policy by the government (*Anadolu Agency*, 12 November 2021; *Daily Sabah*, 11 May 2022). Turkish decision-makers opted for returning to securitisation policies against Greece and the securitisation of Eastern Mediterranean energy resources to protect the rights of the Turkish Cypriots as well as of Turkey. Turkish Foreign Minister Mevlüt Çavuşoğlu spoke about these developments in the region in an interview with the Greek newspaper *Ta Nea* in September 2018:

> Turkey as well as the Turkish Cypriots have warned the Greek Cypriots from the very beginning not to take such irresponsible steps. If they still believe they have nothing to lose, they are mistaken. Turkey will continue to protect the rights of the Turkish Cypriots, as well as its own rights and interests in the Eastern Mediterranean. Our aim is still to ensure peace and stability in the region. As for companies cooperating with the Greek Cypriots in the area of hydrocarbons, they now must review their cost-benefit assessments and re-evaluate the situation. (*Turkish Ministry of Foreign Affairs*, 1 September 2018)

The decision-makers' inclination to utilise securitised policies and practices has further intensified following the initiatives by Greece and the RoC to isolate Turkey in the region as well as to present it as an aggressive actor in international politics. The initiatives by Greece and the RoC, for instance, have paved the way for the EU's strong condemnation of Turkey's activities in the region. Accordingly, the EU has called several times on Turkey to cease its 'illegal drilling activities' in the Eastern Mediterranean, thus reaffirming its full solidarity with the RoC (*Council of the EU*, 22 March 2018 and 20 June 2019). On 11 November 2019, the Council of the EU even adopted a framework for restrictive measures, including imposing sanctions that target 'individuals or entities responsible for or involved in unauthorised drilling activities' in the region (*Council of the EU*, 11 November 2019). It should be noted that Turkey's use of foreign policy as a battle ground for domestic interests, its personalisation and securitisation of foreign policy, and its strained relations with its allies and immediate neighbours have helped both Greece and the RoC in their initiatives.

In the absence of Turkey's dialogue with regional countries, new regional energy and security alliances have begun to emerge. Greece and the RoC have consecutively signed several defence cooperation agreements with regional countries, in addition to their agreements with the US and individual European countries such as France (Dizdaroğlu, 2021). Likewise, the alignment between Israel, Greece and the RoC through deepening their defence relationship has redefined the parameters in the Eastern Mediterranean (Tanchum, 2015, 3–4). Regarding energy, the EAST-MED between Greece, the RoC, Italy, Israel, Egypt, Jordan and Palestine is another development that has left Turkey feeling excluded. During the meeting of the energy ministers of the littoral states – except for Turkey, Syria and Lebanon – in Cairo on 14 January 2019, the parties agreed to establish EAST-MED with the aim to expedite the development of hydrocarbon resources in the region and to transform the region into an energy hub. In return, Turkey conducted the largest ever maritime exercise, which it called Blue Homeland 2019 and which took place between February 27 and March 8 in the Black, Aegean, Mediterranean and Marmara seas (*Milliyet*, 27 February 2019). This practice could also be categorised as a concrete example of the role of certain foreign policy practices in the securitisation process.

The activities of the 'Greek Cypriot-Greek duo' against Turkey have received increasing emphasis by Turkish decision-makers in their official statements. For instance, the Turkish Ministry of Foreign Affairs issued a statement following the joint declaration adopted at the Sixth Summit of the Southern European Union Countries (Med7), held on 14 June 2019:

> This declaration provides yet another regrettable example of how the Greek Cypriot Administration and Greece abuse their EU membership and how some of the members of the EU have become instruments of these acts. [. . .] Turkey's determination to protect its rights within its continental shelf and the equal rights of the Turkish Cypriots over the hydrocarbon resources of the Island continue as before, and Turkey has taken necessary steps to this end and will not hesitate to do so. (*Turkish Ministry of Foreign Affairs*, 15 June 2019)

Similar criticisms were made after the trilateral summits between Greece, the RoC and Egypt in September and October 2019:

Steps with political expediencies aiming to isolate and ignore Turkey and the Turkish Cypriots in the Eastern Mediterranean have no chance of success. Furthermore, it is also insincere on the part of Greece to make baseless claims against Turkey at a time she extends cooperation messages to us. We invite these countries to face the political, economic and geographic realities of the region, and to pursue policies of cooperation in conformity with these realities. [. . .] We will continue to defend resolutely both our and Turkish Cypriots' rights in the Eastern Mediterranean. (*Turkish Ministry of Foreign Affairs*, 28 September 2019)

The maximalist policies of Greek/Greek Cypriot duo, that disregard the principle of 'equity' which is one of the most basic principles of international law and the United Nations Convention on the Law of the Sea (UNCLOS) in maritime boundary delimitation, have led to losses in the past against Egypt's interests regarding its maritime jurisdiction areas. Yet Egypt seems to have turned a blind eye to this abusive treatment by the Greek/Greek Cypriot duo. Turkey will continue to protect resolutely its own rights and the rights of the Turkish Cypriots in the Eastern Mediterrenean. Turkey is ready to talk to all countries in the region, except the GCA, for the delimitation of maritime jurisdiction areas in the Eastern Mediterranean in accordance with the principle of equity [. . .] (*Turkish Ministry of Foreign Affairs*, 9 October 2019)

Aiming to emerge from its regional isolation and prevent EAST-MED, the Blue Homeland discourse has gained popularity; this is in line with Turkey's political strategy to secure its rights in both the Aegean and Mediterranean. The practical applications of these policies include Turkey's largest maritime exercise, an increase in seismic and drilling activities in the region, regular statements regarding the issue and the signing of a memorandum of understanding between Turkey and the UN-backed Libyan Government of National Accord on 27 November 2019 (Çelikpala, 2019; *Turkish Ministry of Foreign Affairs*, 1 December 2019; Baysal and Dizdaroğlu, 2022). As this policy move immediately triggered attempts by Greece and the RoC's to villainise the Turkish-Libyan agreement in the international arena, the issue surrounding the Eastern Mediterranean escalated between Turkey and Greece throughout 2020. In response, the Turkish Ministry of Foreign Affairs offered harsh statements; common accusations include 'the maximalist and unconstructive behaviours of the Greek Cypriot-Greek duo', 'pursuing policies that endanger peace and stability in the region', 'avoiding the legitimate rights of Turkey and Northern Cyprus', and 'Turkey's determination to protect its rights as well as those of the Turkish Cypriots' (*Turkish Ministry of Foreign Affairs* 16 January; 26 March; 21 April; 15 May 2020). When the EAST-MED Gas pipeline agreement was signed at the trilateral summit between Greece, Israel and the RoC in January 2020, the Turkish Ministry of Foreign Affairs similarly described this initiative as 'the latest instance of futile steps, aiming to exclude Turkey and TRNC in the region' (*Reuters*, 2020; *Turkish Ministry of Foreign Affairs*, 2 January 2020).

The Turkish-Libyan agreement on maritime jurisdiction zones that permitted Turkey's research activities in the disputed waters between Cyprus and Crete fuelled the tension in the Eastern Mediterranean, especially in the summer of 2020. The individual moves of both Turkey and Greece escalated the risk of armed conflict. On 21 July 2020, Turkey via NAVTEX (an official alert for exploration activities) announced plans to dispatch the research vessel *Oruç Reis* and additional support vessels to carry out operations in the waters south of the Greek island of Kastellorizo (*Meis*) until 2 August 2020. In response, Greece put its naval forces on alert, heightening for several days the risk of escalation, as evident from a minor collision between a Greek and Turkish vessel on 12 August. Third parties such as Germany served as mediators to de-escalate the tension between the two, given the absence of the US administration, which did not immediately get involved. As result of German Chancellor Angela Merkel's efforts, the Turkish government has suspended its activities in the region as a sign of good intentions. Presidential Spokesperson İbrahim Kalın shared Turkey's position on a TV programme:

> In line with the instructions of our President, we are ready to discuss all issues; the Aegean, continental shelf, islands, airspace, research and screening efforts, and the Eastern Mediterranean along with other bilateral matters with Greece without any precondition. [. . .] Let's be constructive and put efforts on hold for some time. (*Dunya*, 28 July 2020; *Bianet*, 29 July 2020)

Despite Turkey's positive response to the German mediation initiative and its suspension of activities as a gesture of goodwill, Greece and Egypt announced the signing of a maritime delimitation agreement on 6 August 2020. Turkey immediately proclaimed the so-called agreement as 'null and void' by reminding of its determined position on the issue: '[I]t is without a doubt that Turkey will not allow any activity at the area in question and will resolutely continue to defend its legitimate rights and interests as well as those of the Turkish Cypriots in the Eastern Mediterranean' (*Turkish Ministry of Foreign Affairs*, 6 August 2020).

In addition, Turkey re-initiated its exploration activities by issuing a new NAVTEX, between 10 and 23 August, dispatching once again the *Oruç Reis*, accompanied by navy vessels, to the Eastern Mediterranean for exploration (*Hurriyet Daily News*, 10 August 2020). Greece responded by dispatching its own navy to the region, which brought about a face-off between Turkish and Greek warships in the Eastern Mediterranean. While Germany worked to organise direct talks between Turkey and Greece, a Greek military ship, the *Limnos* – according to a Greek defence source – accidentally touched the rear of a Turkish military ship, the *Kemal Reis*, which was escorting the research vessel *Oruç Reis*, on 12 August 2020 (*Independent*, 14 August 2020). After weeks of tension and the risk of escalation in the region, both parties pulled back, and the situation was somewhat pacified thanks to the mediation of Germany and the NATO. Once both sides declared their willingness to start negotiations, both parties withdrew their ships and decided to resume 'exploratory talks' after a five-year hiatus. Accordingly, the sixty-first round of exploratory talks was held in İstanbul on 25 January 2021.

During and after this incident, Turkish decision-makers' statements and policy practices clearly showed the successful securitisation of the issue in their foreign policy. This process of securitisation was initiated and maintained by decision-makers who purposefully made the choice to solve the issue in the security realm rather than in the political sphere. A statement by President Erdoğan on 7 September 2020 represents a concrete example of how the securitised discourse reflected itself in the decision-makers' speeches:

> Those who, disregarding Turkey's rights in the Eastern Mediterranean and the Aegean, try to implement a *fait accompli* without learning their lesson from history will also understand this truth. Let me be very clear, for those who stand against Turkey at the cost of risking their own citizens' security and welfare, that they hopefully will not have to pay a heavy price when the time comes. We say at every opportunity that we are in favour of resolving disputes through discussions, talks, negotiations and reconciliation. I advise that those who defy us with their dilapidated militaries instead of sitting at

the table with us should closely analyse not just history but the diplomatic activities and military operations we have carried out over the past four years [. . .] Turkey, as is the case with its border security, will continue to pursue to the end a determined and active policy regarding its rights in the Eastern Mediterranean as well. (*Presidency of the Turkish Republic*, 7 September 2020)

Apart from the above-mentioned tensions, there existed also several other issues that caused dramatic turns and shifts in bilateral relations, including Turkey's removal of its border restrictions for migrants in late February and the re-opening of the Hagia Sophia for Muslim prayer in late July 2020. An aerial attack by Russian-backed Syrian regime forces, during which at least thirty Turkish soldiers were killed in Idlib in northern Syria on 29 February 2020, paved the way for an influx of migrants towards the Greek border. In reaction to the NATO's and the EU's unwillingness to support Turkey's military campaign in Idlib, President Erdoğan announced that 'Turkey would not stand in the way of refugees and migrants already in the country who hope to head to Europe. We will not close the gates to refugees' (*TRT World*, 29 February 2020). As Romain Örs (2020) has reported, in a matter of two days, tens of thousands gathered at the main checkpoints at the land and sea borders between Turkey and Greece. This humanitarian crisis caused blame-shifting in bilateral relations, as both Turkey and Greece began to accuse each other of 'illegal push-backs' and 'mistreatment' of migrants. The crisis came to end once Greece forcefully prevented migrants from crossing into Greece and the Turkish government decided once more to close its borders due to the COVID-19 pandemic (Kirişci, 2021a). The EU has promised to continue providing financial assistance to Syrian refugees and host communities in Turkey, while also warning against the 'instrumentalization of migrants for political purposes', in line with Greece's insistence (Kirişci, 2021b; Ertan, 2021).

On 10 July 2020, the Turkish Council of State removed any remaining bureaucratic obstacles preventing the Hagia Sophia, which since 1934 had functioned as a state-run museum, from being given the status of a mosque, and President Erdoğan immediately announced that it would be opened for worship on 24 July 2020 (Öztürk, 2020). As Öztürk (2020) has argued, the president's decision has a profound meaning and significant consequences, for himself as well as for the political stance he represents, since most of his supporters see this move as a victory against the Christian West. This political move by the Turkish government also caused a strong reaction in Greece and triggered a spat between Turkish and Greek decision-makers. For instance, the reactions by Greek Prime Minister Kyriakos Mitsotakis, who considered Turkey's move a 'sign of weakness' that will 'create an unbridgeable gap between Turkey and the Christian world' (*EuroNews*, 24 July 2020), received the following response from the Turkish Ministry of Foreign Affairs:

> Greece has once again demonstrated her hostility towards Islam and Turkey under the pretext of reacting to the opening of the Hagia Sophia Mosque to worship. We strongly condemn hostile statements made by members of the Greek Government and Parliament provoking the public opinion and allowing the burning of our glorious flag in Thessaloniki. [. . .] These racist mindsets, who have not drawn the required lessons from history, those who disrespect our glorious Flag should remember their fate in the Aegean. Greece should, from now on, wake up from the Byzantine dream from which she has been unable to wake up for 567 years and get rid of her frustration emanating from it. (*Turkish Ministry of Foreign Affairs*, 25 July 2020)

The frequency of statements by Turkish decision-makers in the post-2016 period show that Greece has constituted one of the major topics in Turkish foreign policy. The two countries have had to deal with numerous crises, large and small, straining relations, ranging from the extradition of the putschist soldiers from Greece to the migration issue, from the conversion of the Hagia Sophia into a mosque to the rising tension in the Eastern Mediterranean. Despite the tendency of Turkish decision-makers to utilise securitisation and prioritise security-oriented policies in the post-2016 period, its repercussions on Turkish–Greek relations only showed themselves explicitly around the Eastern Mediterranean disputes. As reflected in the statements and policy practices by Turkish decision-makers – namely, the securitising actors – regarding the Eastern Mediterranean, the government has instrumentalised successful securitisation in order to solve these issues within the security realm rather than through the normal bargaining process of the political sphere. It is worth to emphasise once more that the post-2016 period in Turkey has witnessed securitisation by civilian authorities rather than by military bureaucrats, as seen during the 1990s. As argued by Baysal and Dizdaroglu (2022), this demonstrates the political nature of securitisation policies that assist the government to consolidate its power within domestic politics.

Notes

1. For a detailed account of the 15 July coup attempt, see Esen and Gumuscu, 2017.
2. For a detailed account of the EU harmonisation process's impact on civil–military relations in Turkey, see Narlı, 2000; Özcan, 2009; Karaosmanoğlu, 2011; Gürsoy, 2012.

7

CONCLUSION: WHAT DOES THE FUTURE HOLD?

Throughout the modern history of Turkish–Greek relations, which dates back as far as to the early nineteenth century, both countries have constructed their national identities in opposition to each other, encumbered by the burden of their past. As the two countries gained their independence by fighting each other, the historical legacy and mutual antipathy between the two nations have had a significant impact on both public perception and the mind-set of decision-makers. This impact has been reflected in both public and elite surveys that are regularly conducted in both countries. As already mentioned, public surveys are useful to capture public perception, which helps to better understand the public's sensitivity. According to one public survey, which has been conducted regularly by a group of scholars since 2010, the Turkish public has considered Greece a threat, even though its ranking has constantly changed in parallel with the up and downs in bilateral relations. In 2020, 49.5 percent of the Turkish public – which presents an increase from 44.5 percent in 2019 – responded that they perceived Greece as a threat to its security (Aydın et al., 2021, 76–77). As 2020 has been the most challenging year – or, in the words of Kirişci (2021a, 3), *annus horribilis* – for bilateral relations because of the emergent crises, measuring the public perception is quite valuable to comprehend these crises' repercussions on public opinion in both countries. The Hellenic Foundation for Foreign and European Policy (ELIAMEP) in partnership with diaNEOsis and the Istanbul Policy Centre conducted the first joint public survey in Greece and Turkey between 19 and 21 February 2021, with the participation of 1,022 Greek and 1,142 Turkish citizens.[1] According to this survey, the bilateral disputes in the Aegean and Mediterranean emerged as the most severe problems, in parallel with the tension in the summer of 2020. What is promising in this research is that the majority of both Greeks (59 percent) and Turks (70 percent) believe that the disputes between the two can be resolved more easily through dialogue and conciliation (Grigoriadis, 2021). However, both countries' decision-makers have preferred to keep in view the historical background of conflict.

It is possible to observe the impact of the historical background on the discourses and practices of both countries' security and foreign policies. The two centuries since the outbreak of the Greek revolt against the Ottoman Empire in March 1821 have been dominated by conflict and competition. Even so, despite the difficult beginnings of the relationship between Turkey and Greece, both countries succeeded in establishing several exceptional periods of cooperation in the course of their relations, under the leadership of responsible and courageous leaders. Apart from the two cooperation periods in the 1930s and 1950s, Turkish–Greek relations entered a golden age with the rapprochement that started in 1999. The consistency of the prudent and affirmative grammar in the Turkish decision-makers' discourses, as seen also during the early cooperation periods of the 1930s and 1950s, has enabled the prevailing friendly atmosphere between the two counties to continue. As already observed in the second part of the book, decision-makers in Turkey refrained from using security grammar or dramatising issues in order to sustain a positive relationship.

The crises in the course of the relationship demonstrate that there is a need for understanding the disputes' historical background and the ways in which decision-makers on both sides handle these disputes. On the eve of the foundation of the Republic of Turkey, during the Lausanne Conference, Turkish decision-makers raised concerns about several issues, such as the sovereignty rights over the Aegean islands and their demilitarised status. Accordingly, İsmet İnönü, the chief negotiator of the Turkish delegation to Lausanne, made quite striking statements about Turkey's stance regarding the Aegean Sea. While explaining the importance of the islands' proximity to Turkey's coast, he clearly emphasised the existential threat to the survival and security of the referent object – that is, Turkey. His dramatisation of the issue by stressing the 'extreme' and 'vital' importance of the islands for the security of Anatolia constituted the backbone of Turkey's official position, and the statements of succeeding decision-makers in Turkey continued to reiterate this notion. Even though İsmet İnönü's speech-acts during the negotiations for the Treaty of Lausanne did not contain the necessary components of an 'existential threat' or 'emergency action', his attempts were transformed into successful securitisation with the help of the security discourse of later decision-makers whenever they encountered crises between Turkey and Greece.

Likewise, the Turkish delegation raised the newly founded Republic's concerns with a particular emphasis on the 'vital importance' of the island of Cyprus for the protection of Turkey's southern coast, even as the Turkish delegation relinquished its rights over the island (Dodd 2010, 3). This emphasis might be considered an early attempt to build a security discourse in Turkish foreign policy. Thereafter, Turkey considered all issues related to Cyprus as belonging to the UK's domestic politics and attempted no involvement, as long as the UK maintained its rule. Turkey did not have a concrete official position on the Cyprus problem until it emerged as an issue in Turkish foreign policy in mid-1955; however, the existential threat that the occupation of the island by a hostile country posed for Turkey's security was clearly pointed out. The lack of a concrete official position precludes any in-depth analysis of the issue at that time, but the developments in the aftermath of the RoC's establishment illustrate its securitisation by the Turkish elite.

Within this context, the emergence of the Cyprus issue in the mid-1950s, as well as developments in international politics and law in the mid-1960s concerning the Aegean Sea (such as the delimitation of maritime boundaries and the continental shelf, the breadth of territorial waters and air space) have not only changed the course of the relationship between Turkey and Greece, but also the discourse of the decision-makers. The dormant source of disputes underlying these issues became apparent especially with the decision-makers' security discourse. The analysis of the statements of securitising actors at that time, with the help of securitisation theory, as presented by Buzan et al., may enable us to comprehend whether, how and to what extent the issues between the two countries were securitised in Turkey. It is possible to interpret the statements of the securitising actors in Turkey regarding Cyprus and other contentious issues in the Aegean Sea, which have been analysed in the book's first part, as successful instances of securitisation.

Turkish decision-makers' statements about Cyprus and issues related to the Aegean Sea were consistent with the early Republican rhetoric that considered both problems through the security lens. Accordingly, Turkish securitising actors viewed all Greek attempts – such as the extension of its territorial waters, the fortification of the islands, the exploration or drilling activities on the disputed continental shelf and finally claims of sovereignty –as existential threats against the security of the referent object, Turkey. The existence of objective security issues between the two countries allowed securitising actors to dramatise the issues. More specifically, the threat posed by Greece has always been in line with Turkey's traditional fear of encirclement. Thus, securitising actors have always stressed in their statements the threat of any change in the balance of power, of cutting off Turkey's access to the open seas as well as the transformation of the Aegean into a 'Greek Lake'; in order to prevent this threat, they have suggested several emergency measures, ranging from declaring a *casus belli*, over taking necessary measures, to using military force.

Regarding Cyprus, there existed a similar pattern in the discourses of securitising actors. As seen during the Cyprus-related crises, Turkish securitising actors raised the issue of the existential threat posed by Greece through destroying the constitutional order on the island and damaging the balance of power in the Eastern Mediterranean, which was evaluated as a direct threat to the security of Turkey, along with the survival of the TRNC. Kaliber (2003, 16) has evaluated the inseparable link between the security of Turkey and of the TRNC in the statements of securitising actors that employ the metaphors of 'motherland' and 'baby land'. The same securitising actors also emphasised emergency measures, including in 1974 an intervention on the island under the name 'Peace Operation', in order to handle the threat. In short order, as seen in the other issues pertaining to the Aegean, Turkish securitising actors took the Cyprus issue outside of the normal political procedure and implemented emergency measures following a successful securitisation. In the cases of both the Aegean and Cyprus, the securitising actors in Turkey were representatives of democratically elected governments; therefore, it is possible to assume an inherent approval by the relevant audience in each of these cases.

This historical background indicates the same pattern in the discourses of the securitising actors. As the focal point of this book consists of the post-Cold War developments, it analyses the divergences between Turkey and Greece on those issues that brought the two countries to the brink of war. The Cold War had a significant impact on both countries' security and foreign policy considerations, as both had to reformulate their priorities in light of new security needs. This period was important for the bilateral relations of the two countries since there occurred a multitude of crises during that time. These crises included Greece's desire to unilaterally extend its territorial waters to twelve miles in the Aegean Sea, Turkey's *casus belli* decision in response, the Kardak (Imia) crisis, the S-300 missile crisis in Cyprus and the capture of Abdullah Öcalan, the leader of the PKK, in the Embassy of Greece in Kenya. An analysis of this period, which constitutes the peak of securitisation in Turkish–Greek relations due to the above-mentioned challenges, within the framework of securitisation theory shows how and to what extent Greece has been securitised by Turkey. In other words, Turkish decision-makers chose to utilise securitisation policies to deal with these crises, rather than handling them in the normal bargaining process of the political sphere. Of course, Turkey's weak coalition governments during that period played an important role in the securitisation policies, which resulted in the consolidation of nationalist votes, thus influencing the country's relationship with Greece.

Before delving into the details, this analysis should once more insist that it is not a scholar's task to determine whether threats raised by securitising actors are indeed legitimate. Rather, scholars try to 'understand who securitizes, on what issues (threats), for whom (referent objects), why, with what results, and, not least, under what conditions (i.e., when securitisation is successful)' (Buzan et al., 1998, 32). Thus, this book does not intend to underestimate the problems between Turkey and Greece or to put the blame on either side. As discussed in the preceding chapters, it aims to show whether, how and to what extent the Turkish elite, like their Greek counterparts, have used securitisation policies in handling various crises, with the help of the methodology and main concepts of securitisation theory as brough forth by the Copenhagen School. By doing so, this study also demonstrates the political nature of securitisation.

In the first crisis of the period, Greece's desires to extend its territorial waters to six miles caused the TGNA's declaration of *casus belli* on 8 June 1995. The declaration by the TGNA was consistent with Turkey's official position regarding the issue, which was first reflected in the statement of then Minister of Foreign Affairs İhsan Sabri Çağlayangil in April 1976. As mentioned in the relevant chapter, Çağlayangil in a letter urged US Secretary of State Henry Kissinger to consider the existential threat against Turkey's rights and interests in the Aegean Sea; he dramatised the issue by specifically referring to Turkey's access to the high seas being obstructed and the possibility of Greek dominance in the Aegean, which he called a 'Greek Lake'. The securitised policy line raised by İhsan Sabri Çağlayangil in 1976 was followed by the TGNA in response to Greek activities in the Aegean Sea in the 1990s. As Greece's intentions to change the status quo in the Aegean became explicit, the Turkish elites evaluated these attempts as instances of *casus belli*. After moving the issue out of the normal bargaining process, the TGNA granted the Turkish government the authority to take emergency measures, 'including military ones', in order to protect and defend the vital interests of the referent object. There existed a similar standpoint among the decision-makers who securitised the issue, as seen in the analysis of their security-related speech-acts within the framework of securitisation theory. The common emphasis reiterated by Turkish decision-makers was on the existential threat mainly posed by 'Greek *fait accompili* attempts' through extending its territorial waters, while the very same decision-makers offered emergency measures (including military ones) to prevent the change of the status quo.

The second breaking point occured due to an incident on 25 December 1995, when a Turkish ship ran aground on an islet in the Aegean. Although the two countries tried to resolve the issue within the bounds of normal politics – that is, by exchanging diplomatic notes between the Ministries of Foreign Affairs – the involvement of the media (which can also be identified as a functional actor) triggered a change in the decision-makers' discourses. The single voice of statements by decision-makers mainly contained a security grammar that included dramatisation, emphasis on an existential threat and emergency actions. Then Prime Minister Tansu Çiller dramatised the issue when she made special reference to the sovereignty and integrity of Turkey. In her statements, she pointed to 'legacy' and the 'sacrificing of lives' in order to protect the country against any *fait accompli*, even if it only concerned Turkish 'pebbles'. The Turkish elites responded with emergency measures such as deploying troops in order to protect Turkey's rights and interests in the Aegean. The similar standpoints of all securitising actors – including the prime minister, the minister of foreign affairs and high-ranking military officers – demonstrates how decision-makers in Turkey handled issues outside the normal bargaining process and securitised them by means of speech-acts. Thus, the security speech-acts of the decision-makers during the Kardak crisis clearly show a successful securitisation of the sovereignty rights in the Aegean: they presenteded and dramatised the existential threat that neighbouring Greece's claim to sovereignty rights over islands, islets and rocks posed against the territorial integrity, sovereignty and national security of the referent object.

Similar to the earlier crises between the two countries, the RoC's desire to acquire S-300 missiles from Russia created tension, since Turkish decision-makers interpreted missiles on the island as an existential threat, not just to neighbouring countries, but also to Turkey and the TRNC. Turkish securitising actors' statements reflected how the RoC's decision – which had been made with the encouragement of the Greek government – posed an existential threat to the security and interests of the referent object since it would alter the military balance in the region. Turkey's determination to prevent the deployment of the missiles to the island and to maintain the regional status quo – even through the use of military force, should it become necessary – represents a clear example of the securitisation process. In the face of a threat, Turkish decision-makers were determined to use emergency measures to 'neutralise the threat' and to maintain the status quo. Likewise, the revelation of Greek politicians' and the EYP's links to the PKK, a terrorist organisation that compromised the unity and sovereignty of Turkey, created more tension between Turkey and Greece. The statements of Ambassador Şükrü Elekdağ, then Under-Secretary of the Ministry of Foreign Affairs, about the Greek government's support to the terrorist organisation clearly emphasised the threat emanating from Greece against the survival and unity of the referent object. Even though the Greek governments denied Turkey's allegations, the capture of fugitive PKK leader Abdullah Öcalan in the Greek Embassy in Kenya revealed the direct link between terrorists and several Greek officials.

While Turkish–Greek relations reached its 'lowest ebb' (Alpogan, 2005, 165; Evin, 2005, 396), the Turkish elites successfully securitised the link between the PKK and Greece by using security grammar in their statements.

Following each of these crises, the decision-makers' statements showed how issues related to Greece were securitised in order to prevent threats against its survival. All securitising actors in Turkey pointed to the 'sovereignty of Turkey', the 'sovereignty of the TRNC', 'peace and security in Cyprus' and, in general, the 'peace in the Aegean and the Eastern Mediterranean'. In the face of imminent and existential threats posed by Greece – through its 'fortification of islands', 'claims to the sovereignty over the islands', 'attempts to extend the breadth of its territorial waters and airspace' and, finally, 'support to terrorist organisations' – the survival and sovereignty of Turkey were commonly raised topics. All securitising actors warned Greece that Turkey would 'take the necessary measures', including military ones, by 'striking the missiles' and even 'beating it [Greece, in the case of war]'. As they cautioned Greece about its actions, Turkish securitising actors also utilised the past to remind Greece of the stakes and costs of such endeavours. For example, during a speech in parliament in January 1997, then Turkish Prime Minister Necmettin Erbakan said: 'The Greeks know our people all too well. They have experience on this matter. They have seen the results of their attempts in 1922 and 1974', in reference to the Turkish War of Independence and the Turkish intervention in Cyprus, respectively (*Milliyet*, 15 January 1997). This 'threatening' and 'hostile' discourse of the Turkish elites was obvious in almost all problems, such as Greece's ratification of the UNCLOS in its parliament, the Kardak incident, the S-300 missile crisis and the revelation of Greek politicians' support for the PKK. Each of these cases contained the components of a successful securitisation, such as 'emergency action' and 'existential threats'.

As seen in the second part of the book, just a few months after Greek officials' connections with the PKK had been revealed, a promising rapprochement between Turkey and Greece was initiated by then Turkish Minister of Foreign Affairs İsmail Cem with a letter to his Greek counterpart, George Papandreou. While the letter, which planted the seeds of friendship and paved the way for desecuritisation, constituted a milestone in the relations between the two countries, it was followed by a combination of factors that assisted in the rapprochement. These factors can be classified under four categories:

the empowerment of civil society in both countries after the earthquakes, the Europeanisation process that affected the two countries' foreign and security policies, the role of İsmail Cem and George Papandreou, and the encouragement of third parties such as the US. Based on these explanations, this book intends to fill a gap in the literature in that it unveils the correlation between the rapprochement process and desecuritisation, with the help of the concept of desecuritisation, as presented by Lene Hansen. Thus, the book aims to show that the rapprochement in Turkish–Greek relations has led to desecuritisation, which might best be explained based on the desecuritisation form of *change through stabilisation*.

Despite the existence of a securitised discourse related to Greece, bilateral relations between Turkey and Greece have ironically transformed into one of cooperation, and this was also reflected in the discourses of the decision-makers who emphasised 'friendship' rather than 'hostility'. During the rapprochement process, there was special prominence given to 'friendship', the 'interests of both peoples' and transforming 'the Aegean Sea into a sea of peace', rather than focusing on the 'existential threat to the referent object'. As argued in the second part, the characteristics of the rapprochement process in Turkish–Greek relations very well match Hansen's (2012, 539) category of *change through stabilisation*. There exists significant evidence to show that decision-makers in Turkey prefer to desecuritise issues by employing various strategies that take these issues outside the military or security sphere.

The reciprocal high-level visits; the establishment of dialogue and cooperation channels in a wide array of fields, including tourism, terrorism, environment, trade, economy, culture and so on; the joint military exercises; the protocols and agreements signed between Turkey and Greece; and the initiation of exploratory talks that aimed to solve long-standing problems between the two countries – these all are signs of the political engagement between two countries, as Hansen (2012, 539) requires it for this form of desecuritisation. After having come to the verge of war over a minor incident in the Aegean Sea only five years ago, the two countries have been focusing on further cooperation, starting with 'low politics' rather than concentrating on the burden of the past. Likewise, decision-makers in both countries have refrained from escalating any potentially dangerous incidents (such as the fighter jets' collision in May 2006) and maintained their careful tone to sustain the rapprochement. The existing political engagement has also been reflected in the security discourse of Turkish decision-makers who prefer to deal with issues within the bounds of diplomacy. Regardless, it bears mentioning once more that the various contentious issues between the two countries persist, despite all attempts at resolution. This is not an obstacle to desecuritisation; Hansen (2012, 529) has underlined that, in this form of desecuritisation, 'the larger conflicts still loom in the background'.

The stabilisation of relations and the focus on cooperation among decision-makers have showed their impact on the affirmative dialogue and partnership in the fields of politics, economy and trade. The break-through high-level diplomatic visits, as well as the increasing interactions in the fields of politics, economy and military, are a result of the decision-makers' continued prudent and positive discourse. Here one may point to the establishment of the Turkish–Greek High-Level Cooperation Council (HLCC) in May 2010, which has gradually boosted the trade volume between Turkey and Greece; this might be evaluated as institutionalisation of bilateral relations. As mentioned above, in contrast to their security speech-acts prior to 1999, the Turkish decision-makers affirmative and prudent stance, in accordance with the détente process, is closely related to desecuritisation through stabilisation. It is obvious that the stabilisation of the relationship between the two countries has provided fruitful ground to sustain the same discourse by Turkish decision-makers.

The positive and promising atmosphere in Turkish–Greek relations post-1999 has gradually begun to deteriorate, however. Even the frequency of statements by Turkish decision-makers post-2016 shows that Greece has once more become a hot topic in Turkey's foreign policy. The subsequent crises – ranging from the putschist soldiers seeking political asylum in Greece, over the rise of tension in both the Aegean and Eastern Mediterranean, to the Turkish government's decisions to open the borders to migrants and to convert the Hagia Sophia into a mosque – caused rising tension in bilateral relations. All these crises emerged in an atmosphere where more than half of the elites (53.5 percent) consider any crises between the two countries within the next five years as 'improbable' or 'rather improbable' (Triantaphyllou and Dizdaroğlu, 2017). Of course, some factors including the tense Turkish politics following the 15 July 2016 coup attempt, Greece's foreign policy alignments causing Turkey's isolation in the region,[2] as well as international developments have paved the way for this deterioration. In the post-2016 period, Turkish decision-makers, or securitising actors, have once more utilised the securitisation policies that accompanied the adjustments in their rhetoric, and this may be evaluated as a reversion to the default settings in Turkish foreign policy. In terms of the coup attempt, this outcome is based on the securitisation policies by the civilian bureaucrats who have consolidated their decision-making powers, rather than by military authorities.

Apart from the other emerging crises (including the tensions due to migration and the Hagia Sophia's coversion), Turkey's official statements and policy practices regarding the Eastern Mediterranean confirmed that Turkish foreign policy has reversed gears. After 2016, the government has used securitisation policies in the region due to a myriad of factors, such as Turkey's isolation in the region and its exclusion from regional alliances. These security-oriented policies have also been triggered by a newly emerging cooperation between the government and the retired military officers who developed the Blue Homeland discourse. Those securitised policies' reflection on Turkish–Greek relations only appeared clearly during the Eastern Mediterranean disputes. As seen during the crises of the 1990s, Turkish decision-makers once more revived the security discourse in their statements by reminding Greece and the RoC to make 'cost-benefit assessments', to consider the potentially 'heavy price' they would have to pay and to contemplate 'lessons from history'. Yet, secTurkey's uritising actors also put emphasis on emergency measures 'to protect the rights of the Turkish Cypriots and its own' and announced that they would 'take necessary steps without any hesitation' in response to the 'maximalist policies of the Greek-Greek Cypriot duo'. The latest problems revealed the political nature of securitisation, which assisted the decision-makers in consolidating their power within domestic politics.

To sum up, the analysis of Turkish–Greek relations in the post-Cold War period based on the concepts of securitisation and desecuritisation as employed by the Copenhagen School enable us to understand whether, how and to what extent the issues related to Greece are securitised and desecuritised by Turkey. The same framework can also be applied to understand Greece's securitisation of Turkey. But such a study necessitates an advanced knowledge of the Greek language in order to analyse the relevant actors' statements. Moreover, the framework of securitisation can provide a tool to comprehend the role of functional actors, such as the media, as seen during the Kardak incident, in shaping countries' foreign and security policy. This book has shown that there exists significant evidence to show that decision-makers may choose to securitise or desecuritise issues and may employ strategies for handling issues in or outside the military/security sphere.

Although the tension in Turkish–Greek relations has somewhat begun to dissipate after the peak point of deterioration in the summer of 2020, even at the time of writing this book, new tensions continue to emerge and damage the dialogue between Turkey and Greece. This might be interpreted as a routine in Turkish and Greek relations, considering the historical background and the burden of the existing problems between the two countries. What has been problematic over the course of this relationship are the policy choices and the ways in which decision-makers on both sides handle the issues. None of the decision-makers on either side want to take responsibility for the reconciliation between Turkey and Greece, due to its political consequences in domestic politics. Although the majority of Greek and Turkish citizens are in favour of resolving bilateral disputes by peaceful means (Grigoriadis, 2021), the decision-makers continue to create obstacles, either through their statements or through their policy practices. Easing bilateral tensions and changing the security-oriented discourse on both sides' foreign and security policies would pave the way for stability and cooperation. As seen in previous periods of cooperation, this is much more beneficial for both Turks and Greeks. In line with the wishes of 68 percent of Greeks and 73 percent of Turks, as reflected in a recent survey (Grigoriadis, 2021), it should be possible to find 'a way of friendly coexistence' between neighbours, despite all major unresolved contentious issues. This would ensure the continuation of a constructive dialogue between Turkey and Greece.

Notes

1. For the detailed findings of this survey, see https://www.eliamep.gr/en/media/η-πρώτη-κοινή-δημοσκόπηση-στην-ελλάδα/.
2. As already mentioned, the reason behind Turkey's isolation is not solely related to Greece's foreign policy preferences. Rather, Turkey's use of foreign policy as a battle ground for domestic interests, the personalisation and securitisation of foreign policy, and the strained relations with its allies and immediate neighbours have helped both Greece and the RoC in their initiatives (Balta, 2021; Tan, 2021; Adar et al., 2021).

BIBLIOGRAPHY

Adamides, C. (2020). *Securitization and Desecuritization Processes in Protracted Conflicts: The Case of Cyprus.* Cham: Palgrave Macmillan.

Adar, S., Aksoy, H. A., Çevik, S. et al. (2021). Visualizing Turkey's Foreign Policy Activism. *SWP Center for Applied Turkey Studies,* https://www.cats-network.eu/topics/visualizing-turkeys-foreign-policy-activism [retrieved 1 November 2021].

Akgönül, S. (2008). *Reciprocity and Greek and Turkish Minorities: Law, Religion, Politics.* Istanbul: Istanbul Bilgi University Press.

Akgül-Açıkmeşe, S. (2008). *Actor, Threat and Policy in Copenhagen School and Realist Security Studies: A Comparative Assessment on European Security.* Unpublished PhD thesis. Ankara: Ankara University Graduate School of Social Sciences.

Akgül Açıkmeşe, S. (2011). Algı mı, Söylem mi? Kopenhag Okulu ve Yeni Klasik Gerçekçilikte Güvenlik Tehditleri [Perception or Discourse? Security Threats in the Copenhagen School and Neoclassical Realism]. *Uluslararası İlişkiler, 8*(30), 43–73.

Akgül Açıkmeşe, S. (2011). EU Conditionality and Desecuritization Nexus in Turkey. *Southeast European and Black Sea Studies, 13*(3), 303–23.

Aksu, F. (2001). Turkish–Greek Relations: From Conflict to Détente the Last Decade. *Turkish Review of Balkan Studies, 1*(1), 167–201.

Aksu, F. (2002). Preservation of Demilitarized Status of the Aegean Islands for the National Security of Turkey. *Turkish Review of Balkan Studies, 1*(1), 107–33.

Aksu, F. (2004). Confidence Building, Negotiation and Economic Cooperation Efforts in Turkish–Greek Relations (1990–2004). *Turkish Review of Balkan Studies, 3*(1), 31–109.

Alexandris, A. (1992) *The Greek Minority of Istanbul and Greek–Turkish Relations*. Athens: Centre for Asia Minor Studies.

Alpogan, Y. (2005). Turkish–Greek Relations: A Key to Stability in the Eastern Mediterranean. In Lino, M. (ed.), *Greek–Turkish Relations: A Key to Stability in the Eastern Mediterranean* (pp. 161–74). Bologna: Libreria Bonomo Editrice.

Amicelle, A. (2007). The Concept of Securitisation as a Tool for Analyzing the Fight Against Terrorist Financing. *Human Security Journal 5*, 62–68.

Anastasakis, O. (2004). Greece and Turkey in the Balkans: Cooperation or Rivalry? *Turkish Studies, 5*(1), 45–60.

Aras, B. (2017). Turkish Foreign Policy After July 15. *Istanbul Policy Center*, https://ipc.sabanciuniv.edu/Content/Images/Document/turkish-foreign-policy-after-july-15-7fc40f/turkish-foreign-policy-after-july-15-7fc40f.pdf [retrieved 1 June 2022].

Aras, B., and Karakaya Polat, R. (2008). From Conflict to Cooperation: Desecuritisation of Turkey's Relations with Syria and Iran. *Security Dialogue 39*(5), 495–515.

Armaoğlu, F. (1963). *Kıbrıs Meselesi: 1954–1959* [The Cyprus Issue: 1954–1959]. Ankara: Sevinc Publication House.

Athanassopoulou, E. (1997). Blessing in Disguise? The Imia Crisis and Turkish–Greek Relations. *Mediterranean Politics*, *2*(3), 76–101.

Åtland, K. (2008). Mikhail Gorbachev, the Murmansk Initiative, and the Desecuritisation of Interstate Relations in the Arctic. *Cooperation and Conflict: Journal of the Nordic International Studies Association, 43*(3), 289–311.

Aydın, M. (1997). Cacophony in the Aegean: Contemporary Turkish–Greek Relations Relations. *The Turkish Yearbook, 27*, 109–40.

Aydın, M. (1999). Determinants of Turkish Foreign Policy: Historical Framework and Traditional Inputs. *Middle Eastern Studies, 35*(4), 152–86.

Aydın, M. (2003). Twenty Years Before, Twenty Years After: Turkish Foreign Policy at the Threshold of the 21st Century. In Ismael, T. Y., and Aydın, M. (eds), *Turkey's Foreign Policy in the 21st Century: A Changing Role in World Politics* (pp. 3–24). Aldershot: Ashgate.

Aydın, M., and Erhan, Ç. (2003). *Turkish-American Relations: Past, Present and Future*. London and New York: Routledge.

Aydın, M., and Ifantis, K. (2004). *Turkish–Greek Relations Relations: The Security Dilemma in the Aegean*. London: Routledge.

Aydın, M., and Akgül Açıkmeşe, S. (2007). Europeanization Through EU Conditionality: Understanding the New Era in Turkish Foreign Policy. *Journal of Southern Europe and the Balkans, 9*(3), 263–74.

Aydın, M., and Dizdaroğlu, C. (2018). Levantine Challenges on Turkish Foreign Policy. *Uluslararası İlişkiler, 15*(60), 89–103.

Aydın, M., Zaim, O., Baybars-Hawks, B., et al. (2015). *Quantitative Research Report: Turkey Trends 2015*. İstanbul: Kadir Has University Turkey Studies Group.

Aydın, M., Kahraman, H. B., Zaim, O., Baybars-Hawks, B., et al. (2016). *Quantitative Research Report: Turkey Trends 2016*. İstanbul: Kadir Has University Turkey Studies Group.

Aydın, M., Çelikpala, M., Yeldan, E., Güvenç, M., et al. (2021). *Quantitative Research Report: Turkey Trends 2020*. İstanbul: Kadir Has University Turkey Studies Group.

Aydınlı, E. (2002). Between Security and Liberalization: Decoding Turkey's Struggle with the PKK. *Security Dialogue, 33*(2), 209–25.

Ayın Tarihi (1955). Statement by Prime Minister Adnan Menderes. *Ayın Tarihi*, 261, 170–73.

Ayman, G. (2002). A Case of Brinkmanship: S-300 Missile Crisis. *Turkish Review of Balkan Studies, 2*(1), 5–34.

Bağcı, H. (1997). Cyprus: Accession to the European Union – A Turkish View. In Axt, H. J., and Brey, H. (eds), *Cyprus and the European Union New Chances for Solving an Old Conflict* (pp. 159–69). München: Südosteuropa-Gesellschaft.

Bahçeli, T. (2001) Turkey's Cyprus Challenge: Preserving the Gains of 1974. In Keridis, D., and Triantaphyllou, D. (eds), *Greek–Turkish Relations in the Era of Globalization* (pp. 208–22). Dulles: Brassay's.

Bahçeli, T. (2004). Turning a New Page in Turkey's Relations with Greece? The Challenge of Reconciling Vital Interests. In Aydın, M., and Ifantis, K. (eds), *Turkish–Greek Relations: The Security Dilemma in the Aegean* (pp. 95–120). London: Routledge.

Balamir Coşkun, B. (2009). *Analysing Desecuritisation: The Case of the Israeli-Palestinian Peace Education and Water Management*. New Castle upon Tyne: Cambridge Scholars Publishing.

Balcı, A., and Kardaş, T. (2012). The Changing Dynamics of Turkey's Relations with Israel: An Analysis of 'Securitisation'. *Insight Turkey, 14*(2), 99–120.

Balta, E. (2021). The 'Pure' Nation against the 'Corrupt' Outsiders: The AKP's Populist Foreign Policy. *Istanbul Political Research Institute (IstanPol) Policy Analysis*, https://en.istanpol.org/post/the-pure-nation-against-the-corrupt-outsiders-the-akp-s-populist-foreign-policy [retrieved 1 November 2021].

Balzacq, T. (2005). The Three Faces of Securitisation: Political Agency, Audience and Context. *European Journal of International Relations, 11*(2), 171–201.

Balzacq, T. (2010). *Securitization Theory: How Security Problems Emerge and Dissolve*. London: Routledge.

Barlas, D. (2005). Turkish Diplomacy in the Balkans and the Mediterranean. Opportunities and Limits for Middle-Power Activism in the 1930s. *Journal of Contemporary History, 40*(3), 441–64.

Baser, B. (2015). KOMKAR: The Unheard Voice in the Kurdish Diaspora. In Christou, A., and Mavroudi, E. (eds), *Dismantling Diasporas: Rethinking the Geographies of Diasporic Identity, Connection and Development* (pp. 113–25). Farnham: Ashgate.

Başeren, S. H. (2006). *Ege Sorunları* [Aegean Problems]. İstanbul: Türk Deniz Araştırmaları Vakfı.

Batur, N. (2004). *Yürekten Gülerekten Yürüdüm* [I Walked Laughing from the Heart]. İstanbul: Dogan Kitap.

Bayar, M., and Kotelis, A. (2014). Democratic Peace or Hegemonic Stability? The Imia/Kardak Case. *Turkish Studies, 15*(2), 242–57.

Baysal, B. (2019). *Securitization and Desecuritization of FARC in Colombia*. Lanham and Boulder: Lexington Books.

Baysal, B. (2020). 20 Years of Securitization: Strengths, Limitations and A New Dual Framework. *Uluslararası İlişkiler, 17*(67), 3–20.

Baysal, B., and Dizdaroğlu, C. (2022). Turkish–Greek Relations after the Cold War: Changing Dynamics of Securitisation and Desecuritisation. In Erdogan, B., and Hisarlıoğlu, F. (eds), *Critical Readings of Turkey's Foreign Policy* (pp. 235–56). Cham: Palgrave Macmillan.

Baysal, B., Karakas, U., and Lüleci-Sula, Ç. (2019). Uluslararası Siyaset Sosyolojisi ve Güvenlik: Küresel Terörizm, Sınır Güvenliği ve Vatandaşlık Örnekleri [International Political Sociology and Security: Global Terrorism, Border Security and Citizenship]. *Ankara University SBF Journal, 74*(4), 1203–31.

Behnke, A. (2006). No Way Out: Desecuritisation, Emancipation and the Eternal Return of the Political – A Reply to Aradau. *Journal of International Relations and Development, 9*(1), 62–69.

Benli Altunışık, M. (2010). Turkey's Changing Middle East Policy. *UNISCI Discussion Papers, 23*, 149–62.

Bigo, D. (2002). Security and Immigration: Toward a Critique of the Governmentality of Unease. *Alternatives, 27*, 63–92.

Bigo, D. (2014). The (In)Securitization Practices of the Three Universes of EU Border Control: Military/Navy-Border Guards/Police-Database Analysts. *Security Dialogue, 45*(3), 209–25.

Bilgel, F., and Karahasan, B. C. (2017). The Economic Costs of Separatist Terrorism in Turkey. *The Journal of Conflict Resolution, 61*(2), 457–79.

Bilgin, P. (2002). Beyond Statism in Security Studies? Human Agency and Security in the Middle East. *Review of International Affairs, 2*(1), 100–18.

Bilgin, P. (2005). Turkey's Changing Security Discourses: The Challenge of Globalisation. *European Journal of Political Research, 44*, 175–201.

Bilgin, P. (2007). Making Turkey's Transformation Possible: Claiming 'Security-Speak' – Not Desecuritisation! *Southeast European and Black Sea Studies, 7*(4), 555–71.

Bilgin, P. (2010). Güvenlik Çalışmalarında Yeni Açılımlar: Yeni Güvenlik Çalışmaları [New Approaches to Security Studies: New Security Studies]. *SAREM Journal of Strategic Studies, 8*(14), 30–52.

Bilsel, C. M. (1998). *Lozan I–II*. İstanbul: Sosyal Yayınlar.

Birand, M. A. (1991). Turkey and the Davos Process: Experiences and Prospects. In Constas, D. (ed.), *The Greek–Turkish Conflict in the 1990s: Domestic and External Influences* (pp. 27–39). New York: St. Martin's Press.

Bonner, A. (2005). Turkey, the European Union and Paradigm Shifts. *Middle East Policy, 12*(1), 44–71.

Boswell, C. (2007). Migration Control in Europe After 9/11: Explaining the Absence of Securitisation. *Journal of Common Market Studies, 45*(3), 589–610.

Bölükbaşı, S. (1992). The Turco-Greek Dispute: Issues, Policies and Prospects. In Dodd, C. H. (ed.), *Turkish Foreign Policy: New Prospects* (pp. 27–54). Huntingdon: The Eothen Press.

Bölükbaşı, S. (1993). The Johnson's Letter Revisited. *Middle Eastern Studies, 29*(3), 505–25.

Bölükbaşı, S. (2004). *Turkey and Greece: The Aegean Disputes, A Unique Case in International Law*. London: Cavendish Publishing.

Buzan, B. (2006). Will the 'Global War on Terrorism' be the New Cold War? *International Affairs, 82*(6), 1101–18.

Buzan, B., and Wæver, O. (2003). *Regions and Powers*. Cambridge: Cambridge University Press.

Buzan, B., Wæver, O., and de Wilde, J. (1998). *Security: A New Framework for Analysis*. Boulder: Lynne Rienner.

Camp, G. (1980). Greek–Turkish Conflict Over Cyprus. *Political Science Quarterly, 95*(1), 43–70.

Carnegie Endowment Discussion Paper (1997). *Greece and Turkey*. Washington, DC: CEIP.

Cem, İ. (2009). *Türkiye, Avrupa, Avrasya* [Turkey, Europe, Eurasia]. İstanbul: Istanbul Bilgi University Press.

Christofis, N., Baser, B., and Öztürk, A. E. (2019). The View from Next Door: Greek–Turkish Relations after the Coup Attempt in Turkey. *The International Spectator: Italian Journal of International Affairs, 54*(2), 67–86.

Cizre, Ü. (1997). The Anatomy of the Turkish Military's Political Autonomy. *Comparative Politics, 29*(2), 151–66.

Clayton, J., and Holland, H. (2015). Over One Million Sea Arrivals Reach Europe in 2015. *UNHCR*, https://www.unhcr.org/news/latest/2015/12/5683d0b56/million-sea-arrivals-reach-europe-2015.html [retrieved 15 April 2016].

Clogg, R. (1980). *Greece in the 1980s*. New York: Palgrave Macmillan.

Clogg, R. (1992). *A Concise History of Greece*. New York: Cambridge.

Constas, D. (1991). *The Greek–Turkish Conflict in the 1990s*. New York: St. Martin's Press.

Coufadakis, V. (1996). Greek Foreign Policy in the Post-Cold War Era: Issues and Challenges. *Mediterranean Quarterly, 7*(3), 26–41.

Criss, N. B. (1995). The Nature of PKK Terrorism in Turkey. *Studies in Conflict & Terrorism*, 18(1), 17–37.

Çarkoğlu, A., and Kirişci, K. (2004). The View from Turkey: Perceptions of Greeks and Greek–Turkish Rapprochement by the Turkish Public. *Turkish Studies, 5*(1), 117–53.

Çarkoğlu, A., and Rubin, B. (2005). *Greek–Turkish Relations in an Era of Détente*. London: Routledge.

Çaycı, S. (2008). Terrorism and Asymmetric Threat: Activities Against Turkey, From the Beginning of the 20th Century to the Present. *Review of Armenian Studies, 18*, 89–99.

Çelenk, A. A. (2007). The Restructuring of Turkey's Policy towards Cyprus: The Justice and Development Party's Struggle for Power. *Turkish Studies, 8*(3), 349–63.

Çelikpala, M. (2019). Türkiye Doğu Akdeniz'deki Senaryoyu Nasıl Değiştirir? [How Does Turkey Change the Scenario in the Eastern Mediterranean?]. *Fikir Turu*, https://fikirturu.com/dogu-akdeniz/turkiye-dogu-akdenizdeki-senaryoyu-nasil-degistirir/ [retrieved 15 September 2020].

Demirözü, D. (2008). The Greek–Turkish Rapprochement of 1930 and the Repercussions of the Ankara Convention in Turkey. *Journal of Islamic Studies, 19*(3), 309–24.

Demirözü, D. (2017). Savaştan Barışa Giden Yol: Atatürk-Venizelos Dönemi Türk Yunan İlişkileri [The Road from the War to the Peace: Turkey-Greece Relations in the Ataturk-Venizelos Era]. İstanbul: İletişim Yayınları.

Denktash, R. R. (1988). *The Cyprus Triangle*. London: K. Rustem & Brothers.
Diez, T., and Tocci, N. (2013). *Cyprus: A Conflict at the Crossroads*. Manchester: Manchester University Press.
Dizdaroğlu, C. (2021). Greek–Turkish Relations at the Crossroads: Cooperation or Rivalry? *Istanbul Political Research Institute (IstanPol) Policy Note*, https://en.istanpol.org/post/greek-turkish-relations-at-the-crossroads-cooperation-or-rivalry [retrieved 1 April 2022].
Dodd, C. (2010). *The History and the Politics of the Cyprus Conflict*. London and New York: Palgrave Macmillan.
Ecevit, B. (2009). *Bir Şeyler Olacak Yarın* [Things Will Happen Tomorrow]. İstanbul: Türkiye İş Bankası Yayınları.
Elekdağ, Ş. (1996). 2 ½ War Strategy. *Perceptions, 1*(4), 33–57.
Eralp, A. (2009). Temporality, Cyprus Problem and Turkey-EU Relationship. *EDAM Discussion Paper Series* 2, 1–10.
Erkaya, G., and Baytok, T. (2001). *Bir Asker, Bir Diplomat* [A Soldier, a Diplomat]. İstanbul: Doğan Kitap.
Ertan, N. (2021). EU Leaders Back Funding but Warn Erdogan Against 'Instrumentalizing' Syrian Migrants. *Al Monitor*, https://www.al-monitor.com/originals/2021/06/eu-leaders-back-funding-warn-erdogan-against-instrumentalizing-syrian-migrants#ixzz7ZZmPBf2E [retrieved 12 June 2022].
Esen, B., and Gumuscu, S. (2017). Turkey: How the Coup Failed. *Democratisation, 28*(1): 59–73.
Evin, A. O. (2004). Changing Greek Perspectives on Turkey: An Assessment of the Post-Earthquake Rapprochement. *Turkish Studies, 5*(1), 4–20.
Evin, A. O. (2005). The Future of Greek–Turkish Relations. *Southeast European and Black Sea Studies, 5*(3), 395–404.
Fırat, M. (1997). *1960–71 Arası Türk Dış Politikası ve Kıbrıs Sorunu* [Turkish Foreign Policy Between 1960–71 and the Cyprus Issue]. Ankara: Siyasal Kitabevi.
Fırat, M. (2002). Soğuk Savaş Sonrası Yunanistan Dış Politikasının Yeniden Biçimleniş Süreci [The Remodelling Process of the Greek Foreign Policy in the Post-Cold War]. In Türkeş, M., and Uzgel, İ. (eds), *Türkiye'nin Komşuları* [Turkey's Neighbours] (pp. 21–73). Ankara: İmge.
Fırat, M. (2006). Soğuk Savaş Sonrası Türk-Yunan İlişkilerinde Değişim [The Change in Turkish–Greek Relations in the Post-Cold War]. In Aydın, M., and Erhan, Ç. (eds), *Beş Deniz Havzasında Türkiye* [Turkey in the Five Sea Basin] (pp. 257–80). Ankara: Siyasal Kitapevi.

Fırat, M. (2010). Relations with Greece. In Oran, B. (ed.), *Turkish Foreign Policy 1919–2006: Facts and Analyses with Documents* (pp. 344–67). Salt Lake City: University of Utah Press.

Floyd, R. (2010). *Security and the Environment: Securitisation Theory and US Environmental Security Policy.* Cambridge: Cambridge University Press.

Ganapati, N. E., Kelman, I., and Koukis, T. (2010). Analyzing Greek–Turkish Disaster-Related Cooperation: A Disaster Diplomacy Perspective. *Cooperation and Conflict, 45*(2), 162–85.

Grigoriadis, I. N. (2003). 'The Changing Role of the EU Factor in Greek–Turkish Relations'. Presented at the London School of Economics and Political Science, Hellenic Observatory, 1st PhD Symposium on Modern Greece, London, 21 June, 1–11.

Grigoriadis, I. N. (2011). The Unripe Fruits of Rapprochement: Greek–Turkish Relations in the Post-Helsinki Era. *International Journal, 67*(1), 119–33.

Grigoriadis, I. N., and Dilek, E. (2019). Securitizing Migration in the European Union: Greece and the Evros Fence. *Journal of Balkan and Near Eastern Studies, 21*(2), 170–86.

Grigoriadis, I. N. (2021). The First Joint Public Opinion Survey in Greece and Turkey: Twelve Introductory Remarks. *Hellenic Foundation for European and Foreign Policy,* https://www.eliamep.gr/en/media/η-πρώτη-κοινή-δημοσκόπηση-στην-ελλάδα/ [retrieved 20 May 2021].

Göktepe, C. (2005). The Cyprus Crisis of 1967 and its Effects on Turkey's Foreign Relations. *Middle Eastern Studies, 41*(3), 431–44.

Gündoğdu, A. (2001). Identities in Question: Greek–Turkish Relations in a Period of Transformation? *Middle East Review of International Affairs Journal, 5*(1), 106–17.

Gürel, Ş. S. (1993a). *Tarihsel Boyut İçinde Türk-Yunan İlişkileri, 1821–1993* [Turkish–Greek Relations in Historical Context, 1821–1993]. Ankara: Ümit Yayıncılık.

Gürel, Ş. S. (1993b). Turkey and Greece: A Difficult Aegean Relationship. In Balkır, C., and Williams A. M. (eds), *Turkey and Europe* (pp. 161–90). London: Pinter Publishers.

Gürsoy, Y. (2012). *Türkiye'de Sivil-Asker İlişkilerinin Dönüşümü* [Transformation of Civil-Military Relations in Turkey]. İstanbul: İstanbul Bilgi Üniversitesi Yayınları.

Güvenç, S. (1998–99). Turkey's Changing Perception of Greece's Membership in the European Union: 1981–1998. *Turkish Review of Balkan Studies, 4,* 103–30.

Güvenç, S. (2004). Beyond Rapprochement in Turkish–Greek Relations. *Exotierika Themata* [Foreign Affairs], *13,* 67–77.

Hale, W. (2002). *Turkish Foreign Policy 1774–2000*. London: Frank Cass.
Hamilton, K., and Salmon, P. (2012). *The Southern Flank in Crisis: 1973–1976*. New York and London: Routledge.
Hannay, D. (2005). *Cyprus: The Search for a Solution*. London: I. B. Tauris.
Hansen, L. (2000). The Little Mermaid's Silent Security Dilemma and the Absence of Gender in the Copenhagen School. *Millennium: Journal of International Studies, 29*(2), 285–306.
Hansen, L. (2011). The Politics of Securitisation and the Muhammad Cartoon Crisis: A Post-Structuralist Perspective. *Security Dialogue, 42*(4–5), 357–69.
Hansen, L. (2012). Reconstructing Desecuritisation: The Normative-Political in the Copenhagen School and Directions for How to Apply it. *Review of International Studies, 38*, 525–46.
Hayes, J. (2009). Identity and Securitisation in the Democratic Peace: The United States and the Divergence of Response to India and Iran's Nuclear Programs. *International Studies Quarterly, 53*, 977–99.
Heper M., and Güney, A. (2000). The Military and the Consolidation of Democracy: The Recent Turkish Experience. *Armed Forces and Society, 26*, 635–57.
Heraclides, A. (2010). *The Turkish–Greek Relations Conflict in the Aegean: Imagined Enemies*. New York: Palgrave Macmillan.
Heraclides, A. (2012). 'What Will Become of Us Without Barbarians?' The Enduring Greek–Turkish Rivalry as an Identity-Based Conflict. *Southeast European and Black Sea Studies, 12*(1), 115–34.
Heraclides, A., and Alioğlu Çakmak, G. (2019). *Greece and Turkey in Conflict and Cooperation: From Europeanization to De-Europeanization*. New York: Routledge.
Hirshon, R. (2004). *Crossing the Aegean: An Appraisal of the 1923 Compulsory Population Exchange Between Greece and Turkey*. New York and Oxford: Berghahn Books.
Hoffmeister, F. (2006). *Legal Aspects of the Cyprus Problem: Annan Plan and the EU Accession*. Leiden and Boston: Martinus Nijhoff Publishing.
Howell, A., and Richter-Montpetit, M. (2020). Is Securitization Theory Racist? Civilizationism, Methodological Whiteness, and Antiblack Thought in the Copenhagen School. *Security Dialogue, 51*(1), 3–22.
Huysmans, J. (1998). Revisiting Copenhagen: Or, On the Creative Development of a Security Studies Agenda in Europe. *European Journal of International Relations, 4*(4), 479–505.
Ifantis, K. (2004). Strategic Imperatives and Regional Upheavals: On the US Factor in Greek–Turkish Relations. *Turkish Studies, 5*(1), 21–44.

İlhan, S. (2002). *Terör: Neden Türkiye?* [Terrorism: Why Turkey?]. Ankara: ASAM Yayınları.

İnan, Y., and Acer, Y. (2004). *The Aegean Disputes*. Ankara: Foreign Policy Institute.

İpek, P., and Gür, T. V. (2021). Turkey's Isolation from the Eastern Mediterranean Gas Forum: Ideational Mechanisms and Material Interests in Energy Politics. *Turkish Studies, 23*(1), 1–30.

Kalaitzaki, T. (2005). US Mediation in Greek–Turkish Disputes since 1954. *Mediterranean Quarterly, 16*(2), 106–24.

Kaliber, A. (2003). *Rearticulation of Turkish Foreign Policy its Impacts on National/State Identity and State Society Relations in Turkey*. Unpublished Ph.D. Dissertation. Ankara: Bilkent University.

Kaliber, A. (2005). Securing the Ground Through Securitised 'Foreign' Policy: The Cyprus Case. *Security Dialogue, 36*(3), 319–37.

Kaliber, A. (2019). 1964 Rum Sürgünü ve Kıbrıs Sorunu: Bir Ötekileştirme Siyaseti Olarak Dış Politika [1964 Expulsions and the Cyprus Problem: Foreign Policy as a Otherisation Policy]. In Romain Örs, I. (ed.), *İstanbullu Rumlar ve 1964 Sürgünleri, Türk Toplumunun Homojenleşmesinde Bir Dönüm Noktası* [Istanbul's Greeks and the 1964 Expulsions: A Turning Point for the Homogenisation of Turkish Society] (pp. 21–29). İstanbul: İletişim Yayınları.

Karakatksanis, L. (2014). *Turkish–Greek Relations: Rapprochement, Civil Society and the Politics of Friendship*. London: Routledge.

Karakaya Polat, R. (2009). The 2007 Parliamentary Elections in Turkey: Between Securitisation and Desecuritisation. *Parliamentary Affairs, 62*(1), 129–48.

Karaosmanoğlu, A. L. (2011). Transformation of Turkey's Civil-Military Relations Culture and International Environment. *Turkish Studies, 12*(2), 253–64.

Kayhan Pusane, Ö. (2015). Turkey's Military Victory over the PKK and Its Failure to End the PKK Insurgency. *Middle Eastern Studies, 51*(5), 727–41.

Kazamias, A. (1997). The Quest for Modernization in Greek Foreign Policy and its Limitations. *Mediterranean Politics, 2*(2), 71–94.

Kazan, I. (2002). Cyprus and the Eastern Mediterranean, Seen from Turkey. In Diez, T. (ed.), *The European Union and the Cyprus Conflict: Modern Conflict Postmodern Union* (pp. 54–69). New York: Manchester University Press.

Keridis, D. (1999). Political Culture and Foreign Policy: Greek–Turkish Relations in the Era of European Integration and Globalization. *NATO Fellowship Report*.

Keridis, D., and Triantaphyllou, D. (2001). *Greek–Turkish Relations in the Era of Globalization*. Dulles: Brassey's.

Ker-Lindsay, J. (2000). Greek–Turkish Rapprochement: The Impact of Disaster Diplomacy? *Cambridge Review of International Affairs, 14*(1), 215–32.

Ker-Lindsay, J. (2007). *Crisis and Conciliation: A Year of Rapprochement Between Greece and Turkey*. London: I. B. Tauris.

Ker-Lindsay, J. (2011). *The Cyprus Problem: What Everyone Needs to Know*. Oxford: Oxford University Press.

Kesgin, B. (2012). Tansu Çiller's Leadership Traits and Foreign Policy. *Perceptions, 27*(3), 29–50.

Keyman, F. (2009). Turkish Foreign Policy in the Era of Global Turmoil. *Seta Policy Brief, 39*, 1–16.

Kirişci, K. (2002). The 'Enduring Rivalry' between Greece and Turkey: Can 'Democratic Peace' Break it? *Alternatives, 1*(1), 38–50.

Kirişci, K. (2009). The Transformation of Turkish Foreign Policy: The Rise of the Trading State. *New Perspectives on Turkey, 40*, 29–57.

Kirişci, K. (2021a). Revisiting and Going Beyond the EU-Turkey Migration Agreement of 2016: An Opportunity for Greece to Overcome Being Just 'Europe's Aspis'. *Hellenic Foundation for European and Foreign Policy, Brookings Institution*, https://www.brookings.edu/research/revisiting-and-going-beyond-the-eu-turkey-migration-agreement-of-2016/ [retrieved 13 May 2022].

Kirişci, K. (2021b). As EU-Turkey Migration Agreement Reaches the Five-Year Mark, Add a Job Creation Element. *Brookings Institution*, https://www.brookings.edu/blog/order-from-chaos/2021/03/17/as-eu-turkey-migration-agreement-reaches-the-five-year-mark-add-a-job-creation-element/ [retrieved 1 June 2022].

Kızılyürek, N. (2005). *Milliyetçilik Kıskacında Kıbrıs* [Cyprus in the Dilemma of Nationalism]. İstanbul: İletişim.

Kollias, C., Manolas, G., and Paleologouc, S. M. (2004). Military Expenditure and Government Debt in Greece: Some Preliminary Empirical Findings. *Defence and Peace Economics, 15*(2), 189–97.

Kurumahmut, A. (1998). *Ege'de Temel Sorun: Egemenliği Tartışmalı Adalar* [The Main Dispute in the Aegean: Islands with Controversial Sovereignty]. Ankara: Türk Tarih Kurumu.

Kutlay, M. (2009). A Political Economy Approach to the Expansion of Turkish–Greek Relations: Interdependence or Not? *Perceptions: Journal of International Affairs, 14*(1), 91–119.

Kutlay, M. (2019). *The Political Economies of Turkey and Greece: Crisis and Change*. Cham: Palgrave Macmillan.

Larrabee, F. S. (2005). Greece's Balkan Policy in a New Strategic Era. *Southeast European and Black Sea Studies, 5*(3), 405–25.

Larrabee, F. S. (2012). Greek–Turkish Relations in an Era of Regional and Global Change. *Southeast European and Black Sea Studies, 12*(4), 471–79.

Leffler, M. P. (1985). Strategy, Diplomacy, and the Cold War: The United States, Turkey, and NATO, 1945–1952. *The Journal of American History, 71*(4), 807–25.

Lesser, I. O. (2001). Turkey, Greece, and the U.S. in a Changing Strategic Environment. *Rand Testimony Series* CT 179, 1–9.

Liargovas, P. (2003). Greek–Turkish Economic Relations. In Kollias, C., and Günlük-Şenesen, G. (eds), *Greece and Turkey in the 21st Century: Conflict or Cooperation* (pp. 133–47). New York: Nova Science Publishers.

Liaropoulos, A. N. (2008). The Institutional Dimension of Greek Security Policy: Is There a Need for A National Security Council? *National Security and the Future, 3*(9), 25–38.

Makovsky, A. (2000). The New Activism in Turkish Foreign Policy. *SAIS Review, 19*(1), 92–113.

McDonald, M. (2008). Securitisation and the Construction of Security. *European Journal of International Relations, 14*(4), 563–87.

McSweeney, B. (1998). Modernity, Identity and Security: A Comment on the 'Copenhagen Controversy'. *Review of International Studies, 24*(3), 435–39.

McSweeney, B. (2004). *Security, Identity and Interests: A Sociology of International Relations*. Cambridge: Cambridge University Press.

Millas, H. (2004). National Perception of the 'Other' and the Persistence of Some Images. In Aydın, M., and Ifantis, K. (ed.), *Turkish–Greek Relations: The Security Dilemma in the Aegean* (pp. 53–66). London: Routledge.

Millas, H. (2016). *Nations and Identities: The Case of Greeks and Turks*. Istanbul: İstanbul Bilgi University Press.

Moustakis, F., and Sheehan, M. (2002). Democratic Peace and the European Security Community: The Paradox of Greece and Turkey. *Mediterranean Quarterly, 13*(1), 69–85.

Moustakis, F. (2003). *The Greek–Turkish Relationship and NATO*. London and New York: Routledge.

Sarıca, M., Teziç, E., and Eskiyurt, Ö. (1975). *Kıbrıs Sorunu* [The Cyprus Issue]. İstanbul: Fakülteler Matbaası.

Müfti, M. (1998). Daring and Caution in Turkish Foreign Policy. *Middle East Journal, 52*(1), 32–50.

Müfti, M. (2009). *Daring and Caution in Turkish Strategic Culture*. Basingstoke: Palgrave Macmillan.

Müftüler-Baç, M., and Güney, A. (2005). The European Union and the Cyprus Problem, 1961–2003. *Middle Eastern Studies, 41*(2), 281–93.

Nachmani, A. (1987). *Israel, Turkey and Greece: Uneasy Relations in the East Mediterranean*. London: Frank Cass.

Nachmani, A. (2001). What Says the Neighbor to the West? On Turkish–Greek Relations. In Rubin, B., and Kirişci, K. (eds), *Turkey in World Politics: An Emerging Multiregional Power* (pp. 71–91). Boulder: Lynne Rienner.

Narlı, N. (2000). Civil-Military Relations in Turkey. *Turkish Studies, 1*(1), 107–27.

Nyman, J. (2013). Securitisation Theory. In Shepherd, L. J. (ed.), *Critical Approaches to Security: An Introduction to Theories and Methods* (pp. 51–62). New York: Routledge.

O'Reilly, C. (2008). Primetime Patriotism: News Media and the Securitization of Iraq. *Journal of Politics and Law, 1*(3), 66–72.

Oğuzlu, T. (2004). How Encouraging is the Latest Turkish–Greek Reconciliation Process? *Journal of Contemporary European Studies, 12*(1), 93–107.

Oran, B. (1991). *Türk-Yunan İlişkilerinde Batı Trakya Sorunu* [The Western Thrace Issue in Turkish–Greek Relations Relations]. Ankara: Bilgi Yayınları.

Oran, B. (2019). 1964 Sürgünleri: Kıbrıs Meselesi mi, 'Prensip' Meselesi mi? [1964 Expulsions: The Issue of Cyprus or the Issue of 'Principle']. In Romain Örs, I. (ed.), *İstanbullu Rumlar ve 1964 Sürgünleri, Türk Toplumunun Homojenleşmesinde Bir Dönüm Noktası* [Istanbul's Greeks and the 1964 Expulsions: A Turning Point for the Homogenisation of Turkish Society] (pp. 21–29). İstanbul: İletişim Yayınları.

Oxford Dictionary (2006). *Oxford English Dictionary*. Oxford: Oxford University Press.

Öniş, Z. (2001). Greek–Turkish Relations and the European Union: A Critical Perspective. *Mediterranean Politics, 6*(3), 31–45.

Öniş, Z., and Yılmaz, Ş. (2008). Greek–Turkish Rapprochement: Rhetoric or Reality? *Political Science Quarterly, 123*(1), 123–49.

Örmeci, O (2011). A Turkish Social Democrat: İsmail Cem. *Turkish Studies, 12*(1), 101–14.

Özcan, N. A. (1999). *PKK (Kürdistan İşçi Partisi): Tarihi, İdeolojisi ve Yöntemi* [PKK (Kurdistan Workers' Party): History, Ideology and Methodology]. Ankara: ASAM.

Özcan, G. (2001). The Military and the Making of Foreign Policy in Turkey. In Rubin, B., and Kirişci, K. (eds), *Turkey in World Politics: An Emerging Multiregional Power* (pp. 13–30). Boulder: Lynne Rienner.

Özcan, G. (2009). Facing its Waterloo in Diplomacy: Turkey's Military in the Foreign Policy-Making Process. *New Perspectives on Turkey, 40*, 83–102.

Özcan, G. (2010). The Changing Role of Turkey's Military in Foreign Policy Making. *UNISCI Discussion Papers, 23*, 23–46.

Özdamar, Ö., and Erciyas, O. (2020). Turkey and Cyprus: A Poliheuristic Analysis of Decisions during the Crises of 1964, 1967, and 1974. *Foreign Policy Analysis, 16*(3), 457–77.

Özel, S. (2004). Rapprochement on Non-Governmental Level: The Story of the Turkish–Greek Relations Forum. In Aydın M., and Ifantis, K. (eds), *Turkish–Greek Relations: The Security Dilemma in the Aegean* (pp. 269–90). London: Routledge.

Özkirimli, U., and Sofos, S. A. (2008). *Tormented by History: Nationalism in Greece and Turkey*. London: Hurst & Company.

Öztürk, A. E. (2020). Turkey's Hagia Sophia Decision: The Collapse of Multiculturalism and Secularism or Something More? *Contending Modernities*, University of Notre Dame, https://contendingmodernities.nd.edu/global-currents/hagia-sophia-multiculturalism/ [retrieved 21 May 2021].

Palley, C. (2005). *An International Relations Debacle: The UN Secretary-General's Mission of Good Offices in Cyprus 1999–2004*. Oxford: Hart Publishing.

Papandreou, G. A. (2001). Principles of Greek Foreign Policy. *Mediterranean Quarterly, 12*(1), 1–10.

Peoples, C., and Vaughan-Williams, N. (2010). *Critical Security Studies: An Introduction*. London and New York: Routledge.

Platias, A. (1991). Greece's Strategic Doctrine: In Search of Autonomy and Deterrence. In Constans, D. (ed.), *The Greek–Turkish Conflict in the 1990s* (pp. 91–108). London: Macmillan.

Robinson, C. (2017). Tracing and Explaining Securitization: Social Mechanisms, Process Tracing and the Securitization of Irregular Migration. *Security Dialogue, 48*(6), 505–23.

Roe, P. (2004). Securitization and Minority Rights: Conditions of Desecuritization. *Security Dialogue, 35*(3), 279–94.

Roe, P. (2012). Is Securitisation a 'Negative' Concept? Revisiting the Normatived Debate over Normal versus Extraordinary Politics. *Security Dialogue, 43*(3), 249–66.

Roth, M. P., and Sever, M. (2007). The Kurdish Workers Party (PKK) as Criminal Syndicate: Funding Terrorism through Organized Crime, A Case Study. *Studies in Conflict & Terrorism, 30*(10), 901–20.

Romain Örs, I. (2019). *İstanbullu Rumlar ve 1964 Sürgünleri, Türk Toplumunun Homojenleşmesinde Bir Dönüm Noktası* [Istanbul's Greeks and the 1964 Expulsions: A Turning Point for the Homogenisation of Turkish Society]. İstanbul: İletişim Yayınları.

Romain Örs, I. (2020). Tensions Mount at Greek Border with Turkey amid Contested History of Migration in the Aegean. *The Conversation*, https://theconversation.com/tensions-mount-at-greek-border-with-turkey-amid-contested-history-of-migration-in-the-aegean-132990 [retrieved 15 June 2022].

Rumelili, B. (2003). The European Union's Impact on the Greek–Turkish Conflict: A Review of the Literature. In *Working Paper Series in EU Border Conflicts Studies 6*. Birmingham: University of Birmingham.

Rumelili, B. (2004). The Talkers and the Silent Ones: The EU and Change in Greek–Turkish Relations. In *Working Paper Series in EU Border Conflicts Studies 10*. Birmingham: University of Birmingham.

Rumelili, B. (2005). Civil Society and the Europeanization of Greek–Turkish Cooperation. *South European Society and Politics, 10*(1), 45–56.

Rumelili, B. (2007). Transforming Conflicts on EU Borders: The Case of Greek–Turkish Relations. *Journal of Common Market Studies, 45*(1), 105–26.

Rychnovska, D. (2014). Securitization and the Power of Threat Framing. *Perspectives, 22*(2), 9–31.

Sezer, D. (1994). *Turkey's Political and Security Interests and Policies in the New Geostrategic Environment of the Expanded Middle East*. Washington, DC: Henry L. Stimson Occasional Paper.

Siegl, E. (2002). Greek–Turkish Relations: Continuity or Change? *Perspectives, 18*(1), 40–52.

Sofuoğlu, M. (2021). How the July 15 Coup Attempt Has Impacted Turkey's Foreign Policy. *TRT World*, https://www.trtworld.com/magazine/how-the-july-15-coup-attempt-has-impacted-turkey-s-foreign-policy-48296 [retrieved 15 May 2022].

Sözen, A. (2017). A Common Vision for a Way Out of the Cyprus Conundrum. *Turkish Policy Quarterly, 15*(4): 27–36.

Stearns, M. (1992). *Entangled Allies: US Policy Toward Greece and Turkey, and Cyprus*. New York: Council of Foreign Relations.

Stritzel, H. (2007). Towards a Theory of Securitisation: Copenhagen and Beyond. *European Journal of International Relations, 13*(3), 357–83.

Stritzel, H. (2011). Security, the Translation. *Security Dialogue, 42*(4–5), 343–55.

Stritzel, H. (2012). Securitization, Power, Intertextuality: Discourse Theory and the Translations of Organized Crime. *Security Dialogue, 43*(6), 549–67.

Tan, N. (2021). Turkey's One-Man Diplomacy. *Yetkin Report*, https://yetkinreport.com/en/2021/10/05/turkeys-one-man-diplomacy/ [retrieved 1 November 2021].

Tanchum, M. (2015). A New Equilibrium: The Republic of Cyprus, Israel, and Turkey in the Eastern Mediterranean Strategic Architecture. *Friedrich Ebert Stiftung and PRIO Cyprus*.

Taş, H. (2019). The Gülenists in Exile: Reviving the Movement as a Diaspora. *GIGA Focus Middle East,* https://www.giga-hamburg.de/en/publications/giga-focus/the-guelenists-in-exile-reviving-the-movement-as-a-diaspora [retrieved 15 May 2022].

TGNA (1995). Genel Kurul Tutanağı [General Assembly Minutes]. 19th Period/4th Legislative Year/121st Session. June 8.

Theodossopoulos, D. (2007). *When Greeks Think About Turks: The View from Anthropology.* London and New York: Routledge.

Triantaphyllou, D. (2005). The Priorities of Greek Foreign Policy Today. *Southeast European and Black Sea Studies, 5*(3), 327–46.

Triantaphyllou, D. (2017). Greek–Turkish Relations and the Perceptions of their Elites. *London School of Economics Hellenic Observatory,* https://blogs.lse.ac.uk/greeceatlse/2017/01/31/greek-turkish-relations-and-the-perceptions-of-their-elites/ [retrieved 15 May 2021].

Triantaphyllou, D., and Dizdaroğlu, C. (2017). Survey on Turkish Elites' Perceptions on Turkish Foreign Policy and Greek–Turkish Relations. *Center for European and International Studies, Academia.edu* https://www.academia.edu/31381301/Survey_on_Turkish_Elites_Perceptions_on_Turkish_Foreign_Policy_and_Greek_Turkish_Relations [retrieved 1 April 2022].

Tsakonas, P. J. (2001a). Turkey's Post-Helsinki Turbulence: Implications for Greece and the Cyprus Issue. *Turkish Studies, 2*(2), 1–40.

Tsakonas, P. J. (2001b). Post-Cold War Security Dilemmas: Greece in Search of the Right Balancing Recipe. In Yallourides, C. P., and Tsakonas, P. J. (eds), *Greece and Turkey After the End of the Cold War* (pp. 145–66). New York: Caratzas.

Tsakonas, P. J., and Dokos, T. P. (2004). Greek–Turkish Relations in the Early Twenty-First Century: A View from Athens. In Martin, L., and Keridis, D. (eds), *The Future of Turkish Foreign Policy* (pp. 101–26). Cambridge, MA: MIT Press.

Tsarouhas, D. (2009). The Political Economy of Greek–Turkish Relations. *Southeast European and Black Sea Studies, 9*(1–2), 39–57.

Tuğtan, M. A. (2016). Cultural Variables in Foreign Policy: İsmail Cem and Ahmet Davutoğlu. *Uluslararası İlişkiler, 13*(49), 3–24.

Tulça, E. (2003) *Atatürk, Venizelos ve Bir Diplomat Enis Bey* [Atatürk, Venizelos and a Diplomat Mr Enis]. İstanbul: Simurg.

Turan, I. (2010). Zero Problems with Greece: Grounds for Optimism. *On Turkey.* The German Mashall Fund of the United States, 1–3.

Tür, Ö. (2011). Economic Relations with the Middle East under the AKP-Trade, Business Community and Reintegration with Neighbouring Zones. *Turkish Studies, 12*(4), 589–602.

Türkeş-Kılıç, S. (2019). Accessing the Rapprochement in its Second Decade: A Critical Approach to the Official Discourse between Turkey and Greece. In Heraclides, A., and Alioğlu Çakmak, G. (eds), *Greece and Turkey in Conflict and Cooperation: From Europeanization to de-Europeanization* (pp. 181–93). New York: Routledge.

Türkmen, F. (2009). Turkish-American Relations: A Challenging Transition. *Turkish Studies, 10*(1), 101–29.

UNHCR (2016). Refugees and Migrants Sea Arrivals in Europe – Monthly Data Update: December 2016. *Reliefweb*, https://reliefweb.int/report/greece/refugees-migrants-sea-arrivals-europe-monthly-data-update-december-2016 [retrieved 9 November 2020].

Uslu, N. (1997). The Cooperation Amid Problems: Turkish-American Relations in the 1980s. *The Turkish Yearbook, 27*, 13–30.

Uzgel, İ. (2003). Between Praetorianism and Democracy: The Role of the Military in Turkish Foreign Policy. *The Turkish Yearbook, 34*, 177–211.

Varouhakis, M. (2009). Greek Intelligence and the Capture of PKK Leader Abdullah Ocalan in 1999. *Studies in Intelligence, 53*(1), 1–7.

Verney, S. (1997). Greece: A New Era. *Mediterranean Politics, 2*(1), 193–200.

Volkan, V. D. (1979). *Cyprus: War and Adaptation: A Psychoanalytic History of Two Ethnic Groups in Conflict*. Charlottesville: Virginia University Press.

Wæver, O. (1995). Securitisation and Desecuritisation. In Lipschutz, R. D. (ed.), *On Security* (pp. 46–86). New York: Columbia University Press.

Wæver, O. (1996). European Security Identity. *Journal of Common Market Studies, 34*(1), 103–32.

Wæver, O. (2000). The EU as a Security Actor: Reflections from a Pessimistic Constructivist on Post-Sovereign Security Orders. In Kelstrup, M., and Williams, M. C. (eds), *International Relations Theory and the Politics of European Integration* (pp. 250–94). London: Routledge.

Wæver, O. (2003). Securitisation: Taking Stock of a Research Programme in Security Studies. Unpublished manuscript.

Wæver, O., and Buzan, B. (2020). Racism and Responsibility: The Critical Limits of Deepfake Methodology in Security Studies – A Reply to Howell and Richter-Montpetit. *Security Dialogue, 51*(4), 386–94.

Warner, J., and Boas, I. (2020). Securitization of Climate Change: How Invoking Global Dangers for Instrumental Ends can Backfire. *Environment and Planning C: Politics and Space, 37*(8), 1471–88.

Wilkinson, C. (2007). The Copenhagen School on Tour in Kyrgyzstan: Is Securitisation Theory Useable Outside Europe? *Security Dialogue, 38*(1), 5–25.

Williams, M. C. (2003). Words, Images, Enemies: Securitisation and International Politics. *International Studies Quarterly, 47*(4), 511–31.
Wilson, A. (1979/1980). The Aegean Dispute. *Adelphi Papers 155*. London: The International Institute for Strategic Studies.
Yavuz, M. H., and Özcan, N. A. (2006). The Kurdish Question and Turkey's Justice and Development Party. *Middle East Policy, 13*(1), 102–19.

OFFICIAL DOCUMENTS

Brussels Joint Communique, 31 May 1975.
Constitution of the Republic of Turkey, 1982.
Convention on the Continental Shelf, 1958.
Council of the European Union, 22 March 2018, https://www.consilium.europa.eu/en/press/press-releases/2018/03/23/european-council-conclusions-22-march-2018/ [retrieved 15 May 2021].
Council of the European Union, 20 June 2019, https://www.consilium.europa.eu/en/press/press-releases/2019/06/20/european-council-conclusions-final-20-june-2019/ [retrieved 15 May 2021].
Council of the European Union, 11 November 2019, https://www.consilium.europa.eu/en/meetings/fac/2019/11/11/ [retrieved 15 May 2021].
European Council Press Release, 144/16, 18 March 2016.
Helsinki Summit Presidency Conclusion, 10–11 December 1999, http://www.europarl.europa.eu/summits/hel1_en.htm [retrieved 12 January 2016].
Presidency of the Turkish Republic, 7 December 2017.
Presidency of the Turkish Republic, 7 September 2020.
Turkish Ministry of Foreign Affairs, 10 January 1997.
Turkish Ministry of Foreign Affairs, 12 February 1998.
Turkish Ministry of Foreign Affairs, 23 October 2000.
Turkish Ministry of Foreign Affairs, 14 August 2007.
Turkish Ministry of Foreign Affairs, 21 September 2011.
Turkish Ministry of Foreign Affairs, 10 October 2012.
Turkish Ministry of Foreign Affairs, 15 February 2013.
Turkish Ministry of Foreign Affairs, 5 June 2018.
Turkish Ministry of Foreign Affairs, 5 August 2018.
Turkish Ministry of Foreign Affairs, 1 September 2018.
Turkish Ministry of Foreign Affairs, 15 May 2019.
Turkish Ministry of Foreign Affairs, 15 June 2019.
Turkish Ministry of Foreign Affairs, 28 September 2019.

Turkish Ministry of Foreign Affairs, 9 October 2019.
Turkish Ministry of Foreign Affairs, 1 December 2019.
Turkish Ministry of Foreign Affairs, 2 January 2020.
Turkish Ministry of Foreign Affairs 16 January 2020.
Turkish Ministry of Foreign Affairs 26 March 2020.
Turkish Ministry of Foreign Affairs 21 April 2020.
Turkish Ministry of Foreign Affairs 15 May 2020.
Turkish Ministry of Foreign Affairs, 25 July 2020.
UN Convention on the Law of the Sea (1982).
UN General Assembly 54th Session (6 December 1999) UN A/RES/54/30.
UNSC Resolution 353 (20 July 1974) UN Doc S/RES/353.
UNSC Resolution 367 (12 March 1975) UN Doc S/RES/367.
UNSC Resolution 395 (25 August 1976) UN Doc S/RES/395.
UNSC Resolution 541 (18 November 1983) UN Doc S/RES/541.
UNSC Resolution 1092 (23 December 1996) UN Doc S/RES/1092.
The Madrid Joint Declaration (8 July 1997), http://www.hri.org/MFA/thesis/summer97/section.html [retrieved 10 December 2015].

NEWSPAPERS
Anadolu Agency
BBC
BiaNet
Cumhuriyet
Daily Sabah
Dunya
Ekathimerini
EuroNews
Guardian
Hurriyet Daily News
Hürriyet
Independent
Millet
Milliyet
New York Times
NTV
Reuters
Sabah

The Directorate General of Press and Information
Turkish Daily News
Turkish Official Newspaper
Washington Post
Yeni İstanbul

INDEX

Aegean Sea, 5, 16, 25, 31–9, 42–8, 51–2, 54, 56–8, 60–3, 73, 77, 122–3, 127–9, 130, 136–9, 141–2, 150, 155, 166–70, 173
airspace, 5, 31–2, 40, 47, 76, 127, 160, 172
AKP, 114, 118, 131, 135, 153
Anatolia, 3, 11, 34, 49, 50, 65, 77, 84–5, 88, 129, 135, 167
Atatürk, M. K., 4, 65–6

balance of power, 12, 32, 39, 52, 64, 68, 91, 110, 120, 168
Berne Agreement, 35–6, 38
Blue Homeland, 155, 158–9, 175

casus belli, 12, 25, 29, 39, 40, 42, 44–6, 62, 74, 141, 168–70
Cem, İ., 62, 78, 92–4, 98, 105, 107–8, 113, 116–19, 125–31, 142, 172–3
change through stabilisation, 17, 99, 101, 126, 140, 142, 144, 173

civil society, 6, 16, 98, 103–4, 106–8, 116, 173
Cold War *see* post-Cold War
Confidence Building Measures (CBMs), 40, 117, 129–30, 142–3
continental shelf, 5, 16, 31, 33–6, 38–41, 43, 52, 143, 156, 158, 160, 167–8
Copenhagen School, 7–10, 19, 99–100, 140, 169, 175
coup, 17, 68, 70–2, 91, 121, 132, 150–1, 153–4, 174
Cyprus problem, 5, 16, 19, 41, 64–7, 69, 73–4, 80, 110, 120–2, 156, 167
Çiller, T., 57–61, 75–6, 88, 170

Davos, 40, 90, 107
Davutoğlu, A., 114, 136–7
delimitation, 5, 16, 31, 33–4, 36, 38, 56, 156, 159–60, 167
demilitarisation, 16, 47–54, 153

Demirel, S., 35, 37, 54, 59, 62, 68, 79, 89–90, 104
dialogue, 7, 19, 27, 36–8, 40, 57, 62, 90–1, 93, 97–9, 106–7, 112, 116–19, 122, 127–9, 132, 134–42, 144, 149, 155, 158, 166, 173
discourse, 8–9, 11–12, 16–19, 26, 28, 32, 42, 45–6, 51, 60–1, 65, 71, 79–80, 87, 82, 94, 99–102, 108, 114, 125–9, 131, 135–6, 139–41, 144, 155, 159, 161, 166–76
Dodecanese, 47–8, 51

earthquake, 6, 98, 103–5, 107, 115
Eastern Mediterranean, 5, 7, 17, 47, 64, 66, 70, 75, 77–9, 120, 127–9, 131–2, 135, 149–50, 154–63, 168, 172–5
elite, 2, 8, 12, 16–19, 28, 32, 74, 98, 132, 134, 139, 141, 149, 153, 155, 165–7, 169–74
emergency measures, 8, 38, 42, 45, 53–4, 58, 61, 71, 76–9, 90, 168, 170–1, 175
energy, 97, 120, 155–8
Enosis, 19, 67–71
Erdoğan, R. T., 115, 131, 134–8, 140–1, 150–3, 161–2
Europeanisation, 6, 16, 98, 103, 109, 111–15, 144, 173
existential threat, 8, 11–2, 17, 25–9, 32, 38, 42, 45–6, 50, 52–9, 61–2, 71, 75–8, 80, 87, 90, 114, 129, 166–8, 170–3

fait accompli, 42, 46, 56–8, 69–70, 161, 171
FETO, 91, 150–2
friendship, 4, 17, 88, 105–6, 118, 126–9, 132, 139, 141, 172–3

Hagia Sophia, 7, 17, 149, 162–3, 174–5
Hansen, L., 9–10, 16–17, 19, 94, 99, 101–2, 140–3, 173–4
Helsinki Summit, 6, 14, 92, 98, 108, 111–12, 127–8, 153
High-Level Cooperation Council, 114, 132, 135–7, 174

Imia, 25, 29, 54–63, 109, 122–3, 129, 140–1, 169, 171–2, 175
International Court of Justice (ICJ), 34–6, 113–15
İnönü, İ., 4, 49–51, 68, 121, 166–7

Karamanlis, C., 34–5, 37, 73, 140
Kardak *see* Imia

mediation, 34, 68, 114, 121, 123, 128, 160–1
migration, 7, 9, 17, 23, 68, 125, 132, 137–9, 145, 149, 151, 163, 175
militarisation *see* demilitarisation
mistrust, 1–2, 11, 66, 106
Montreux, 37, 47, 49

National Security Council (NSC), 13–14, 20, 28, 57, 70–1, 76–7, 84, 135–6, 153–4

NATO, 4–5, 24, 40, 60, 62, 66, 73, 75, 81, 110, 117–22, 128–30, 139, 161
negotiation, 34–6, 48, 56, 60, 69, 72–4, 86, 109, 112–15, 118, 126, 131, 135–8, 145, 161, 167

Ottoman Empire, 1–3, 11, 18, 47–8, 50, 83, 166
Öcalan, A., 25, 82–3, 85–92, 110, 140, 152, 169, 171
Özal, T., 24, 37, 39–40, 107

Papandreou, A., 35, 37–40, 55, 87, 107, 118
Papandreou, G., 67, 92–4, 98, 107, 116–19, 125–7, 130, 132, 172–3
Paris Peace Treaty, 47–8, 51
Paris School, 9, 46, 150
PASOK, 35, 37, 55, 87, 91
perception, 1–3, 11, 15, 24, 32, 44, 51, 53, 55, 80, 110, 130, 142, 165
PKK, 12, 25, 82–93, 110, 152, 169, 171–2
population exchange, 3, 4
post-Cold War, 7, 15–16, 23–5, 29, 32, 101, 120, 122–3, 142, 169, 175

rapprochement, 2, 4, 6–7, 16–17, 40, 94, 97–9, 102–3, 107, 116, 120, 124, 127, 132, 136, 139–44, 155, 166, 172–3
referent object, 8, 11–12, 25–8, 32, 46, 49–54, 59, 61, 71, 75–80, 87, 90, 129, 167–73

S-300 missile, 25, 29, 64, 74–5, 77–8, 122–3, 169, 171–2

securitising actors, 8, 11–15, 19, 26–8, 32, 41–2, 45–6, 50, 52–3, 56–62, 71, 75, 77–80, 82, 86–9, 141, 149, 163, 166–9, 171–2, 175
Simitis, C., 25, 55, 62, 80, 90–2, 109–10, 117, 123, 132
sovereignty, 16, 29, 31–3, 43, 45–8, 50, 56–9, 61–2, 65–6, 71–2, 130, 156, 166, 168, 170–2
Soviet Union, 4–5, 23–4, 72, 110, 120, 122, 142–3
speech act, 8, 10, 12–14, 16, 25–9, 46, 61, 74, 77, 80, 99–100, 155, 167, 170–1, 174
status quo, 25, 45–6, 65, 68, 79–80, 122–3, 170–1

territorial waters, 5, 12, 16, 25, 29, 31–3, 38, 40–6, 54–6, 140, 167–70
terrorism, 6, 9, 16, 82, 84–6, 89–90, 92–3, 125–6, 139, 152, 173
tourism, 84–6, 93, 97, 106, 125, 127, 137, 139, 144, 173
Treaty of Lausanne, 5, 41, 45, 47–9, 57, 64, 68, 167
Turkish Ministry of Foreign Affairs, 38, 46, 52, 75, 78, 88, 92, 117–18, 128–9, 136, 151–2, 156–63
Twelve Islands *see* Dodecanese

unilateral, 36, 41, 43–4, 52, 56, 62, 68, 71–3, 90, 155, 169
UN Security Council (UNSC), 35–6, 69, 72, 74–5
UNCLOS, 29, 41–6, 63, 159, 172

EU representative:
Easy Access System Europe
Mustamäe tee 50, 10621 Tallinn, Estonia
Gpsr.requests@easproject.com

www.ingramcontent.com/pod-product-compliance
Lightning Source LLC
Chambersburg PA
CBHW051125160426
43195CB00014B/2341